Edward E. Cohen

Ancient
Athenian
Maritime
Courts

THE LAWBOOK EXCHANGE, LTD.
Clark, New Jersey

ISBN-13: 978-1-58477-661-1

Lawbook Exchange edition 2010

THE LAWBOOK EXCHANGE, LTD.
33 Terminal Avenue
Clark, New Jersey 07066-1321

*Please see our website for a selection of our other publications
and fine facsimile reprints of classic works of legal history:*
www.lawbookexchange.com

Library of Congress Cataloging-in-Publication Data
Cohen, Edward E.
  Ancient Athenian maritime courts / Edward E. Cohen.
    p. cm.
  Originally published: Princeton, N.J. : Princeton University Press,
  [1973].
  Includes bibliographical references and indexes.
  ISBN 1-58477-661-7 (alk. paper)
  1. Maritime law--Greece--Athens--History. 2. Courts--Greece--
Athens--History. 3. Maritime law (Greek law) I. Title.

KKE4980.26.C64 2005
343.38'5096--dc22   2005002596

Edward E. Cohen

Ancient Athenian Maritime Courts

PRINCETON
UNIVERSITY PRESS
Princeton, New Jersey

L.C. Card: 65-17135
ISBN: 0-691-09227-3

Publication of this book
has been aided by a grant
from the
Center for Ancient History,
University of Pennsylvania

This book has been
composed in Linotype
Caledonia

Printed in the
United States of America
By
Princeton University Press,
Princeton, New Jersey

Contents

Preface

Vᴀʀɪᴏᴜs causes have prevented the early appearance of this book, which is based to a considerable extent on my doctoral dissertation which was completed in 1963 and has since circulated in microfilm form. Some of the alterations in the book reflect more recent work by other scholars, including some whose own work has incorporated findings and discussions contained in the dissertation.

I have attempted to make this work in its present form accessible to students of legal history and others who may have only a limited, or even no knowledge of Greek. This has entailed compromise. For example, I have tried to translate in a neutral fashion passages where various interpretations are sometimes possible. Again I have cited as "Demosthenes" those speeches usually included in the Demosthenic corpus and as "Aristotle" those works similarly included in the Aristotelian corpus. This implies no judgment as to authorship; it is only an effort to avoid paleographical and historical issues irrelevant to my subject. A further example: instead of transliterating Greek or employing the adjective "mercantile," which in English does not convey a "maritime" implication, I have used the adjective "emporic" to refer to the congeries of business transacted in or through the Peiraeus market.

At an early stage I profited much from discussions with Professors Wesley Thompson and Michael Jameson. Professor Martin Ostwald, whose constant interest in this project never went unappreciated, has read the manuscript and saved me from a number of errors. Dr. Dimitri Gofas has reviewed those areas pertaining to modern Greek law. Professor J. V. A. Fine read my early drafts critically and most helpfully. Many others offered useful aid on critical points, but of course I claim sole responsibility for all remaining deficiencies.

Dr. Walter Snyder, at an early stage, and Dr. Penelope Fullard, at a later, rendered signal service in the checking of citations, proofreading, and indexing. I am most grateful to Ms. Gail Filion, of the Princeton University Press staff, for invaluable and patient advice.

EEC

Philadelphia
January 1973

Abbreviations

Amit–M. Amit, *Athens and the Sea*, Brussels, 1965.

Andreades–A. Andreades, *A History of Greek Public Finance*, tr. by C. N. Brown, I, Cambridge, 1933.

Ashburner–W. Ashburner, *The Rhodian Sea-Law*, Oxford, 1909.

Ath. Pol.–Aristotle's *Constitution of the Athenians*.

ATL–B. D. Meritt, H. T. Wade-Gery, M. F. McGregor, *The Athenian Tribute Lists*, 4 Vols., Cambridge, 1939-1953.

Beauchet–L. Beauchet, *Histoire du droit privé de la république athénienne*, 4 Vols., Paris, 1897.

BGU–*Berliner griechische Urkunden*.

Blass–F. Blass, *Die attische Beredsamkeit*, 4 Vols., Leipzig, 1887-1898.

Bogaert–R. Bogaert, *Banques et banquiers dans les cités grecques*, Leyden, 1968.

Bo.-Sm.–R. J. Bonner and G. Smith, *The Administration of Justice from Homer to Aristotle*, 2 Vols., Chicago, 1930, 1938.

Bu.-Sw.–G. Busolt and H. Swoboda, *Griechische Staatskunde*, 2 Vols., Munich, 1920, 1926.

Calhoun, *Business Life*–G. M. Calhoun, *The Business Life of Ancient Athens*, Chicago, 1926.

Charles, *Statutes of Limitations*–J. F. Charles, *Statutes of Limitations at Athens*, Chicago, 1938.

Cl. Phil.–Classical Philology.

Clerc, *Les Métèques*–M. Clerc, *Les Métèques athéniens*, Paris, 1893.

Davies–J. K. Davies, *Athenian Propertied Families, 600-300 B.C.*, Oxford, 1971.

Dem.–Demosthenes.

DS–C. Daremberg and E. Saglio, *Dictionnaire des antiquités grecques et romaines*, 5 Vols., Paris, 1877 and thereafter.

Gernet, *REG* 1938–L. Gernet, "Sur les actions commerciales en droit athénien," *Revue des études grecques*, 51 (1938), pp. 1-44.

Gernet, *Budé Demosthenes*–L. Gernet, *Démosthène, Plaidoyers Civils* (Collection des Universités de France), 4 Vols., Paris, 1954-1960.

Gilbert–G. Gilbert, *Handbuch der Griechischen Staatsalterthümer* (Erster Band: *Der Staat der Lakedaimonier und der Athener*), second edition, Leipzig, 1893.

Gofas–Δ. Χ. Γκόφας, Δεῖγμα: ἱστορικὴ ἔρευνα ἐπὶ τοῦ Ἑλληνικοῦ Δικαίου τῶν συναλλαγῶν, Athens, 1970.

Gomme, *Essays*–A. W. Gomme, "Traders and Manufacturers," *Essays in Greek History and Literature*, Oxford, 1937, pp. 42-67.

Harrell, *Public Arbitration*–H. C. Harrell, *Public Arbitration in Athenian Law* (*University of Missouri Studies*, XI, no. 1), Columbia, 1936.

Harrison, *Family and Property*–A. R. W. Harrison, *The Law of Athens—The Family and Property*, Oxford, 1968.

Harrison, *Procedure*–A. R. W. Harrison, *The Law of Athens—Procedure*, Oxford, 1971.

Hasebroek, *Trade and Politics*–J. Hasebroek, *Trade and Politics in Ancient Greece*, tr. by L. M. Fraser and D. C. MacGregor, London, 1933.
Hignett–C. Hignett, *A History of the Athenian Constitution*, Oxford, 1952.
Hill–G. F. Hill, *Sources for Greek History between the Persian and Peloponnesian Wars* (revised edition), Oxford, 1951.
IG–*Inscriptiones Graecae.*
Jacoby, *FGH*–F. Jacoby, *Die Fragmente der griechischen Historiker*, Berlin, 1923 onward.
Jones, *Legal Theory*–J. W. Jones, *The Law and Legal Theory of the Greeks*, Oxford, 1956.
Knorringa, *Emporos*–H. Knorringa, *Emporos: Data on Trade and Trader in Greek Literature from Homer to Aristotle*, Amsterdam, 1926.
Lipsius, *AR*–J. H. Lipsius, *Das attische Recht und Rechtsverfahren*, 3 Vols., Leipzig, 1905-1915.
Lofberg, *Sycophancy in Athens*–J. O. Lofberg, *Sycophancy in Athens*, Chicago, 1917.
Meyer-Laurin–H. Meyer-Laurin, *Gesetz und Billigkeit im attischen Prozess*, Weimar, 1965.
Michell–H. Michell, *Economics of Ancient Greece*, second edition, Cambridge, 1957.
MSL–M. H. E. Meier and G. F. Schömann, *Der attische Process*, neu bearb. von J. H. Lipsius, Berlin, 1883-1887.
Paley-Sandys–F. A. Paley and J. E. Sandys, *Select Private Orations of Demosthenes*, 2 Vols., second edition, Cambridge, 1886.
Paoli, *SDA*–U. E. Paoli, *Studi di diritto attico*, Firenze, 1930.
Paoli, *SPA*–U. E. Paoli, *Studi sul processo attico*, Padova, 1933.

Pringsheim, *GLS*–F. Pringsheim, *The Greek Law of Sale*, Weimar, 1950.

RE–*Paulys Real-Encyclopädie der klassischen Altertumswissenschaft*, rev. G. Wissowa et al., Stuttgart, 1894- .

RIDA–*Revue internationale des droits de l'antiquité*.

Rostovtzeff, *SEHHW*–M. Rostovtzeff, "The Ancient World in the Fourth Century B.C.," Chapter II, Vol. I of *The Social and Economic History of the Hellenistic World*, Oxford, 1941.

Sandys, *Ath. Pol.*²–J. E. Sandys, *Aristotle's Constitution of Athens*, second edition, London, 1912.

Schäfer–A. Schäfer, *Demosthenes und seine Zeit*, 3 Vols., second edition, Leipzig, 1885-1887.

SEG–*Supplementum Epigraphicum Graecum*.

SZ–*Zeitschrift der Savigny-Stiftung für Rechtsgeschichte*, pt. 2, romanistische Abteilung.

Weiss–E. Weiss, *Griechisches Privatrecht auf rechtsvergleichender Grundlage*, Leipzig, 1923.

Wilamowitz, *A & A*–U. von Wilamowitz-Moellendorff, *Aristoteles und Athen*, 2 Vols., Berlin, 1893.

Wolff–H. J. Wolff, *Die attische Paragraphe*, Weimar, 1966.

Ziebarth, *Beiträge*–E. Ziebarth, *Beiträge zur Geschichte des Seeraubs und Seehandels im alten Griechenland*, Hamburg, 1929.

Ancient
Athenian
Maritime
Courts

1

PROCEDURAL CHARACTERISTICS

G REEK law failed of fruition. It was Roman legal science that could judge "every national law, with the exception of our own, disordered and almost absurd."[1] Influenced by Greek philosophy, responsive to the challenge of vast empire, the Roman jurists developed a unique law of objective and humane magnificence. When in the sixth century A.D. Greek-speaking lawyers at Constantinople codified their law, it was Roman law written in Latin that became the world-influencing Corpus Iuris Civilis.[2] The classical legal heritage revived by the Glossators and Commentators of medieval and renaissance Western Europe was Roman. The Byzantine law that took root in Eastern Europe was Roman.[3] The law that lives today even in modern Greece,

[1] "omne ius civile, praeter hoc nostrum, inconditum ac paene ridiculum" (Cicero, *De Orat.* 1.44.197). On the singular development of classical Roman law, see F. Pringsheim, *Journal of Roman Studies*, 34 (1944), pp. 60-64.

[2] On the question of Greek influence and interpolation, see W. W. Buckland, "Interpolations in the *Digest*: A Criticism of Criticism," *Harvard Law Review*, 54 (1940-41), pp. 1273-1310, where he convincingly refutes the arguments of E. Albertario (*Introduzione storica allo studio del diritto romano giustinianeo*, Part I, Milan, 1935) on the Oriental influence in the *Digest*. Buckland's general conviction affirms the position of S. Riccobono: "the law of Justinian, handed down by the glossators to modern Europe, was in essentials a Roman law."

[3] The late Byzantine *Hexabiblos* of Harmenopoulos (1345) has had wide influence on legal developments in Eastern Europe until quite recently. (See S. Sakellariadēs, "Περὶ Ἀρμενοπούλου

under the Civil Code of 1940, is Roman, albeit enriched
or adulterated by later developments in the Roman
civil-law codes of Byzantium and Germany.[4]

In this vast evolution and extension of Roman law,
one branch alone preserves ancient Hellenic influence.[5]

κ.τ.λ." in 'Αρχεῖον 'Ιδιωτικοῦ Δικαίου, 12 (1945), pp. 191 ff., and
more recently, K. Triantaphyllopoulos, 'Η 'Εξάβιβλος τοῦ 'Αρμενο-
πούλου καὶ ἡ νομικὴ σκέψις ἐν Θεσσαλονίκῃ κατὰ τὸν δέκατον τέταρτον
αἰῶνα, Thessaloniki, 1960.) The earlier Isaurian *Ecloga* is the
basis of the Serbian *Zacon* ("Laws") and of the Bulgarian *Zacon
Soudni lioudem* ("Laws of the People"). The same *Ecloga* influenced Russian law through the *Ruscaja Pravda.* (See C. Spul-
ber, *L'Eclogue des Isauriens,* Cernautzi, 1929, pp. 103 ff.) P. J.
Zepos, *Greek Law,* Athens, 1949, pp. 11-45, sketches well the
later history of the Roman law in Eastern Europe, although not
always clearly differentiating between Roman institutions and
their unconnected ancient Greek parallels.

[4] Modern Greek legal science relies heavily on the comparative
method. Byzantine law remains however the historical basis of
the legal system. Since the time of G. L. von Maurer, German
lawyer and member of the Bavarian regency in Greece (from
1833), German law has predominated. A large number of Greek
jurists continue to be German-trained, and more than anything
else Western, the *Bürgerliches Gesetzbuch* is the basis of the
Civil Code of 1940. The Commercial Code however is heavily
influenced by French law. The commercial maritime law in
particular was heavily Gallic, prior to the code of 1958, but is
now free of any one dominant influence. Petropoulos has well
characterized the great impact of pure Roman law in the development of Greek law since the Revolution: "Χαρακτηριστικὸν
τῆς περιόδου ταύτης [μετὰ τὸ 1821] ἀποτελεῖ ἡ ἐν πολλοῖς βιαία καὶ
παρὰ πᾶσαν λογικὴν ἐπιβολὴ τοῦ ρωμαϊκοῦ δικαίου, τοῦ Corpus Iuris
Civilis ὡς ἰσχύοντος ἐν Ἑλλάδι δικαίου διὰ τοῦ παραμερισμοῦ τοῦ ἐθνι-
κοῦ ἑλληνικοῦ . . . ." ('Ιστορικὴ εἰσαγωγὴ εἰς τὰς πηγὰς τοῦ 'Ελληνι-
κοῦ Δικαίου, Athens, 1961, p. 9.)

[5] In the area of family law (οἰκογενιακὸν δίκαιον) the legal institution of the dowry (προῖκα) may represent a similar continuity.
The influence of the ancient Greek law concerning προίξ upon

4

The principles of Greek maritime commerce, operating during the Roman period through the famed Rhodian Sea Law and continuing in the mercantile legislation of the medieval age,[6] now constitute the germinal cells of the complex modern international law of maritime commerce.[7]

---

the Roman *dos* is still somewhat unclear. Under the Greek Civil Code of 1940, articles 1412 and ff., dotal immovables remain the largely inalienable property of the wife, the husband's interest being restricted to administration and usufruct. This is contrary to the general Roman principle that the husband is owner of the dowry, although conforming to ancient Greek doctrine and Byzantine practice. Cf. P. J. Zepos, *Journal of Comparative Legislation*, 27 (1946), pp. 56 ff. The fundamental legal rules governing the family and its relationship to society were substantially altered, however, as early as the time of Alexander the Great. Cf. W. K. Lacey, *The Family in Classical Greece*, London, 1968, p. 223.

[6] D. Gofas in two pioneering studies has demonstrated the continuity from Hellenic times of legal principles in two areas of maritime commerce, the transportation of cargo on deck and the use of the sample (τὸ δεῖγμα). See D. Gofas, ἡ φόρτωσις ἐπὶ τοῦ καταστρώματος, Athens, 1965, and Δεῖγμα—ἱστορικὴ ἔρευνα ἐπὶ τοῦ Ἑλληνικοῦ Δικαίου τῶν συναλλαγῶν, Athens, 1970.

[7] On the importance of earlier maritime codes in shaping contemporary admiralty law, see C. John Colombos, *International Law of the Sea*, London, 1959, pp. 29-35; F. R. Sanborn, *Origins of the Early English Maritime and Commercial Law*, New York, 1930, p. 5. W. McFee, *Law of the Sea*, London, 1951, p. 36, terms the Rhodian Sea Law "the foundation of modern maritime jurisprudence." Absolutely no validity adheres to the contention of R. D. Benedict, author of the classic American work on admiralty, that the Rhodian Sea Law is a myth based on a spurious fifteenth century document. Benedict, writing in *Yale Law Journal*, 18 (1908-9), pp. 223 ff., ignores scholarship more recent than Story's *Literature of the Maritime Law* (1818). Ashburner shortly thereafter established beyond doubt the Sea Law's Hellenic authenticity.

5

This should not be surprising. The Greeks relied heavily on the sea for transportation and communication. The maintenance of services and supplies depended upon adequate attention to the relationships, mutual and separate, among those using the sea and those making that use possible. This concern, in juridical form, constituted the commercial law codes of the Greek waters.

In Hellenic times Athens was the mercantile giant of the Aegean. Pericles in his funeral address could claim that Athenian greatness made available from everywhere everything, that it was the happy lot of the Athenians to enjoy as their own the goods of other lands no less than those of Attica.[8] The Old Oligarch adds that command of the sea had gathered into Athens "everything desirable whether it be in Sicily or in Italy or in Cyprus or in Egypt or in Lydia or in Pontos or anywhere else."[9]

In the fourth century, imperial power gave way to commercial supremacy, an emporic influence built upon geographical and mercantile reality, assisted by the ever-present political and maritime reality of the Athenian fleet. Her naval stranglehold broken forever in the Great Harbor at Syracuse in 413, Athens nonetheless maintained through most of the fourth century a fleet seldom paralleled by any and excelled by none. Of all peoples she depended most on imported foodstuffs

[8] ἐπεσέρχεται δὲ διὰ μέγεθος τῆς πόλεως ἐκ πάσης γῆς τὰ πάντα καὶ ξυμβαίνει ἡμῖν μηδὲν οἰκειοτέρᾳ τῇ ἀπολαύσει τὰ αὐτοῦ ἀγαθὰ γιγνόμενα καρποῦσθαι ἢ καὶ τὰ τῶν ἄλλων ἀνθρώπων (Thucydides 2.38.2).

[9] ὅ τι ἐν Σικελίᾳ ἡδὺ ἢ ἐν Ἰταλίᾳ ἢ ἐν Κύπρῳ ἢ ἐν Αἰγύπτῳ ἢ ἐν Λυδίᾳ ἢ ἐν τῷ Πόντῳ ἢ ἐν Πελοποννήσῳ ἢ ἄλλοθί που, ταῦτα πάντα εἰς ἓν ἤθροισται διὰ τὴν ἀρχὴν τῆς θαλάττης (2.7). For similar sentiment (in a humorous vein), cf. Hermippos Fr. 63 (Edmonds) preserved at Athenaeus 1.27.e-f.

(Dem. 20.31). In turn she exported silver and agricultural specialties, especially wine and olive oil.[10] The Peiraeus, with its three harbors and central location, was the port of call for much or most of Aegean trade.[11] Her coinage continued its triumphant march around the Mediterranean world.[12] Workshops flourished.[13] The world's first private banks developed.[14] A prosperous

[10] See J. Beloch, "Die Handelsbewegung im Altertum," *Jahrbücher für Nationalökonomie und Statistik*, 1899, pp. 626-631; K. Bucher, *Beiträge zur Wirtschaftsgeschichte*, 1922, pp. 17 ff.; Knorringa, *Emporos*, pp. 132-139. It seems probable that manufactured goods were not of great significance in Athenian trade.

[11] Her natural geographical advantages have never changed. οὐκ ἂν ἀλόγως δέ τις οἰηθείη τῆς Ἑλλάδος καὶ πάσης δὲ τῆς οἰκουμένης ἀμφὶ τὰ μέσα οἰκεῖσθαι τὴν πόλιν . . . ὁπόσοι τ' ἂν αὖ βουληθῶσιν ἀπ' ἐσχάτων τῆς Ἑλλάδος ἐπ' ἔσχατα ἀφικέσθαι, πάντες οὗτοι ὥσπερ κύκλου τόρνον τὰς Ἀθήνας ἢ παραπλέουσιν ἢ παρέρχονται (Xenophon, *Poroi*, 1.6). The same author says of the harbor-facilities: ναυσὶ καλλίστας καὶ ἀσφαλεστάτας ὑποδοχὰς ἔχει (3.1). The utilization of these facilities followed naturally: ἐμπόριον γὰρ ἐν μέσῳ τῆς Ἑλλάδος τὸν Πειραιᾶ κατεσκευάσατο [αἱ Ἀθῆναι] τοσαύτην ἔχονθ' ὑπερβολὴν ὥσθ' ἃ παρὰ τῶν ἄλλων ἐν παρ' ἑκάστων χαλεπόν ἐστι λαβεῖν, ταῦθ' ἅπαντα παρ' αὐτῆς ῥᾴδιον εἶναι πορίσασθαι (Isocrates, *Panegyricus*, 4.42 [49]).

[12] Athenian coins down to the time of Alexander were the accepted currency of a large part of the Mediterranean world. Not all Attic "owls" from hoards buried in the fourth century are "imitations," as Milne has contended ("Trade Between Greece and Egypt," *Journal of Egyptian Archaeology*, 1939, pp. 177-183). For a detailed study and interpretation of the composition of eastern Mediterranean coin-hoards, see my unpublished "Circulation of Athenian Coins in the Eastern Mediterranean before Alexander," available at the American Numismatic Society, New York City.

[13] For the fourth century, see Dem. 36.4, 37.9 ff., 48.12; Xen., *Mem.* 2.7.6; Plato, *Laws*, 846E; Aeschines 1.97; Lykurgos, *Against Leokrates* 58.

[14] The money-changers of the early Middle East never ma-

middle class and a wealthy group of nouveaux riches flaunted and increased their possessions.[15]

In this commercial metropolis of fourth-century Hellas, maritime commerce reached maturity. Here there developed the naval loan (ναυτικὸν δάνεισμα) with its special characteristic of required repayment only on successful completion of a journey, and its utilization of ship or cargo as security. And here there developed the *dikai emporikai* (δίκαι ἐμπορικαί), special commercial maritime courts.

At Athens in the fourth century particular offenses or disputes were handled in various courts clearly delineated and definitely limited in jurisdiction. But distinct from the multitude of separate civil categories stand the *dikai emporikai*, in procedure quite unique. Concerned only with cases arising from maritime commerce, in certain respects they are the juridical counterparts of the ἐπιμεληταὶ ἐμπορίου,[16] the administrative officials of the harbor. In contrast to the general rule that "a foreigner has no rights," these courts were open to individuals of varied citizenship. Special provisions were available for assuring a defendant's appearance at the ensuing trial, and uniquely strong measures could be taken to enforce the judgment of the maritime tribunals. The courts were summary in procedure, rendering rapid decisions. In short, the commercial maritime courts of fourth-century Athens were marked by *rapidity, supranationality* and *rigor*.

---

tured into true bankers. See Calhoun, *Business Life*, pp. 81-87. Athens too had her money-changers in the fifth century. See Bogaert, p. 61.

[15] E.g. Pasiōn's son Apollodōros, who in Dem. 50 explains how he met his trierarchic duties φιλοτίμως.

[16] Cf. *Ath. Pol.* 51.4; Dem. 35.51; 58.8, 9.

RAPIDITY

The statement that the commercial maritime courts offered an especially rapid procedure generally is taken to mean that the *dikai emporikai* were *dikai emmēnoi* (δίκαι ἔμμηνοι).[17] As usually defined, *dikai emmēnoi* are cases in which final adjudication must occur within 30 days of the initiation of the action.[18] To expedite summer trade these cases were heard only during the

[17] The term δίκη, not employed definitively in ancient Greek law (cf. Jones, *Legal Theory*, pp. 24ff.), has been further complicated in modern terminology. It remains a pressing task for Greek legal scholarship to ascertain exactly which of the multitudinous *dikai* mentioned in the literary sources actually had juridical existence in the fourth century. To say that *dikai emporikai* were *dikai emmēnoi* is necessary and correct, but confusing. It is true that Aristotle (*Ath. Pol.* 52.2) lists a number of cases in the category δίκαι ἔμμηνοι. But no complaint was ever headed *dike emmēnos*. Hence the case category is juridically non-existent—it is simply a descriptive appellation properly to be ascribed to a number of cases (*dikai*). Further confusion arises when scholars persist in speaking of *dikai emporikai* themselves under other case names. Thus Bo.-Sm. II, pp. 115-116, in discussing the δίκη βλάβης, speak of "mercantile suits of this type," specifying Dem. 33, 37, and 56. Since the speech describing the case in 33 was delivered at a paragraphic hearing, one might in recent scholarship encounter this case (*Against Apatourion*) in the classes παραγραφή, δίκη ἐμπορική, δίκη ἔμμηνος, δίκη βλάβης. But necessarily the complaint fell into a single category, either δίκη βλάβης or δίκη ἐμπορική depending on the (unknown) practice in the emporic courts. Similar considerations hold for 37 and 56.

[18] Cf. thus *MSL*, p. 525; Beauchet IV, p. 100; Reinach, *DS*, s.v. ἔμμηνοι δίκαι; Lipsius, *AR*, p. 901; Thalheim, *RE*, s.v. ἔμμηνοι δίκαι; Calhoun, *Business Life*, p. 165; Bo.-Sm. II, pp. 91 and 116; Charles, *Statutes of Limitations*, p. 2; Andreades, p. 386, n. 1; Michell, p. 349; M. A. Levi, *Commento storico alla Respublica Atheniensium di Aristotele*, II, Milan, 1968, p. 376; Harrison, *Procedure*, pp. 16, 154.

winter: αἰ δὲ λήξεις τοῖς ἐμπόροις τῶν δικῶν ἔμμηνοί εἰσιν ἀπὸ τοῦ βοηδρομιῶνος μέχρι τοῦ μουνιχιῶνος, ἵνα παραχρῆμα τῶν δικαίων τυχόντες ἀνάγωνται (Dem. 33.23). [The complaints for the cases involving maritime merchants are "monthly" from Boēdromion until Mounichion, so that attaining their rights they might sail without delay.] Thus Athenian commercial maritime law was in accord with various modern systems that in practice offer procedural time-preference for certain commercial actions.[19]

Delay in The Courts

The Athenian courts otherwise were subject to long delays.[20] The litigation over the "crown," subject of the great speech by Aeschines and the greater by Demosthenes, came to trial some seven years after initiation of prosecution (Aeschines 3.219,254).[21] While the statutory time limitation (προθεσμία) appears normally to have been five years (Dem. 36.26-27), the case discussed at Dem. 38 allegedly came into court fourteen years after the relevant agreement had been made. Less spectacularly, Dem. 21 was argued some two years after the offense (§13),[22] and Dem. 30 three years after the

[19] In urban courts in the U.S.A. even where the forms of actions have been abolished, actions sounding in "contract" rather than in "tort" will often proceed far more rapidly to trial. For New York State, e.g., cf. Zeisel, Kalven and Buchholz, *Delay in the Court*, Boston, 1959, p. 7.

[20] Cf. Charles, *Statutes of Limitations*, pp. 9-10; Reinach, DS, s.v. ἔμμηνοι δίκαι, believed that "En réalité . . . il arrivait presque toujours que la décision était différée fort au delà du terme légal."

[21] Cf. Schäfer III, p. 84, n.2, p. 224, n.1.

[22] The incident giving rise to the original suit apparently took place in 364/63. The speech was published about 347/46. See Harrison, *Procedure*, p. 156, n.4.

10

plaintiff had come of age (§§15-16). The speaker at Dem. 43 (§67) defends the long time that had passed before final adjudication, speaking of ἀναγκαῖαι διατριβαί (unavoidable delays). With the exception of the litigation on the crown, however, all these cases are explicable on the basis of non-juridical considerations, e.g. unwillingness to prosecute immediately. The crown litigation is a baffling business, but political considerations certainly predominated.

There are, however, numerous other instances of delay in Athenian courts *even after institution of suit.* Thus Dem. 39 was delivered in all probability one year after the case originally went to arbitration.[23] The speaker in Dem. 40 mentions an undesired wait of 11 years and a continuing delay.[24] Even early in the fourth century (c. 397) the same situation prevailed: πέρυσι μὲν οὖν διεγράψαντό μου τὰς δίκας, ἔμποροι φάσκοντες εἶναι. νυνὶ δὲ λαχόντος ἐν τῷ Γαμηλιῶνι μηνὶ οἱ ναυτοδίκαι οὐκ ἐξεδίκασαν. [Last year they had my suit quashed by claiming that they were maritime merchants; now the *nautodikai* have not adjudicated my complaint of the month Gamēlion] (Lysias 17.5). In public prosecutions the situation was no better: γραφὴν δ' ὕβρεως γράφομαι πρὸς τοὺς θεσμοθέτας αὐτόν. χρόνου δὲ γιγνομένου, καὶ τῆς μὲν γραφῆς ἐκκρουμένης, δικῶν δ' οὐκ οὐσῶν, γίγνονται παῖδες ἐκ τούτου τῇ μητρί. [I indicted him for "outrage" be-

---

[23] The speaker was taxiarch in 350/49. His speech was delivered in 349/48. He was not able to introduce into evidence at the trial the events cf 350/49, owing to the rule that evidence was not admissible at the trial that had not been submitted at the arbitration. Cf. §17: ταῦτα δ' εἰ μὴ σεσημασμένων ἤδη συνέβη τῶν ἐχίνων, κἂν μάρτυρας ὑμῖν παρεσχόμην. See Paley-Sandys I, pp. 139-140; Gernet, Budé *Demosthenes,* II, pp. 14-15.

[24] ἵνα, ὥσπερ καὶ πρότερον ἕνδεκα ἔτη διήγαγε κακουργῶν, οὕτως καὶ νῦν . . . τὴν δίκην ταύτην ἐκκρούῃ (43).

11

fore the *thesmothetes*. But with time passing, the indictment being evaded, but still no trials, children have been born to him by my mother] (Dem. 45.4). And in the second speech of Apollodōros against Stephanos, a law is reported at 46.22: κληροῦν δὲ τὸν ἄρχοντα κλήρων καὶ ἐπικλήρων, ὅσοι εἰσὶ μῆνες, πλὴν τοῦ σκιροφοριῶνος. [Let the archon set hearing dates for inheritances and heiresses every month except Skirophorion.] The citation is significant, for it alludes clearly to the archon's inability to complete the hearing before leaving office, Skirophorion being the final month of the Attic year. A month was not enough to complete a hearing.

The Monthly Suits

In the *dikai emmēnoi* (as defined) a decision supposedly had to be reached before a month's passage. The cases known to have been *emmēnoi* are of great variety, from different areas of the law, and concerned with diverse matters. Thus Aristotle (*Ath. Pol.* 52.2) terms "*emmēnoi*" the following cases:[25]

> ΠΡΟΙΚΟΣ [Dowry] (ἐάν τις ὀφείλων μὴ ἀποδῷ) available both in aid of the divorced woman whose husband failed to return the dowry, and the widow deprived by the heirs of her dotal interest.[26]

[25] κληροῦσι δὲ καὶ εἰσαγωγέας ε̄ ἄνδρας, οἳ τὰς ἐμμήνους εἰσάγουσι δίκας, δυοῖν φυλαῖν ἕκαστος.

[26] Cf. Dem. 27.17; 59.52; Isaeus 3.9, 78. As to whether this action was available to a husband or a prospective husband seeking to enforce a withheld dowry payment see Wolff, *RE*, s.v. προίξ, 144 ff.; Harrison, *Family and Property*, pp. 50-51.

12

ΔΑΝΕΙΟΝ [LOAN]   (κἄν τις ἐπὶ δραχμῇ δανεισάμενος ἀποστερῇ) only those satisfied with a return not in excess of 12 percent (cf. Aeschines 3.104) could avail themselves of the expeditious procedure.[27]

ΑΦΟΡΜΗ [CAPITAL]   (κἄν τις ἐν ἀγορᾷ βουλόμενος ἐργάζεσθαι δανείσηται παρά τινος ἀφορμήν.) suits on loans made to establish a business in the agora.[28]

ΑΙΚΕΙΑΣ [ASSAULT]   a suit for violence done to the person of an individual similar to the γραφὴ ὕβρεως, but leading to collection of damages by the plaintiff (see below).

ΕΡΑΝΙΚΑΙ   Either suits arising from "friendly loans" or cases involving disputes in an ἔρανος, or both.[29]

[27] Cf. Dem. 27.23, 35. The ancient world's concern with abolishing or controlling interest rates is justified by Aristotle, *Politics* 1257a, ff. Rates higher than 12% are often encountered in the orators: cf. for example Dem. 53.13 (16%); Isaeus, fr. 23 (33 and 1/3%) from Harpocration, s.v. ἐπιτρίταις; Aeschines, 1.107 (18%). On the legal implications of the varying interest rates, see J. H. Lipsius, *Leipziger Verhandlungen*, 1891, p. 57n.

[28] No such case is recorded by the orators. Dem. 36 is termed by Libanios a δίκη ἀφορμῆς and cited as such by Lipsius, *AR*, pp. 725 ff. But that case underwent public arbitration and hence was not *emmēnos*. Gernet considers it a δίκη βλάβης (*Budé Demosthenes*, I, pp. 201-202).

[29] Pollux' references (8.37, 144) to ἐρανικαὶ δίκαι are as indefinite as Aristotle's. To Beauchet (IV, pp. 267-268, 357-358)

13

ΚΟΙΝΩΝΙΚΑΙ	suits involving "partnership" disputes or perhaps suits against "corporations."[30]
ΑΝΔΡΑΠΟΔΩΝ	a suit involving slaves. Its precise nature is unknown (see below).
ΥΠΟΖΥΓΙΩΝ	a suit involving beasts of burden or draught. It is generally thought to parallel the "slave" suits, but its precise nature is no better known.
ΤΡΙΗΡΑΡΧΙΚΑΙ	"trierarchic" (naval command) suits. Again their precise nature is unknown.[31]

"paraît plus naturel d'appliquer les δίκαι ἐρανικαί à tous les cas d'érane, qu'il s'agisse d'un prêt ou d'une société . . ." (358) But there is really no basis from which to determine the scope of the δίκαι ἐρανικαὶ ἔμμηνοι. On the legal nature of the ἔρανος as organization, see Jones, *Legal Theory*, pp. 170-173.

[30] See Sandys, *Ath. Pol.*², who terms them "suits against corporations." To the contrary, Beauchet translates "actions entre associés" (IV, p. 353; cf. IV, p. 100). A guide to the extensive bibliography on the subject of Greek corporations or associations is given by N. Pantazopoulos in Αἱ Ἑλληνικαί "Κοινωνίαι," Athens, 1946, pp. 1-4. See especially E. Ziebarth, *Das griechische Vereinswesen*, Leipzig, 1896; P. J. T. Endenburg, *Koinoonia en Gemeenschap van Zaken bij de Grieken in den Klassieken Tijd*, Amsterdam, 1937.

[31] Gernet, *REG*, 1938, p. 7. His discussion on pp. 7-8 of the Polyklēs case (Dem. 50) is vitiated by our lack of knowledge concerning admission of cases to δίκαι τριηραρχικαὶ ἔμμηνοι. No more certain is Gernet's statement that these cases must involve "une demande d'un particulier contre un particulier à l'occasion d'une triérarchie." See Lipsius, *AR*, pp. 774 ff. Paragraph 17 of Dem. 50 is no argument for the case's being a δίκη ἐμπορική—cf. Pringsheim's convincing demonstration that no bottomry loan is

ΤΡΑΠΕΖΙΤΙΚΑΙ   banking cases.[32]

He continues (52.3): οὗτοι μὲν οὖν ταύτας δικάζουσιν ἐμμήνους εἰσάγοντες, εἱ δ᾽ ἀποδέκται τοῖς τελώναις καὶ κατὰ τῶν τελωνῶν,[33] τὰ μὲν μέχρι δέκα δραχμῶν ὄντες κύριοι, τὰ δ᾽ ἄλλ᾽ εἰς τὸ δικαστήριον εἰσάγοντες ἔμμηνα. [The eisagōgeis thus judge these cases, introducing them "monthly," but the apodektai (have jurisdiction over) cases for and against tax farmers, being competent in those up to ten drachmai, and introducing the others into court "monthly."]

Also among the dikai emmēnoi were of course the dikai emporikai and the dikai metallikai, the famed "mining cases."[34]

---

here involved (Der Kauf mit fremdem Geld, Leipzig, 1916, pp. 18-22). The "Secular Law on the Trierarchy" unearthed in the Athenian Agora excavations tells us little because of the fragmentary nature of the stone. See J. H. Oliver, "Greek Inscriptions," Hesperia, 4 (1935), pp. 14-19.

[32] Isocrates 17 may be a good example of such a case. But it is very early in the fourth century, and there is no reference to monthly procedure. The cases involving Apollodōros (Dem. 36, 49, 52) are not clear examples of "banking" matters of any type, since the questions involved are complicated by considerations of inheritance and partnership. Cf. Bogaert, pp. 63-77.

[33] Tax laws in Athens (τοὺς νόμους τοὺς τελωνικούς, Dem. 24.101) equipped the tax-farmer with a number of legal weapons including the φάσις (see Gilbert, pp. 394-395). On "the farming out of public revenues," see Andreades' discussion with source reference, pp. 159-161. For the ἀποδέκται, cf. Lipsius, AR, pp. 100 ff.

[34] The scope of the dikai metallikai is defined at Dem. 37.35-38. As Nikoboulos there remarks, "κἂν ἄλλο τι ἀδικῇ τις περὶ τὰ μέταλλα καὶ τούτων εἰσὶν ἕand but as he further shows, not all "mining disputes" were admissible as "dikai metallikai emmēnoi." The starting point for all investigation of Attic mining remains E. Ardaillon, Les mines du Laurion dans l'antiquité,

Despite the range of cases subject to *emmēnoi* provisions, modern scholarship has tended to avoid the question of ultimate purpose of the *dikai emmēnoi*—it has been satisfied to note the speedy procedure without ascertaining the reason for the speedy procedure.[35] However, there has been a parallel tendency toward assuming a commercial origin for the monthly suits,[36] despite the clear separation of a number of *dikai emmēnoi* from the commercial category.

The δίκη αἰκείας[37] [action of assault] stands out immediately as a suit belonging not to mercantile but to

---

Paris, 1897. Much information has been gained from the fragmentary mining leases unearthed by the excavations in the Athenian Agora; see M. Crosby, "The Leases of the Laureion Mines," *Hesperia*, 19 (1950), pp. 189-312, with full bibliography on important studies prior to that date. Historically oriented, R. J. Hopper's "The Attic Silver Mines in the 4th-cent. B.C.," *Annual of the British School at Athens*, 48 (1953), pp. 200-254, is invaluable.

[35] This phenomenon can be seen best in the encyclopedia articles: Thalheim in *RE*, s.v. ἔμμηνοι δίκαι; Reinach in *DS*, s.v. ἔμμηνοι δίκαι. Throughout his massive work Beauchet makes such statements as "Ces actions étaient considérées comme présentant un caractère particulier d'urgence et, à ce titre, elles étaient comprises parmi les *dikai emmēnoi*" (IV, p. 267, in reference to ἐρανικαὶ δίκαι), but offers no study of the *dikai emmēnoi* as a class.

[36] Thus Bonner and Smith (II, p. 5) muse: "The development of the monthly suits themselves must have been due to commercial reasons. They, like δίκαι ἀπὸ συμβόλων, could have been of consequence only after Athens had become an important trading center." Cf. L. Gernet, *Droit et société dans la Grèce ancienne*, Paris, 1955, p. 6.

[37] The spelling αἰκίας is certainly an erroneous form of the well-attested αἰκείας (cf. Lipsius, *AR*, p. 643, n. 25).

16

personal law. Harpocration defines it as a private suit arising from personal injury with variable damages.[38]

However the *dikē aikeias* had not always been *emmēnos*. About 346/5 the Forty had jurisdiction over these suits.[39] Accordingly the case described in Dem. 54 was submitted to public arbitration and was not heard under *emmēnos* provisions.[40] About 355, Dem. 43, also involving a *dikē aikeias*, was handled in the usual way, with required public arbitration and hence no rapid procedure. But by the time Aristotle's *Constitution of the Athenians* was composed, the *dikē aikeias*, in no way a commercial case, was included among the *dikai emmēnoi*.[41]

[38] εἶδος δίκης ἐστὶν ἰδιωτικῆς ἐπὶ πληγαῖς λαγχανομένης, ἧς τὸ τίμημα ἐν τοῖς νόμοις οὐκ ἔστιν ὡρισμένον, ἀλλ᾽ ὁ μὲν κατήγορος τίμημα ἐπιγράφεται ὁπόσου δοκεῖ ἄξιον εἶναι τὸ ἀδίκημα, οἱ δὲ δικασταὶ ἐπικρίνουσιν (s.v. αἰκίας). It was available against ὁπότερος ἦρξεν χειρῶν ἀδίκων (Dem. 47.7). Cf. Isocrates 20.1; Dem. 23.50; Dem. 47.15,40.

[39] ἡ αἴκεια . . . πρὸς τοὺς τετταράκοντα (Dem. 37.33). Cf. Scholiast, Plato, *Rep.*, 464E. On the date of Dem. 37, see Gernet, *Budé Demosthenes*, I, p. 229.

[40] For the date, see Paley-Sandys II, pp. 229 ff.; Gernet, *Budé Demosthenes*, III, pp. 100-101.

[41] The ultimate purpose of *emmēnoi* procedure aside, the reason for the transfer of the δίκη αἰκείας to the *emmēnos* category is not difficult to imagine, if all monthly suits were subject to the ἐπωβελία, as were the *dikai emporikai* (see below, p. 83). The *dikē aikeias* seems to have been available in roughly the same areas as the γραφὴ ὕβρεως. Thus the speaker in Dem. 54 (§1) says: πάντων . . . ἔνοχον μὲν φασκόντων αὐτὸν ἐκ τῶν πεπραγμένων εἶναι καὶ τῇ τῶν λωποδυτῶν ἀπαγωγῇ καὶ ταῖς τῆς ὕβρεως γραφαῖς, συμβουλευόντων δέ μοι καὶ παραινούντων μὴ μείζω πράγματ᾽ ἢ δυνήσομαι φέρειν ἐπάγεσθαι . . . ἰδίαν ἔλαχον δίκην. For the speaker, however, the real advantage of the *dikē* over the *graphē* was that the resulting damages from the private *dikē* were awarded

ANCIENT ATHENIAN MARITIME COURTS

The δίκη προικός [dowry action] also has no necessary connection with commerce, and it too may have become *emmēnos* at a late date. The case discussed in Dem. 40 concerns προῖκα [dowry] but underwent public arbitration (§§16-17), as did that in Dem. 41 (§12). Hence as late as 347 the δίκη προικός appears not to have been a monthly suit.⁴² Its inclusion in the category by the time of Aristotle shows further the ultimate non-commercial nature of the *dikai emmēnoi*.

The δίκη ἀνδραπόδων in some fashion concerns slaves. Traditionally it has been connected with the Solonian law holding an individual subject to double damages for harming a slave (οἰκῆος βλάβης τὴν διπλῆν ὀφείλειν).⁴³

---

to the private individual bringing suit, whereas generally in the public *graphai* assessed financial penalties went to the state. Further, in the *graphai* failure to take one-fifth of the votes meant a 1,000 drachmai fine. In normal private procedure no such danger loomed. Hence the young man's desire not to shoulder risks μείζω ἢ δυνήσομαι φέρειν. With the penalties, as Harpocration says, not being fixed, it was possible in the *dikē aikeias* to seek extremely large damages without personal danger. Hence, an invitation to συκοφαντία. A transfer to the *dikai emmēnoi* and the consequent danger of *epōbelia* (fine of one-sixth sum in litigation upon failure to take one-fifth of the votes) would militate against excessively large demands and against rash introduction of cases.

⁴² It is possible however that the δίκη ὑπὲρ προικός or περὶ προικός (vulg.) represented by these two cases is not the same thing as the δίκη προικός mentioned by Aristotle. If so, Dem. 40 and 41 offer no evidence for the monthly suits. See Harrison, *Family and Property*, pp. 50-52; Wolff, *RE*, s.v. προίξ (1957). The δίκη προικός is not to be confused with the δίκη σίτου, a suit against the husband for maintenance, not against dotal capital. Cf. Gernet, *Budé Demosthenes*, I, p. 37; Lipsius, *AR*, pp. 496-497.

⁴³ Lysias 10.19. Cf. Sandys, *Ath. Pol.*², note on 52.2. The so-

18

Similarly the δίκη ὑποζυγίων may be connected with damages done by beasts of burden. These cases are thus non-commercial.[44]

The other suits are similarly varied. Tax collections are not necessarily mercantile. *Eranikai* might refer to "friendly loans" or to associations of individuals. *Koinō-*

---

called *vindicatio servi* has also been offered as an explanation of the suit, the claim of a third party to ownership of the slave in question. See Beauchet II, p. 513; Lipsius, *AR*, p. 640.

[44] Pringsheim, *GLS*, pp. 472 ff., esp. p. 476, connects them with warranties against latent defects. Thus the δίκη ἀνδραπόδων would lie for restitution of the sales price where unseen defects known to the seller were not revealed at time of sale. The situation would be parallel in the δίκη ὑποζυγίων, *mutatis mutandis*. But if so, why the 30-day limit on completion of legal proceedings, instead of a 30-day *prothesmia* (time limitation) on the action dating from the time of sale? With the lapse of time, it would become more difficult to determine if the latent defect had already existed at the time of sale or was of later origin. Pringsheim sees the difficulty and seeks for this *dikē emmēnos* a different meaning than the one usual for the term, viz. an action "to be brought within a month of the sale of the slave" (p. 477). But this interpretation of *dikē emmēnos* would mean an impossibly short statute of limitations in most of the other monthly suits. In some of the other case categories, e.g. *eranikai* or *koinōnikai*, there would be difficulty in determining from what date the limitation ran (from the date of the purported wrong, from the date of its discovery?). Pringsheim also sees this difficulty and states, "I do not assert that my interpretation holds good for all the *emmēnoi dikai*" (p. 477, n. 4). The problem being such, it seems better to consider Aristotle's grouping of cases a homogeneous one, at least in respect to procedure: whatever definition is adopted for *emmēnos dikē* should be applicable to all such cases. Furthermore it seems likely that the action for unrevealed latent defects in slaves was a δίκη ἀναγωγῆς, not a δίκη ἀνδραπόδων. Cf. Caillemer, *DS*, s.v. *anagogēs dikē*; Beauchet IV, pp. 150-156; Lipsius, *AR*, pp. 744-45.

niai could lead to disputes non-mercantile in nature. It is hard to classify disagreements about trierarchic duties in the category of commercial litigation.

Speculation on Motivation Underlying Monthly Suits

What factor then unites the monthly suits? Why were certain cases singled out for special handling? Surprisingly, aside from a vague feeling of mercantile motivation, no suggestion has been offered for the existence of the *dikai emmēnoi.* There is, of course, no reason to posit a logical grand scheme for the origin and continuation of this summary procedure. In view, however, of the extensive and sharp Athenian delineations of trial procedure and magisterial jurisdiction, it seems reasonable to assume that the cases subject to *emmēnoi* provision were for some reason considered individually or as a group especially suited to summary action.

Our lack of knowledge concerning most of the monthly cases makes it impossible to determine whether the various suits shared procedural similarities other than speed. If, for example, the *epōbelia* was typical of *emmēnoi dikai,* the *dikē aikeias* might well have been placed in the category of monthly suits to discourage sycophancy by subjecting *aikeias* plaintiffs to the same risks of financial loss as in the public γραφαὶ ὕβρεως.[45] It is possible then that the *dikai emmēnoi* arose from some specific cause, perhaps mercantile commerce,[46] and that thereafter individual suits were added to the category, as experience showed that the monthly procedure would be beneficial in a particular type of dispute. Hence arose the phenomenon of cases that earlier

[45] See above, n. 41.
[46] See Gernet, *REG* 1938, pp. 10 ff., and below, pp. 158 ff.

in the fourth century had not been *emmēnoi* but had become so by the time of Aristotle (αἰκείας, προικός, ἐμπορικαί). The Athenians with their practical freedom from, or perhaps lack of, philosophical jurisprudence would have needed no Justice Holmes to teach them that "the life of the law has not been logic; it has been experience."[47]

Nonetheless, two factors seem to link the various suits in the *dikai emmēnoi*. One of course is commercial. Certain mercantile cases demand an expedient procedure in a court situation subject to long delays—in some areas business cannot be conducted unless disputes can be resolved with reasonable rapidity. Thus Calhoun notes for the mining cases, "The intent was obviously the speedy settlement of disputes that might hinder or retard the working of the mines, and it shows clearly the importance the state attached to this particular industry."[48]

The state, however, attached importance not only to industries and enterprises but to ethical norms as well.[49] Hence it is possible that certain offenses deemed of exceptional ethical importance were subject to summary procedure. Wrongs involving dowry, loans made between friends without interest, and assaults upon the person might be included in this category.

Rapid procedure claimed the attention even of philosophers and would-be reformers. Plato was against it: he saw extended litigation and repeated consideration

---

[47] *The Common Law*, Boston, 1881, p. 1.

[48] *Business Life*, p. 165.

[49] We need note in this regard only the existence of the γραφὴ ἀσεβείας (indictment for impiety). See Peter Fischer, *Die Asebieklage des attischen Rechts*, Erlangen, 1967.

as a prerequisite to a clear understanding of the dispute.[50] Xenophon in the *Poroi* appeals for a swift procedure in maritime commercial disputes: . . . τῇ τοῦ ἐμπορίου ἀρχῇ ἆθλα προτιθείη τις, ὅστις δικαιότατα καὶ τάχιστα διαιροίη τὰ ἀμφίλογα. . . . [Prizes should be offered to the harbor magistrate who most justly and quickly resolves disputes] (*Poroi*, 3.3).

The attempt to isolate the teleology of the *dikai emmēnoi*, however, must remain speculative, uncertain, and perhaps unavailing. There are many commercial categories, e.g., sale and hire, that could have utilized a rapid procedure but were not among the monthly suits. In the same way there are moral infractions prior in objectionability to dowry-disputes—murder, for example[51]—that were not subject to the summary procedure.

One conclusion is sure: cases in the monthly category were placed there because *some* advantage was expected from their admission to summary procedure. From the evidence now available, more cannot be determined.

[50] σαφὲς δὲ ἀεὶ τὸ ἀμφισβητούμενον χρεὼν γίγνεσθαι παρ' ἑκατέρων, ὁ δὲ χρόνος ἅμα καὶ τὸ βραδὺ τό τε πολλάκις ἀνακρίνειν πρὸς τὸ φανερὰν γίγνεσθαι τὴν ἀμφισβήτησιν ξύμφορον. (Laws, 766D-E.)

[51] In dealing with murder, the Athenians in fact showed great temperance in allowing an extended procedure. See Chapter 2, n. 114. But the moderation of procedure in homicide cases may have resulted from the likelihood that "the Greeks were not nearly so concerned with the taking of human life as with other crimes that we look upon today as far less heinous . . . among the Hellenes the punishment of homicide (was not) 'das Centrum des Criminalrechts.'" (G. M. Calhoun, *Growth of Criminal Law in Ancient Greece*, Berkeley, 1927, p. 85.) Long periods sometimes elapsed between death and prosecution. See D. M. MacDowell, *Athenian Homicide Law in the Age of the Orators*, Manchester, 1963, p. 10.

Basic Significance of "Emmēnos Procedure"

The *dikai emporikai* then were *emmēnoi* together with a number of other cases, all of which for no known single reason had been placed in a special category subject to rapid procedure. Unfortunately the nature of this rapid procedure has not received from scholars the careful treatment it merits.[52]

In fact the commonly accepted and often-repeated definition of the *emmēnos* procedure, cases that "had to be brought to trial within a month,"[53] is difficult to justify. Repeated since the earliest periods of scholarship on Attic legal antiquities,[54] the definition has not gained the strict acceptance even of its proposers, who postulate delays and exceptions to the monthly limit. Hence the "time limit" is considered not really to have been absolute.[55] Our sources however tell of no such exceptions.[56]

[52] Pringsheim is not unduly harsh in charging that the *emmēnoi dikai* have been defined "without precise formulation." *GLS*, p. 476.

[53] Bo.-Sm. II, p. 91.

[54] Thus *MSL* prior to the first publication of the *Ath. Pol.* are matter-of-factly defining "Klagen . . . die in Monatsfrist entschieden werden mussten . . ." (1887, p. 525).

[55] Thus Pringsheim, summarizing scholarly judgment, notes that "it seems to be the common opinion . . . that this period could be prolonged by agreement" (*GLS*, p. 476). Beauchet, in regard to *dikai emporikai* in particular, simply states that "Il est peu probable, du reste, que malgré le voeu de la loi, le jugement de l'affaire ait toujours pu intervenir le trentième jour de la demande au plus tard. Dans nombre d'affaires maritimes, en effet, il fallait aller chercher très loin les preuves nécessaires à la découverte de la vérité, et l'on ne pouvait matériellement arriver à juger la demande dans le délai imparti par la loi" (IV, p. 101). Cf. Caillemer, in *DS*, s.v. foenus, p. 1223.

[56] Thalheim, *RE*, s.v. ἔμμηνοι δίκαι, "Von einer Abweichung des Verfahrens bei diesen Klagen ist nichts überliefert."

It is imperative then to examine in detail the fundamental concept of *emmēnos* (monthly). For doing so, two roads lie open, and both must be taken. First, the basic meaning of the word itself must be explored, and then an attempt must be made *precisely* to understand the resulting definition in the context of fourth-century legal procedure at Athens.

The term *emmēnos* moves between two variant but closely connected meanings, as does the English word "monthly" and the modern Greek ἔμμηνος.[57] If something is *emmēnos* (monthly), it may "recur at monthly intervals" or it may "encompass a monthly period." Semantic difficulty however results from the possibility that something that lasts precisely a month, i.e. encompasses a monthly period, might happen more than once: when this condition presents itself, both meanings are at the same time necessary and appropriate, for from different aspects the same thing can be either "lasting a month" or "recurring at monthly intervals."

Thus the Liddell-Scott Lexicon (9th edition) offers two fundamental definitions of ἔμμηνος: "lasting a month" or "done *or* paid every month, monthly." But of the examples offered to illustrate the former meaning, the majority are equally applicable (or more so) to the latter. Thus Timaios of Lokroi speaks of a lunar period as *emmēnos* (ἁ μὲν ὦν σελάνα ποτιγειοτάτα ἐᾶσα ἔμμηνον τὰν περίοδον ἀποδίδωτι . . .) (96d). But this is a most indecisive citation, for a lunar "cycle" is the example *ne plus ultra* of the indivisible connection in real meaning between the two apparently disparate usages of the

[57] Ἔμμηνος is defined by the Modern Greek Τὸ Σύγχρονον Λεξικὸν Ἑλληνικῆς Γλώσσης, Athens, 1961, as an adjective of ancient origin employed in the modern καθαρεύουσα ("pure") language with the meaning "ὁ κατὰ μῆνα γινόμενος."

word *emmēnos*. Similarly a passage from Plutarch is cited to illustrate the definition "lasting a month": ἐμμήνοις ἡμερῶν περιόδοις κ. τ. λ. (Moralia, 2.495d), in reference to menstruation. The passage has been correctly translated, "it is nature's custom and care to discharge the blood at monthly periods,"[58] the basic meaning opposed to the one that the Lexicon is trying to illustrate. The problem is the same: the menstrual period occurs every month but also, from another aspect, lasts a month. What is sure is that the flow of blood itself does not last a month, a point that will be important in considering the time allowed for trial in the *dikai emporikai*.

Other occurrences are no less equivocal. Plato in the *Laws*, 956A refers to ὑφὴν δὲ μὴ πλέον ἔργον ἢ γυναικὸς μιᾶς ἔμμηνον [an amount of woven material not more than a month's production by one woman], again either the product of labor consuming one month, or, given the production in successive monthly periods, the output *each month*.

Of the citations meant to illustrate that which is "done *or* paid every month" most show the same duplicity of connotation. Thus Sophocles in the *Electra* (l. 281) mentions θεοῖσιν ἔμμην' ἱερὰ τοῖς σωτηρίοις [monthly sacrifices to the saving gods], for which variant scholia exist, illustrating both connotations of the word ἔμμηνος, but here mutually contradictory, κατὰ μῆνα (occurring monthly) and μηνὸς Γαμηλιῶνος (referring to a specific month).[59] Plato again in the *Laws* (828C) offers an example identical to that of Sophocles, and no more specific in possible suggestion: θύοντας τούτων ἑκάστοις

[58] Helmbold in the Loeb volume of Plutarch's *Moralia*.

[59] Manuscript R reads μηνὸς Γαμηλιῶνος, while L is less helpful or sensible with τὰ μηλίων.

25

ἔμμηνα ἱερά [performing monthly sacrifices to each of them].

The same is true of all similar references generally taken to illustrate the sense of "done every month." The distribution of grain in Rome was monthly, but was it meant to last a month or only to occur every month? Unless it were both, the people were being short-changed (cf. the σιτηρέσιον ἔμμηνον of Plutarch, *Caesar* 8.4, also mentioned by Pollux at 1.59). Theocritus says (16.35): ἁρμαλιὴν ἔμμηνον ἐμετρήσαντο [drew their measured rations month by month].[60] But the connotation is the same as that of the Roman σιτηρέσιον.

Nor are the medical writers of assistance in clarifying the usage. They make a substantive of the epithet and use it regularly for "the menses of women" (τὰ ἔμμηνα). Here too it must have both the connotation of "done every month" and the dual characteristics of "lasting a whole month" (the period) and "not lasting a whole month" (the flow).[61]

It is difficult immediately to see the connection between the two prime meanings of *emmēnos* and its supposed technical legal sense of suits "in which judgment must be given within thirty days."[62] A *dikē emmēnos* should be by linguistic analogy either a suit occurring every thirty days or a suit lasting thirty days. In fact, the former is the preferable meaning, and close attention to the implications of *dikai emmēnoi* occurring at monthly intervals does much to explain the procedural operations of Athenian courts.

As for the scholarly definition which has been handed

[60] Gow, *Theocritus*, I, Cambridge, 1952.

[61] Cf. Dioskorides "Medicus" 3.36 and elsewhere; Soranos IV.19 (τὸ ἔμμηνον).

[62] Liddell-Scott's definition.

down, we must note that it rests on no ancient evidence and is rather an extrapolation from the ancient sources, not a totally false one, but not a totally true one, and in some ways misleading. A preferable definition of *dikai emmēnoi* would be "suits for which complaints (λήξεις) were accepted at monthly intervals and expeditiously decided by a shortened procedure."

Neither of these definitions occurs as a lexicographical entry in the books of the later Greek authors normally responsible for our understanding of Attic legal antiquities. Harpocration and Pollux, generally the most reliable of the lexicographers, are of little help. Harpocration says only: EMMHNOI ΔIKAI : αἵ τε ἐμπορικαὶ καὶ ἐρανικαί· Δημοσθένης καὶ Ὑπερείδης. [*dikai emmēnoi: dikai emporikai* and *dikai eranikai.* Demosthenes and Hypereides.] while Pollux simply mentions ἐμπορικαὶ δὲ δίκαι ἔμμηνοι [*dikai emporikai emmēnoi*] (8.63). The *Lexica Segueriana* (237.33) does suggest strongly that the *dikai emmēnoi* were expeditious in procedure, for under the entry *dikē emporikē* we read: ἦσαν δὲ αὗται ἔμμηνοι ὑπὲρ τοῦ μὴ τρίβεσθαι αὐτοὺς δικαζομένους καὶ ἀργεῖν τῆς ἀγορᾶς [these were *emmēnoi* so that they might not be engrossed in litigation and be absent from the market]. Finally the late Byzantine compilation ἡ Σοῦδα, or Suidas, defines ἔμμηνα as κατὰ μῆνα, quoting Sophocles' *Electra*, 281, in clarification, precisely the indecisive passage considered above.

The likelihood remains then that the lexicographers were never concerned to determine exactly what a "monthly suit" was in fourth-century procedure. Either they did not know or did not care. A "monthly" suit is a "monthly" suit, and everyone knows what *emmēnos* means. Only Suidas caters to those given to overly fine distinctions and tells us that *emmēnos* means κατὰ μῆνα.

27

As for κατὰ μῆνα, when used by the orators or when otherwise appearing in a legal context, it seems clearly to have the notation of "month-by-month" rather than "lasting a month." In the fragments of the Code of Nikomachos (late fifth-century), discovered in the Athenian Agora excavations, there appears twice the "ek-rubric," ἐκ τῶν κατὰ μῆνα, necessarily meaning "month-by-month" in reference to sacrifices.[63] A similar citation, ἐκ τῶν κατὰ μῆνα, is known from an earlier fragment published by A. Hauvette-Besnault.[64] Again at Dem. 50.10, pay that has to be given month-by-month is termed τοὺς μισθοὺς οὓς ταῖς ὑπηρεσίαις καὶ τοῖς ἐπιβάταις κατὰ μῆνα ἐδίδουν [the pay which I gave monthly to the rowers and the marines]. Identically at 50.25 reference is made again to τούς τε μισθοὺς τοὺς τῇ ὑπηρεσίᾳ καὶ τοῖς ἐπιβάταις κατὰ μῆνα διδομένους [the pay given monthly to the rowers and the marines].[65]

Much later the Oxyrhynchus Papyri preserve the same definition in reference to payments to be made month-by-month (275, l. 18, 66 A.D.): here κατὰ μῆνα refers to a payment εἰς λόγον διατροφῆς δραχμὰς πέντε [a monthly payment of five drachmai on account of sustenance]. Again in a legal context, Pollux says of the Areopagos: καθ᾽ ἕκαστον δὲ μῆνα τριῶν ἡμερῶν ἐδίκαζον... [each month for three days they judged] (8.117). Since

[63] See J. H. Oliver, "Greek Inscriptions," *Hesperia*, 4 (1935), pp. 21-23; S. Dow, "The Law Codes of Athens," *Proceedings of Massachusetts Historical Society*, 71 (1953-57), pp. 15, 19-20.

[64] *Bulletin de correspondance hellénique*, 3 (1879), pp. 69-73.

[65] That it was a repetitive month-by-month affair is made clear by the immediately following reference to the two months μόνον when pay had been taken from the generals: παρὰ τῶν στρατηγῶν σιτηρέσιον μόνον λαμβάνων, πλὴν δυοῖν μηνοῖν μόνον μισθὸν ἐν πέντε μησὶν καὶ ἐνιαυτῷ.... (Dem. 50.10)

the number of days is separately noted (τριῶν ἡμερῶν), the κατὰ μῆνα must mean month-by-month.

The single most illuminating reference to emmēnoi procedure occurs however at Dem. 33.23: αἱ δὲ λήξεις τοῖς ἐμπόροις τῶν δικῶν ἔμμηνοί εἰσιν ἀπὸ τοῦ βοηδρομιῶνος μέχρι τοῦ μουνιχιῶνος, . . . [The complaints for the cases involving maritime merchants are "monthly" from Boēdromion until Mounichion, . . .] The passage is translated by Paoli: "le istanze per le cause dei commercianti debbono essere evase entro un mese nel periodo che va dal mese di boēdromione al mese di munichione."[66] This rendering carries the especially technical but purportedly correct meaning of dikai emmēnoi over into a case where the word emmēnoi stands alone and describes not dikai but lēxeis (λήξεις, i.e. complaints). This is an artificial transfer, and, as we have seen, there is little real support even for the translation of dikai emmēnoi as "cases in which judgment must be given within thirty days." It would be far more natural to translate "the complaints are [accepted] every thirty days, from. . . ."

Paoli himself observes the difficulties that result from treating the lēxeis as citations for cases that must be decided within a month. There is simply no reason for the supplying of information as to the months (ἀπὸ τοῦ βοηδρομιῶνος μέχρι τοῦ μουνιχιῶνος).[67] Paoli is correct in noting that such a translation conveys the suggestion that the commercial maritime courts were "emmēnoi" only during the months mentioned, but during the remainder of the year followed the usual procedure. The suggestion is untrue, for we learn later in the speech

[66] SPA, p. 177.
[67] SPA, p. 178.

29

(at §26) that these courts were active only part of the year.

This is the all-important matter: the passage as a whole makes sense only if we interpret *emmēnoi* in the natural sense of that word in legal context—occurring month-by-month. If the *lēxeis* were admissible month-by-month but only in *certain* months, then it must be stated what those months are. The speaker has no reason to conceal this information and gives us this important citation. It is a natural statement, if only *emmēnos* be given its natural interpretation.

The speaker in Dem. 7 (342 B.C.) opposes making commercial agreements (σύμβολα) with Macedonia, claiming that such agreements were not necessary in the past and are not necessary now especially since formerly the *dikai emporikai* were not regularly recurrent: ἐμπορικαὶ δίκαι οὐκ ἦσαν, ὥσπερ νῦν, ἀκριβεῖς, αἱ κατὰ μῆνα, ποιοῦσαι μηδὲν δεῖσθαι συμβόλων . . . (§12). The passage's contribution to a correct understanding of *emmēnos* is heightened because it does not define the *dikai emporikai* by the adjective in question (*emmēnoi*) but rather by the descriptive κατὰ μῆνα. In this context it is vital to note the adjective ἀκριβεῖς among whose meanings is that of "returning precisely at its time." Thus for the medical writers, ἀκριβεῖς describes a recurrent symptom. For example, Hippocrates in the *Epidēmiai* (1.24) speaks of a fever as τριταῖος ἀκριβής. This meaning of "recurring at a regular time" is exactly what would be demanded of monthly trials that are "held each month." Thus here both the "κατὰ μῆνα" and the "ἀκριβεῖς" argue for a simple and proper interpretation of *dikai emmēnoi*, not trials in which judgment must be given within 30 days, but trials recurring in a monthly pattern.

30

Another important passage is Dem. 37.2, which again is more consistent with a recurrent monthly trial procedure than with the accepted scholarly definition. There Nikoboulos insists that if Pantainetos had a valid case he would have brought it while the contract was in force since they were both in the jurisdiction and the courts were *emmēnoi*: εἰ μὲν οὖν ἐπεπόνθει τι τούτων Πανταίνετος ὧν νῦν ἐγκαλεῖ, κατ᾽ ἐκείνους ἂν τοὺς χρόνους εὐθὺς ἐφαίνετό μοι δικαζόμενος, ἐν οἷς τὸ συμβόλαιον ἡμῖν πρὸς ἀλλήλους ἐγένετο, οὐσῶν μὲν ἐμμήνων τούτων τῶν δικῶν, ἐπιδημούντων δ᾽ ἡμῶν ἀμφοτέρων. . . . In establishing the possibility of prosecution it is not germane to give a technical description of the *dikai metallikai*. What is vital is not a statement that the trials were subject to decision within thirty days, but that the complaints were being accepted at monthly intervals. The speaker says that (μὲν) the trials were occurring month after month, and (δὲ) we were both present in the city. The mention of repetitive opportunities for prosecution is more natural than the description of a particular judicial procedure, even if expedient.

The close connection of λῆξις with monthly procedure is further illustrated by the well-known reference to ἔμμηνα (monthly) procedure in the fifth century, IG I².65, ll. 47-49 (*ATL* II, D8).[68] In this citation we face public not private cases, and the fifth, not the fourth, century. Officials known as ἐπιμεληταί, restored with fair certainty from the preceding preserved text, are the administrators of the procedure. The ἐπιμεληταί are, however, nowhere else connected with monthly suits.[69]

[68]
47   Hο[ι δὲ ἐπιμελεταὶ ἐσαγό]
48   ντον ἔμμεϝα ἐς τὸ δ[ικαστέριον ἐπειδὰν Hοι κ]
49   λετêρες ἔκοσι. . . .
[69] Cf. below Chapter 3.

Nonetheless, the traditional interpretation has been put on the passage: "Cases . . . to be introduced . . . within a month."[70]

A more precise understanding of the text comes however only from observing the nearness of [κ]λητῆρες and ἔμμηνα in the preserved portion of the inscription. The κλητῆρες in Attic procedure witnessed delivery to the defendant of the summons to court,[71] the πρόσκλησις. Their connection with the monthly provision here indicates that the monthly period was connected with the lēxis in some way, as they normally might be liable for testimony at the hearing on the lēxis. The incomplete nature of the document together with an absence of explanatory materials makes it necessary to rely upon interpretations based upon otherwise known procedure. But if that other knowledge has been imprecisely stated, then the interpretation of the monthly provisions in the text of IG I².65 must be similarly imprecise. In formulating an exact interpretation of monthly suits, observation must be made of the connection shown in this fifth-century text between the presence of the κλητῆρες and the monthly provision. A wider conclusion goes beyond the evidence.

Another connection between the lēxis and possible monthly procedure is preserved in the seventeenth speech of Lysias, §5, a passage that demands our attention often in the study of the dikai emporikai: πέρυσι μὲν οὖν διεγράψαντό μου τὰς δίκας, ἔμποροι φάσκοντες εἶναι · νυνὶ δὲ λαχόντος ἐν τῷ Γαμηλιῶνι μηνὶ οἱ ναυτοδίκαι οὐκ ἐξεδίκασαν. [Last year they had my suit quashed by

[70] B. D. Meritt, Documents on Athenian Tribute, Cambridge, 1937, pp. 39-40.

[71] On κλητῆρες, see Lecrivain, DS, s.v., p. 826; Lipsius, AR, pp. 804 ff.; Harrison, Procedure, pp. 85-86.

claiming that they were maritime merchants; now the *nautodikai* have not adjudicated my complaint of the month Gamēlion.] The great importance of this citation is that it is symptomatic: it shows the difficulty inherent in the use of the regular trial procedure for commercial disputes and the fault that a rapid procedure might ameliorate. The case itself was of the type that later would have been subject to the commercial maritime monthly procedure [δίκη ἐμπορικὴ ἔμμηνος].[72] The *lēxis* here had been introduced in the month of Gamēlion, but some time later the case had not been completed. In other words, *the delay in maritime procedure had taken place after the introduction of the lēxis.* If procedure was to be expedited, then we might expect that the attack would be raised against the formidable battery of legal steps that had to be taken after the introduction of the *lēxis* before the presiding magistrate, in this case the *nautodikēs.* Again the mention of a specific month in reference to the hearing of the *lēxis* should be noted.

The *lēxis* then constitutes a fixed point in trial procedure. As Dem. 33.23 reports, the *lēxeis* are *emmēnoi.* As our sources show, the meaning of *emmēnoi* is probably "recurring every month."

The *nautodikai*, in their other role as presiding officials in γραφαὶ ξενίας, accepted the *lēxis* at recurring monthly intervals. Hence Harpocration quotes (s.v. ναυτοδίκαι) an inscription from the collection of Krateros authorizing the *nautodikai* to accept indictments against those usurping Athenian citizenship *on the last day of each month during the periods when the courts are in session*: ἐὰν δέ τις ἐξ ἀμφοῖν ξένοιν γεγονὼς φρατρίζῃ, διώκειν δεῖ τῷ βουλομένῳ Ἀθηναίων, οἷς δίκαι εἰσὶ, λαγ-

[72] For the equation of the court of the *nautodikai* with the emporic jurisdiction, see Chapter 3, pp. 176 ff.

33

χάνειν δὲ τῇ ἕνῃ καὶ νέᾳ πρὸς τοὺς ναυτοδίκας. It is difficult to suppress the suspicion, to which we seem inexorably led, that such a γραφή [prosecution] would have been termed *emmēnos*. Opportunity to submit a *lēxis* recurred monthly (κατὰ μῆνα)—this was the essential characteristic. Whether the further proceedings were or were not expeditive is superfluous to the definition of δίκαι (or γραφαί) ἔμμηνοι. Similarly the emporic cases heard by the *nautodikai* might have been termed *emmēnoi* if the mention of the month Gamēlion indicates that here too the *lēxis* was accepted monthly at an early period.

It seems likely that even in the fifth century the *lēxis* in δίκαι χρέως [actions of debt] also was received only once a month on a specific date, again the last day of the lunar period. Aristophanes several times suggests that the summons to court (πρόσκλησις) required an appearance before the magistrate on the last day of the month.[73]

To look more closely at specific procedure: the *lēxis* had been introduced, a trial date was set. But even in cases known to have been monthly, there was still some

[73]

Clouds:

1189	ἐκεῖνος οὖν τὴν κλῆσιν εἰς δύ᾽ ἡμέρας
1190	ἔθηκεν, εἴς γε τὴν ἕνην τε καὶ νέαν,
1191	ἵν᾽ αἱ θέσεις γίγνοιντο τῇ νουμηνίᾳ.

Clouds:

1220	. . . καλοῦμαι Στρεψιάδην.
	ΣΤΡΕΨ. τίς οὑτοσί;
1221	ΠΑΣ:
	ἐς τὴν ἕνην τε καὶ νέαν.

Birds:

1047	καλοῦμαι Πισθέταιρον ὕβρεως ἐς τὸν
	Μουνιχιῶνα μῆνα.

interval between the bringing of the case and the hearing of the arguments, enough to allow the parties to entrust the case to a private arbitrator and bypass the impending official litigation.[74] In cases that were not "monthly,"[75] there was generally a public arbitrator (διαιτητής),[76] who apparently was subject to no time

[74] Μελλούσης δὲ τῆς δίκης εἰσιέναι εἰς τὸ δικαστήριον ἐδέοντο ἡμῶν ἐπιτρέψαι τινί · καὶ ἡμεῖς ἐπετρέψαμεν Θεοδότῳ . . . (Dem. 34.18).

[75] An unconvincing attempt to connect arbitrators with dikai emmēnoi was made by T. D. Goodell, American Journal of Philology, 12 (1891), pp. 323-325. The whole concept of the expeditious procedure, no matter how precisely defined, makes public arbitration with its inherent and unregulated delay impracticable. Cf. Lipsius, AR, p. 228, n. 32. The emporic speeches, among the few pleadings considered with certainty to have been delivered at monthly suits, show no evidence of public arbitral proceedings. H. C. Harrell believes that the method employed for introducing evidence at Isocrates 17.37-38 shows that this "monthly" case could not have been heard before an arbitrator (Harrell, Public Arbitration, p. 36). Isocrates 17 however may not have been a monthly suit. At any rate, there exists no reason for inclusion of the dikai emmēnoi among the arbitrated cases.

[76] Cf. Ath. Pol. 53.1-7, which shows the wide range of cases coming before the Forty and the immediate relationship of the arbitrators to the Forty. Harrell summarizes the situation: "in, or shortly after, 403 B.C. . . . the public arbitrators were instituted, and a law was passed making arbitration compulsory for most civil suits" (Public Arbitration, p. 8). On the institution of δίαιτα in general, see B. Hubert, De Arbitris Atticis et Privatis et Publicis, Leipzig, 1885; B. Matthiass, Das griechische Schiedsgericht, Stuttgart, 1892; A. Pischinger, De Arbitris Atheniensium Publicis, Munich, 1893; R. J. Bonner, "The Institution of Athenian Arbitrators," Cl. Phil., 11 (1916), pp. 191-195; A. Steinwenter, Die Streitbeendigung durch Urteil, Schiedsspruch und Vergleich nach griechischem Rechte, Munich, 1925; L. Gernet, "L'institution des arbitres publics à Athènes," REG, 52 (1939), pp. 389-414; Harrison, Procedure, pp. 64-68.

limitation in rendering his decision—even the annual tenure of the position provided no check on the public arbitrator's employment of his "time prerogative." Aristotle specifically reports that in case of adjournments an arbitrator had to complete a case even though his year of service was otherwise completed.[77] A private arbitrator, once entrusted with a dispute, apparently was also free to consume as much time as he might like. Apollodōros complains of an arbitrator's delaying judgment until one of the parties died (at Dem. 52.15).[78] Hence a procedure that would eliminate the arbitral requirements would be *ipso facto* expeditious.

Fundamental Steps in Monthly Procedure

The usual private procedure (δίκη) involved:

1-ἡ πρόσκλησις (summons) (*prosklēsis*)
2-ἡ λῆξις (complaint) (*lēxis*)
3-ἡ ἀνάκρισις (examination) (*anakrisis*)
4-ἡ δίαιτα (arbitration) (*diaita*)
5-ἡ εὐθυδικία (trial proper) (*euthydikia*)

In contrast the monthly suits proceeded as follows:

A plaintiff instituted a *dike emmēnos* through the πρόσκλησις, calling the defendant or defendants to trial by a summons witnessed through κλητῆρες. Since the summons had to be served on the person of the defendant, the monthly suit could not even be instituted if the defendant was away from Athens and could not be served.[79]

---

[77] *Ath. Pol.* 53.5: ἀναγκαῖον ἃς ἂν ἕκαστος λάχῃ διαίτας ἐκδαιτᾶν.

[78] ἐπιτρέψαντος δὲ τοῦ πατρός, ὃν μὲν χρόνον ἔζη ὁ πατήρ, ὅμως καίπερ οἰκείως ἔχων τούτοις ὁ Λυσιθείδης (the Arbitrator) οὐκ ἐτόλμα οὐδὲν εἰς ἡμᾶς ἐξαμαρτάνειν.

[79] This was probably generally true in cases other than δίκαι

Once service was attained, the *lēxis* had to be drawn.[80] This statement of the issues seems to have been the essential "monthly" feature of the *dikai emmēnoi—ai lḗξεις εἰσὶν ἔμμηνοι.* On one day of each month the magistrate would accept (or reject)[81] the *lēxis.* Since the *anakrisis*, and not the presentation of the *lēxis*, encompassed the preliminary hearing or preliminary examination, an extremely large number of *lēxeis* could have been handled on the same day, as was apparently

---

ἐμπορικαί. But there were exceptions, as in the summons by εἰσαγγελία served on Alkibiades after the mutilation of the Hermai (Thuc. 6.61).

[80] The *lēxis* was a "complaint," somewhat similar to the classical Roman *formula*, although certainly more flexible in wording. A typical *lēxis* is that to which Stephanos offered his ἀντιγραφή in the δίκη ψευδομαρτυρίων brought against him by Apollodōros. We read: Ἀπολλόδωρος Πασίωνος Ἀχαρνεὺς Στεφάνῳ Μενεκλέους Ἀχαρνεῖ ψευδομαρτυρίων, τίμημα τάλαντον. τὰ ψευδῆ μου κατεμαρτύρησε Στέφανος μαρτυρήσας τὰ ἐν τῷ γραμματείῳ γεγραμμένα. <Στέφανος Μενεκλέους Ἀχαρνεὺς> τἀληθῆ ἐμαρτύρησα μαρτυρήσας τὰ ἐν τῷ γραμματείῳ γεγραμμένα. [Apollodōros, son of Pasión, of Acharnai v. Stephanos, son of Menekles, of Archarnai. Action for perjury. Damages: one talent. Stephanos gave false testimony, attesting to that contained in the memorandum.] And the answer: [I gave true testimony, attesting to that contained in the memorandum] (Dem. 45.46).

Another complaint is that found in the speech of Nikoboulos against Pantainetos (Dem. 37). It is, however, incomplete. It was read in portions (§§22, 25, 26, 28, 29) of which the final part is attested only by the rubric ἔγκλημα. Cf. also the γραφή preserved in Dionysios of Halikarnassos, *On Deinarchos*, 635. The most sensible discussion of written complaints (Die Klagschriften) in Athenian procedure is still that of Lipsius, *AR*, pp. 816 ff.

[81] As to the magistrate's powers when presented with a *lēxis* see Lipsius, *AR*, p. 845; Bo.-Sm. II, p. 75, n. 2; Calhoun, *Cl. Phil.*, 14 (1919), pp. 338 ff.; Harrison, *Procedure*, pp. 89-91.

the case with the δίκαι χρέως of Aristophanes' time. The date for the main trial could then have been set, and all the cases in the monthly category might have proceeded one after the other to hearing.

In all likelihood the sole delay in the Athenian system occurred between the receipt of the *lēxis* and the trial proper. The problem did not lie in an inadequate number of magistrates presiding over an extremely large volume of court business. The monthly trials, varied and vital, were almost entirely handled by the *eisagō-geis* (*Ath. Pol.* 52.2), and the *eisagōgeis*, unlike the other boards, which comprised ten men, numbered only five. There is no reason to assume that the trial itself was time-consuming. The speeches preserved are uniformly brief (by modern standards), and the very watching of forensic time by the water-clocks argues for a pressing concern with expediting procedure once the trial had begun.[82] In fact, it is generally believed that the hearing of any action that came before a court had to be completed in a single day.[83]

Delay in the courts thus arose at some point between the introduction of the *lēxis* and the opening of the trial proper (εὐθυδικία). An expeditious procedure hence must control in some way the arbitrator's unlimited time allowance—it must confound the opportunity for delay implicit in the *anakrisis*.

[82] There was certainly no shortage of jurors under normal circumstances: hence, the intricate process by which successful applicants for jury service were selected (*Ath. Pol.* 63 ff.). Only on extraordinary occasions did the courts run into difficulty in maintaining their normal operations. For suspension of private cases in the chaos toward the end of the Peloponnesian War, see Lysias 17.3. For a similar occurrence in the fourth century (caused by lack of funds), cf. Dem. 39.17.

[83] Lipsius, *AR*, p. 912; Harrison, *Procedure*, p. 161.

Possible obstructions aside, the vital point for an understanding of the monthly suits lies in the realization that they were monthly because their *lēxeis* were monthly. Why they were expedient, assuming that they were, arises from considerations apart from their name. We can no longer simply contradict normal philological usage and substitute for evidence our own ideas of necessary legal nature—we cannot define cases whose *lēxeis* were *emmēnoi*, cases that occurred κατὰ μῆνα, as "cases in which decision had to be rendered within 30 days."

It is highly likely that the decision normally was rendered within 30 days of the introduction of the complaint, probably within an even shorter period. In the cases definitely known to have been monthly (in particular those reported in the speeches, Dem. 32, 33, 34, 35, 37, 56) there is much discussion of the admissibility of the particular suit and of the legal concomitants ringing the dispute (except in 56, which is a straightforward argument on the facts, embellished only by rhetoric). While there are other reasons for this attention to juridical detail,[84] the factor compelling close oratorical attention to basic questions of venue and jurisdiction seems to lie in the lack of a previous preliminary hearing.

Gomme has correctly observed that the essential aim in an arbitral hearing was not the reconciliation of the disputants but the sifting of the facts.[85] All cases that went to arbitration nonetheless received an *anakrisis*. But with the long, involved, detailed arbitral hearing in the background, the *anakrisis* in the fourth century was basically a formality in cases subject to arbitration

[84] See below, Chapter 2, pp. 145 ff.
[85] A. W. Gomme, *Classical Review*, 50 (1936), p. 232

—the *diaita* replaced in effect the *anakrisis*. The arbitrator thus offered the possibility of a leisurely investigation, a full and generous procedure—precisely the barrier to expeditious procedure. The rapidity of the monthly suits arose from the removal of the arbitrator. Perhaps even the *anakrisis* was dispensed with, but for this we have no evidence.

The *lēxeis* then were necessarily accepted each month. There was no long wait before introducing a case—the opportunity was specific and recurred regularly. Once the *lēxis* was entered, the juridical procedure moved quickly. The case was not farmed out to an arbitrator for extensive and time-consuming investigation. And it is clear that if the procedure were to work well, the cases from one month would have to be finished prior to the acceptance of the *lēxeis* for the next month. The magistrate was under a powerful stimulus to complete his business, i.e. the trials, "within 30 days." He no doubt did. But this is not the same as defining the cases themselves as "suits in which judgment must be rendered within 30 days." The *dikai emmēnoi* were rather cases in which the *lēxis* was accepted monthly, where the procedure was expeditious through the absence of arbitration provisions, where the smooth workings of the court demanded that one month's cases be completed before the next cycle began.

ΑΙ ΤΡΙΑΚΟΣΤΑΙΑΙ ΔΙΚΑΙ

Similar only in name, the few "30-day cases" (τριακοσταῖαι δίκαι) known to us from the area outside Athens provide no suggestion as to the nature of the Athenian "monthly suits." Rather the fourth-century B.C. Tabula Heraclea and the fifth-century B.C. law for the Opountian Lokrians illustrate the exceptional conditions under which known "monthly provisions" occurred in other places.

The Tabula Heraclea speaks of τριακοσταίας δίκας whose precise nature is unknown.[86] It is clear, however, that they dealt with sacred law and with problems of land-tenure, two areas with which the Athenian monthly trials had no connection.[87]

Under the law establishing an Opountian Lokrian colony at Naupaktos,[88] a magistrate must bring to trial within 30 days those seeking to destroy the new colony through unconstitutional actions.[89] Again there is no

[86] R. Dareste, B. Haussoulier & T. Reinach, *Recueil des inscriptions juridiques grecques*, Paris, 1895, I, pp. 196 and 214:

FACE I:

48 . . . ταύταν τὰν γᾶν κατεσώισα-
49 μες ἐγδικαξαμένοι δίκας τριακοσταίας τοῖς τὰν ἱαρὰν γᾶν Ϝι
50 δίαν ποιόνταςσιν . . .

FACE II:

26 . .καὶ τοὶ μὲν ἐριξάντες ἀπέσταν, τοῖς δὲ ἐδικαξάμεθα δίκας
27 τριακοσταίας. . .

[87] In the ancient world to be sure the separation of the sacred and the secular law was not so great as in present Western law. See F. Jacoby, *Atthis*, Oxford, 1949, passim; S. Dow, "The Law Codes of Athens," *Proceedings of Massachusetts Historical Society*, 71 (1953-57), pp. 8-9, p. 35n.

[88] *Recueil des inscriptions juridiques grecques*, supra n. 86, I, p. 184 (XI, Face B).

[89] The provisions
"Οστις κα τὰ ϜεϜαδερότα διαφθείρει τέχνᾳ καὶ μαχανᾷ κα
ὶ μιᾷ, ὅτι κα μὲ ἀνφοτάροις δοκέει, Ὀποντίον τε χιλίον πλέθ-
ᾳ καὶ ΝαϜπακτίον τὸν ἐπιϜοίϙον πλέθᾳ, ἄτιμον εἶμεν καὶ χρέματα παματοφαγεῖσται. τὸνκαλειμένοι τὰν δίκαν δόμεν τὸν ἀρ-
χὸν ἐν τριάϙοντ' ἀμάραις δόμεν, αἴ κα τριάϙοντ' ἀμάραι λείποντ-
αι τᾶς ἀρχᾶς· αἴ κα μὲ διδôι τôι ἐνκαλειμένοι τὰν δίκαν, ἄτιμον εἶμεν καὶ χρέματα παματοφαγεῖσται, τὸ μέρος μετὰ Ϝο-
ικιατᾶν. . . .

connection with Athenian procedure. Everything is different—the law is public, not private; the concept of *lēxis* is absent; the case is as exceptional as the action it is meant to suppress.

A look at the situations envisioned by these Italian and Western Greek provisions reveals the variety of procedure that can be masked by similar terminology.

Emporic Cases Heard in the Winter

A knowledge of the procedure followed in the monthly suits explains a citation seemingly clear but recently the object of considerable discussion. The passage has been previously noted in other context, Dem. 33.23: αἱ δὲ λήξεις τοῖς ἐμπόροις τῶν δικῶν ἔμμηνοί εἰσιν ἀπὸ τοῦ βοηδρομιῶνος μέχρι τοῦ μουνιχιῶνος ἵνα παραχρῆμα τῶν δικαίων τυχόντες ἀνάγωνται. [The complaints for the cases involving maritime merchants are "monthly" from Boēdromion until Mounichion, so that attaining their rights they might sail without delay.] The emporic courts then were "monthly" only in the winter period: *lēxeis* for the cases were accepted by the magistrate only in the months from Boēdromion to Mounichion (c. September-c. April). Hence the merchants could trade unhampered throughout the summer sailing period while litigating during the winter. The passage and the purpose are reflected by the *Lexica Segueriana* (237.33) in its definition of the emporic process.[90]

The reference at 33.23 is confirmed by the invaluable citation at Lysias 17.5 telling of a *lēxis* introduced in the month Gamēlion in a case purported to be emporic: πέρυσι μὲν οὖν διεγράψαντό μου τὰς δίκας, ἔμποροι φάσκον-

---

[90] . . . ἔμμηνοι ὑπὲρ τοῦ μὴ τρίβεσθαι αὐτοὺς δικαζομένους καὶ ἀργεῖν τῆς ἀγορᾶς.

τες εἶναι, νυνὶ δὲ λαχόντος ἐν τῷ Γαμηλιῶνι μηνὶ οἱ ναυτοδίκαι οὐκ ἐξεδίκασαν. [Last year they had my suit quashed by claiming that they were maritime merchants; now the *nautodikai* have not adjudicated my complaint of the month Gamēlion.] At this time, early in the fourth century, the emporic courts did not yet possess an expeditious procedure (such as omission of arbitration). Still the *lēxis* was introduced in the winter. Taken with Dem. 33.23, it suggests that very early in the fourth century commercial maritime suits were being introduced during the non-sailing period.

The passage Dem. 33.23, seemingly so sensible and so secure,[91] has however been attacked as self-contradictory and full of "absurdities." Paoli has attempted to win from the citation a meaning precisely the opposite of that which the passage carries.[92] This feat is accomplished by reversing the names of the months and reading: αἱ δὲ λήξεις τοῖς ἐμπόροις τῶν δικῶν ἔμμηνοί εἰσιν ἀπὸ τοῦ μουνιχιῶνος μέχρι τοῦ βοηδρομιῶνος. The text thus altered announces that complaints were accepted for the commercial maritime courts only "from April to Sep-

[91] The classic statement of the seasonal pattern of the *dikai emporikai* is H. F. Hitzig's: "Für die *dikai emporikai* waren besondere Monate vorgesehen, die Wintermonate Boedromion bis Munychion; mit Beginn der Sommerszeit sollten die Fremden ihre Reise antreten können (ἵνα κ. τ. λ.)." SZ, 28 (1907), p. 228. For other phrasings of this orthodox position, see Lipsius, AR, p. 630; Thalheim, RE, s.v. ἐμπορικαὶ δίκαι. Prior to 1929 the passage provoked no controversy. See F. Meulemans and M. Verschueren, "Het nautikon daneisma te Athene," RIDA (3rd Ser. 12) (1965), pp. 164-165.

[92] See "Zur Gerichtszeit der δίκαι ἐμπορικαί im attischen Recht" in SZ, 49 (1929), pp. 473-477, reprinted as "Sul periodo di attività dei tribunali commerciali in Atene," in SPA, pp. 177-186.

tember" and that being "monthly" these cases were decided then "from May to October."[93]

Paoli's reversal of the text is a bold and unwarranted step. Against a clear, soundly attested textual reading, he suggests a highly unsatisfactory interpretation of what the judicial situation in the fourth century might have been, could have been, should have been. No consensus of modern authorities, however, can alter the necessity that not modern scholarship but ancient Athenians enacted the laws of fourth-century Athens, and that the scholar's task is to discover, not to write ancient Hellenic law.

Paoli however reversed the months solely on the basis of what he supposed to be a contradiction. The textual tradition, however, is totally opposed, and nowhere does Paoli offer a paleographical explanation for the initial reversal he attributes to the text as transmitted.[94] In fact, the alteration he proposed arises from a false understanding or at least imprecise definition of the *dikai emmēnoi*. The contradiction he discerned disappears if the monthly procedure of the emporic courts is correctly understood, and if their seasonal activity is interpreted in the correct context of the monthly suit.

The essential contradiction as seen by Paoli is the conflict between the courts' functioning in the winter and the purpose given for the winter operation—to make it possible for the merchants to sail without delay.[95] On the strength of this paradox and his reparatory

[93] *SPA*, p. 178.

[94] He says, "Io ritengo che la notizia sia degna di fede" and "Scarsa importanza ha la questione . . . se le parole . . . siano genuine o interpolate" (*SPA*, p. 178).

[95] "Scopo della *dikē emmēnos* è che il commerciante possa partir subito: παραχρῆμα ἀνάγεσθαι. Ma questo non è possibile se

reversal, Paoli's view has gained wide acceptance, virtually become orthodox.[96]

But the seeming contradiction is not in fact even a paradox. The manuscript reading is internally consistent—the best way the sea lanes could be kept open during the summer in the interest of merchants and traders was to hold emporic trials in the winter. The manuscript reading is externally buttressed: commercial trials in the winter are consistent with all else known about the emporic process. This can best be shown by a consideration of the external citations sup-

---

non nel caso in cui l'istanza sia presentata nei mesi dell'anno navigativo" (*SPA*, pp. 178-179).

[96] Thus Paoli in his republication (1933) of the original *SZ* article observed that his own view had now become "il comune insegnamento" because "le mie conclusioni non sono state combattute." Gernet in his recent Budé edition of Demosthenes comments on 33.23: "Nous avons interverti les deux noms de mois qui sont donnés par les manuscrits. Il y a lieu de penser que c'était pendant la saison de la navigation (entre avril et septembre) que les procès commerciaux se jugeaient: la raison d'être d'une procédure rapide instituée dans l'interêt des commerçants navigateurs ne peut guère se comprendre qu'à ce moment-là." Harrison, *Procedure*, p. 86: "Paoli has convincingly argued . . . that the passage should be emended . . . ." Typical of the view adopted by economic historians is that of Michell: "From a passage in one of the cases prepared by Demosthenes we hear that such cases were heard in the winter months. But (Paoli) has given excellent reasons to suppose that this was not so, and that the names of the months have been transposed." (pp. 349-350) Paoli's transposition has not yet penetrated to all non-specialist circles: cf. "Aperçu historique du droit maritime grec," *XXVᵉ Conférence du Comité Maritime International*, Athens, 1962, p. 2: "Ces procès . . . sont confiés à des cours speciales siègeant par ailleurs seulement pendant l'hiver, c'est à dire durant la période de l'interruption de la navigation."

posedly or actually relating to Dem. 33.23, and by an examination of the passage itself.

Certain references in ancient literature have been alleged to argue in favor of emporic trials held in the summer, specifically Plato, *Laws*, 915 C-D, Dem. 32.9, Dem. 33.25. Antithetically, certain references in Aristophanes' *Birds* have been considered to refer to commercial maritime courts as functioning in the winter. In fact, none of these passages is decisive. As a whole they are of slight importance in determining the season of activity in the emporic courts.

Plato, *Laws*, 915 C-D (termed by Paoli, "the strongest support for my view"): ἐὰν δὲ ὡς αὑτοῦ ἐφάπτηται ζῷον καὶ ὁτουοῦν ἢ τινος ἑτέρου τῶν αὑτοῦ χρημάτων, ἀναγέτω μὲν ὁ ἔχων εἰς πρατῆρα ἢ τὸν δόντα ἀξιόχρεών τε καὶ ἔνδικον ἤ τινι τρόπῳ παραδόντα ἄλλῳ κυρίως, εἰς μὲν πολίτην ἢ καὶ μέτοικον τῶν ἐν τῇ πόλει ἡμερῶν τριάκοντα, εἰς δὲ ξενικὴν παράδοσιν πέντε μηνῶν. ἧς μέσος ὁ μὴν ἐν ᾧ τρέπεται θερινὸς ἥλιος εἰς τὰ χειμερινά. [If anyone claims as his own the beast of any other man, or any other of his chattels, the man who holds it shall refer the matter to the person who, as being its substantial and lawful owner, sold it or gave it, or made it over to him in some other valid way; and this he shall do within thirty days, if the reference be made to a citizen or metic in the city, or, in the case of a foreign delivery, within five months, of which the middle month shall be that which includes the summer solstice.][97]

[97] A good neutral rendering by R. G. Bury (*Plato, Laws II* ("Loeb"), Cambridge, 1926). The passage is full of problems and has been, as Paoli notes, "molto variamente interpretato" (*SPA*, p. 181). The chief difficulties linguistically lie in the construing of ἀξιόχρεών τε καὶ ἔνδικον (see in particular Pringsheim, *GLS*, p. 435) and the interpretation of παράδοσιν. As

The passage certainly concerns cases of restitution involving defective ownership.[98] As such it has no connection with *dikai emporikai*. A time limitation for reference by "good-faith transferees" to their transferors is here established. In the case of "foreign delivery" the limit will apparently be two months after the month containing the summer solstice. This is a simple recognition that sailing is easier in the summer, and that restoration or reference in foreign cases takes longer than domestic transfers. To extrapolate from this passage anything decisive for the *dikai emporikai* is impossible. Not only are we in a different legal area but Plato's legislation in the *Laws* is far from a mere restatement of the law then prevailing in Athens.[99]

Another passage allegedly arguing for summer *dikai emporikai* is Dem. 32.9: τῶν ἀρχόντων τῶν ἐν τῇ Κεφαλλη-

England remarks in *The Laws of Plato*, II, London, 1921, p. 516, "It is, however, too much after stretching the meaning of παράδοσιν one way, to ask us to believe that ἧς—of which delivery—stands here for 'of which delivery-*period*.' I would suggest that ἧς is a mistake for οἷς. The utmost limit of time allowed for restitution would thus be two and a half months after the summer solstice."

[98] On such cases, see Pringsheim, *GLS*, "Warranty against eviction and against secret defects," pp. 429 ff.

[99] Paoli makes allowance for "qualche mutamento nei particolari," but concludes that "Nel libro XI Platone espone diritto patrimoniale attico, senza badare se questo si accorda o no con gli ordinamenti generali della futura colonia" (*SPA*, p. 182). Morrow's interpretation seems preferable in his description of Plato's "idealized Hellenic city, a city expressing as nearly as human institutions can, the type of character and of social life that the native gifts and long established traditions of his people, as he saw them, point to as the goal of their aspiration," an Athens only insofar as the real city met these ideals. *Plato's Cretan City*, Princeton, 1960, p. 592.

νίᾳ γνόντων ᾿Αθήναζε τὴν ναῦν καταπλεῖν, ὅθενπερ ἀνήχθη. . . .
[with the officials in Kephallēnia deciding that the ship should sail back to Athens, whence it set out.] Paoli asks why a commercial dispute would be settled in Kephallēnia in the summer and in Athens in the winter.[100]

The decision in question, however, appears not to have been juridical but administrative: hence the officials are termed ἄρχοντες (translated by Amit as "authorities").[101] The dispute involved is precisely of the sort that at Athens the ἐπιμεληταὶ ἐμπορίου would handle. Obviously the day-to-day settling of difficulties would be met from day to day, at Athens or at Kephallēnia, by the responsible officials. The Athenian *dikai emporikai*, of highly limited although extremely important scope,[102] were not necessarily subject to the same regulations as the acts of the administrative officials (harbor police?) at Kephallēnia.

The speaker at Dem. 33.25 refers to his adversary's failure to take prompt court action, and speculates on the causes for the delay: ἀλλὰ νὴ Δία εὐπόρως διέκειτο, ὥστ᾿ ἐνεδέχετο αὐτῷ καὶ ὕστερον ἐπ᾿ ἐμὲ ἐλθεῖν, τότε δ᾿ ἀσχόλως εἶχεν περὶ ἀναγωγὴν ὤν. [But, by Zeus!, he was well off, so that it was possible for him even later to proceed against me, and at the time he was busy about sailing off.] The reference is humorous and sarcastic, as Paoli himself says.[103] The irony increases if commercial trials actually were held in the winter: the defendant's excuse, unacceptable and impossible and for that reason sug-

[100] "non si vedono le ragioni per cui le decisioni di una controversia commerciale a Cefalonia dovessero avvenire d'estate e in Atene d'inverno" (*SPA*, p. 183).
[101] Amit, p. 134.   [102] See Chapter 2 below.
[103] *SPA*, p. 183.

gested by his opponent, would be yet more untenable. If commercial maritime trials were held in the summer, the defendant—even though poverty had deprived him of his possessions and forced him to sell his ship[104]— might still have been able to find some work at sea or perhaps have engaged in trade employing another's craft. Only if commercial maritime trials were held in the winter is the statement a perfect thrust.

So much for the passages allegedly demanding *dikai emporikai* during the summer; the citations quoted on the other side of the argument should be introduced. Unfortunately they are no more decisive.

The passage from Lysias 17.5, quoted above at p. 42, although not compelling, suggests that commercial courts were held in the winter. Two scholia to Aristophanes' *Birds* are important, but in a context different from that which has been given them. Thus the scholiast to *Birds*, ll. 1478-81, in explaining his author's comic remarks on the "Kleōnymos tree" and its respective summer and winter fruits indicates that during the "spring month" of Mounichion cases "against foreigners" were judged: τῷ γὰρ Μουνιχιῶνι μηνὶ τοῦ ἔαρος δικάζονται αἱ πρὸς τοὺς ξένους δίκαι. The month Mounichion falls at the beginning of the sailing season: its mention can argue either for or against winter cases concerning non-Athenians. However these cases πρὸς τοὺς ξένους, whatever they may have been (possibly *dikai* ἀπὸ συμβόλων or "citizenship cases"), imply nothing about *dikai emporikai*.

At l. 1047, *Birds*, Aristophanes writes: καλοῦμαι Πισθέταιρον ὕβρεως ἐς τὸν Μουνιχιῶνα μῆνα. [I summon Pisthetairos (to answer) for outrage in the month Mou-

---

[104] δι' ἀπορίαν ἐξειστήκει τῶν ἑαυτοῦ καὶ τὴν ναῦν ἐπεπράκει (§25).

49

nichion.] The scholiast insists, however, that Maimak-tērion was the month in which foreigners were summoned to trial.

The scholiast's correction has been questioned,[105] but inscriptional evidence of the fifth century supports the scholiast, not the author. Thus in a highly restored, but probably correct version of *IG.* I².63,[106] concerning tribute assessment for 425/4, it is commanded that it be announced in the cities that "ambassadors" should be present in the month of Maimaktērion: Ηοῦτ[οι δὲ ἀνει-πόντον ἐν τοῖ] κοινοῖ Η[εκάστες τὲς πόλ]εος πα[ρὲναι πρέ-σβες τõ Μαι] μακτεριõν[ος μενός (*ATL* II, A9, ll. 6-7). The hearing of tribute cases by the fifth-century Empire during the late fall-early winter in itself had no necessary influence on the procedure adopted at Athens in the fourth century for dealing with *dikai emporikai*. But it does establish the possibility that people could get from one place to another in Greece during the winter, as does the scholiast's statement at *Birds* 1047. While summer was the preferable time for sailing and certainly

---

[105] Paoli: "non c'è ragione di ritenere che l'errore di diritto sia imputabile ad Aristofane e non allo Scoliaste . . . lo Scoliaste non si appella a una personale conoscenza di diritto attico. . ." (*SPA*, p. 185).

[106] The probability arises from the persuasively sensible nature of the process envisioned by the total inscription as restored (*ATL*, II, A9). While on so fragmentary a stone a particular restoration at random is quite speculative, the entire text as restored makes good procedural sense and hence each part increases the likelihood of correct restoration of another section —provided that the entire process and each particular conform to the "control" of the letters remaining and to the sense of the entire decree. Our particular citation is required by the procedure involved, while the name of the month is on the stone. For a conception of the process envisioned by the document as a whole, see *ATL*, III, pp. 77 ff.

constituted the "trading season," there is little reason to suppose that all communication by sea ceased during the winter months.[107] In southern Greece and in Attic waters, the seas do not as a rule become monstrously rough during the winter. From the time of Hesiod on, the sailing season, as presented in our literary sources, is progressively extended.[108] Certainly some travel continued, and that is why tribute assessments could demand the presence of foreign ambassadors at Athens in the month of Maimaktērion. If necessary, merchants and shipowners could arrive in the same fashion. A good example is offered by the experience of Nikoboulos and his voyage to the Pontos in "March" 347: πραχθέντων δὲ τούτων ἐλαφηβολιῶνος μηνὸς ἐπὶ Θεοφίλου ἄρχοντος, ἐγὼ μὲν ἐκπλέων εἰς τὸν Πόντον εὐθὺς ᾠχόμην (Dem. 37.6). Conversely it must be assumed that he would have been able to come from the Pontos to Athens for the *dikai emporikai* functioning in that month.

Similarly the emporic contract cited at Dem. 35.10-13 envisions a return voyage from the Pontos commencing

[107] In the medieval period, for commercial purposes, the sea was "officially closed" from November to February. Cf. "Statutes of Pera, Ancona" (in W. McFee, *Law of the Sea*, London, 1951, p. 56). No such closing took place in the classical age. In fact, in Hellenic times, even the fragile triremes of the Athenian fleet were able, where necessary, to function during the winter. See A. J. Gomme, *Commentary on Thucydides*, II, Oxford, 1956, p. 709; Amit, p. 28.

[108] Hesiod's recommended sailing season is July-August. See *Works and Days*, ll. 663 ff.:

'Ήματα πεντήκοντα μετὰ τροπὰς ἠελίοιο,
ἐς τέλος ἐλθόντος θέρεος καματώδεος ὥρης
ὡραῖος πέλεται θνητοῖς πλόος κ. τ. λ.

Spring was a dangerous time for a voyage, and Hesiod advises against it (*Works and Days*, l. 686).

even after "the rising of Arktouros in the month Boē-dromion."[109] An actual Pontic voyage after Arktouros is mentioned at Dem. 50.19.[110]

In all probability, however, the great bulk of traders and merchants using the Attic market resided in Attica.[111] For them commercial trials in the winter would be pure boon. While the absence of reliable statistics makes it extremely difficult to arrive at a clear picture of the residence pattern of ancient merchants, the great number of metics living at Athens, the large number of preserved inscriptions dealing with *symbola* arrangements between Athens and other Greek cities, the practical exigencies of carrying on trade—all argue for a winter residence in Athens of numerous merchants and traders.

The Athenians were not unaware of the benefits to be gained through the permanent residence of useful foreigners in Attica. Long after the philo-metic policy of Pericles, Xenophon's *Poroi* argues for a positive correlation between mercantile prosperity and the number of foreigners arriving and settling in Athens.[112]

At least some foreign traders are known to have resided in Athens. The orators make the point that X could have sued Y in the emporic courts at an earlier

---

[109] Dem. 35.10: . . . ἐὰν δὲ μετ᾽ Ἀρκτοῦρον ἐκπλεύσωσιν ἐκ τοῦ Πόντου ἐφ᾽ Ἱερόν, ἐπὶ τριακοσίαις τὰς χιλίας. . . .

[110] καὶ ἐκεῖ περιέμεινα πέντε καὶ τετταράκοντα ἡμέρας, ἕως ὁ ἔκπλους τῶν πλοίων τῶν μετ᾽ ἀρκτοῦρον ἐκ τοῦ Πόντου ἐγένετο.

[111] Amit (p. 81) even suggests that since "the actual maritime activities were concentrated in Piraeus . . . people working in the harbor would prefer to live near the place of their occupation," rather than to live in the city (ἄστυ) of Athens itself.

[112] ὅσῳ γε μὴν πλείονες εἰσοικίζοιντό τε καὶ ἀφικνοῖντο, δῆλον ὅτι τοσούτῳ ἂν πλέον καὶ εἰσάγοιτο καὶ ἐξάγοιτο καὶ ἐκπέμποιτο καὶ πωλοῖτο καὶ μισθοφοροῖτο καὶ τελεσφοροίη (3.5).

period and had no excuse for not doing so, since both resided in the city at the time when the courts were functioning. When the orators indicate that X or Y is a foreigner, it is clear that the foreigner was in Athens during the winter, since during the summer sailing season a foreign trader would be engaged in his commerce and could not be normally characterized as "living in Athens."[113] Of course, a foreigner's coming to Athens for the trials is not ruled out by the statements of the orators, but the stress is rather upon the ease of litigation for those resident in the city.

A more concrete example is described in Dem. 56, where a case is brought against individuals who failed to honor a contract calling for delivery of Egyptian grain to Athens. They halted their journey at Rhodes. Their opponents charge that had they come to Athens, the winter would have overtaken them, and they would have had to reside at Athens instead of profitably continuing their trade by the Egypt-Rhodes route, which remained open throughout the winter.[114] Equity aside, the point remains: they were foreigners but they might winter in Athens.[115]

The use at Dem. 56.30 of the participle ἐπιδημήσαντας with the connotation of "wintering" should be noted. The same concept and the same terminology are applied to Apatourios, of Byzantine citizenship, whose suit is discussed in the paragraphic speech Dem. 33. His resi-

[113] An individual merchant might be away on voyages most of the year. Dem. 58.15: ταχύ γ᾽ ἂν οὗτος . . . ἀνθρώπων ὀλίγων φροντίσειεν ἢ τῶν τὸν πλεῖστον τοῦ χρόνου πλεόντων, ὥσπερ ὁ Μίκων
. . . .

[114] ἐκεῖσε μέν γε ἀεὶ ἀκέραιος ὁ πλοῦς, καὶ δὶς ἢ τρὶς ὑπῆρχεν αὐτοῖς ἐργάσασθαι τῷ αὐτῷ ἀργυρίῳ· ἐνταῦθα δ᾽ ἐπιδημήσαντας παραχειμάζειν ἔδει καὶ περιμένειν τὴν ἁραίαν . . . (30).

[115] Cf. Blass III.1, p. 583.

dence in the city at the time when the emporic courts were functioning is stressed, and the verb employed is ἐπιδημῶ. Thus, §25: διὰ τί πέρυσιν ἐπιδημῶν, μὴ ὅτι δικάσασθαι, ἀλλ᾽ οὐδ᾽ ἐγκαλέσαι μοι ἐτόλμησεν; καίτοι προσῆκεν . . . προσελθεῖν αὐτόν μοι ἔχοντα μάρτυρας καὶ ἀπαιτῆσαι τὴν ἐγγύην, εἰ μὴ πρωπέρυσιν, ἐν τῷ ἐξελθόντι ἐνιαυτῷ. [Why residing here last year did he not only not dare to go to trial against me, but not even to make a demand on me? Indeed it was proper . . . that he come to me with witnesses and demand the sum guaranteed, if not the year before last, then the year just past.] And at §26: ὅτι δ᾽ ἐπεδήμει πέρυσιν, ὅτε αἱ δίκαι ἦσαν, λαβέ μοι τὴν μαρτυρίαν. [To prove that he was here last year, when the courts were in session, read the deposition for me.]

The basic meaning of ἐπιδημῶ is to "remain" or "abide," not to "visit." This signification is especially clear when it is used of people who "come to a place to stay there," as at Dem. 59.37 and Aeschines 2.154. Similarly it is used of foreigners who come to stay or reside in a city (Xen., *Mem.* 1.2.61).[116] Hence merchants who ἐπιδημοῦσι can be expected to stay through the winter— they will be in Athens when the courts are open.

Winter residence could serve many purposes. The labors of trade do not cease when mercantile traffic enters its winter lull. Financing is to be arranged; plans to be made for the coming season. All this would be done most naturally in the economic center, Athens. Furthermore it is possible that merchants disposed of goods in retail trade during their winter sojourn in Athens.[117]

---

[116] The discussion in the Liddell-Scott Lexicon, s.v. ἐπιδημῶ, is clear. Cf. Thucydides 1.136; Plato, *Theaitetos*, 173E; Andocides 1.132, ἐ. τρία; Dem. 35.16, ἐ. Ἀθήνησιν; etc.

[117] Cf. Thucydides 3.74.2; Aristophanes, *Acharnians*, 974;

There is then no theoretical ground for anticipating the hearing of *dikai emporikai* during the summer. There remains accordingly only the text of Dem. 33.23 telling us that they were held in the winter.

The passage itself seems at first glance sensible—for that reason, no doubt, it went unchallenged for a hundred years. Any commercial litigation during the summer naturally interferes with trade—the less litigation, the less interference, and hence the conclusion that the most sensible arrangement for *dikai emporikai* would be to hold them in the winter.

Difficulties arise only if one insists on construing the participle τυχόντες in an emphatic sense of previous time, as does Paoli: "le istanze per le cause dei commercianti debbono essere evase . . . affinchè, ottenuta giustizia, possano subito rimettersi in mare" (*SPA*, p. 177). There rises to mind then a particular case: a merchant comes to trial, finishes the litigation by expedient procedure, and thereafter immediately (παραχρῆμα) goes to his ship in order to sail off (ἵνα ἀνάγωνται). The comic denouement: he can't, because it is winter. The trading season is over. The merchant has been tricked. This is a useless expeditious procedure.

Such a vignette is not however the subject of our citation. General procedure—not an individual case—is under discussion. The participle τυχόντες, like all participles in ancient Greek, does not primarily indicate time-relationship between the subordinate and the main actions—it could, but need not, and here does not, emphasize aspect. The picture drawn is a general one—

Aristotle, *Oeconomica*, 1347b; Dem. 35, passim. See M. I. Finkelstein, "Ἔμπορος, Ναύκληρος and Κάπηλος," *Cl. Phil.*, 30 (1935), pp. 335-336. On the mechanics of retail trade at Athens see Gofas, pp. 41-49.

merchants are both able to sail the seas without losing time *and* to solve their legal problems. The purpose served by the monthly introduction of the *lēxis* from Boēdromion to Mounichion is, "in order that attaining their rights they might sail without delay." We may either consider the participle as without time implication (neither present, past, nor future) or we may entirely reverse the meaning of the citation by transposing the months without textual, historical, or legal justification. The former course seems preferable.

The passage is thus consistent: it envisions the long-term process of merchants obtaining justice (during the winter) and sailing without impediment (during the summer). This is why the *lēxeis* were monthly from "September to April," and it is the "from September to April" that the "*ἵνα*-clause" attempts to explain. The passage makes perfectly good sense and contains no inconsistency. Athens has provided an extremely advantageous device for merchants using her port—winter commercial trials, meeting the dual purposes of maximum trade and minimum legal interference with that trade.

It is here that an understanding of the *dikai emmēnoi* procedure clarifies the functioning of winter *dikai emporikai*. The normal quarrels and differences, inevitably arising in the conduct of trade no less than in other human activities, were handled through the disciplinary action of the administrative officials of the harbor, ἐπιμεληταὶ ἐμπορίου. Non-maritime disputes arising among commercial people were subject to the otherwise prevailing judicial channels at Athens. The complicated questions of finance, in litigation arising from a written contract providing for transportation of goods to or from

Athens, were alone admissible to the *dikai emporikai*.[118]
These cases, extremely important but limited in nature,
were handled in the winter. There would be no halting
of trade while creditor and borrower litigated—even
assuming that *dikai emmēnoi* could be completed within a month, the loss of thirty days from a sailing season
only five months long would be a harsh interference
with commercial activity. Heard in the winter, with
complaints introduced each month and the magistrates
impelled to rapid solution of the cases, all commercial
disputes of the type admissible as *dikai emporikai* would
be settled during the off-season.

It is probable that non-Athenians could be held to
bail in commercial cases.[119] It is not true, however, that
winter commercial maritime cases meant possible
months in prison for an alien awaiting commercial trial.
Since the *dikai emporikai* could not be initiated during
the summer, no merchants could be held to bail for
long periods, awaiting winter trial for summer offenses.[120]

Now we see the full subtlety of the procedure. To
effect a foreigner's presence at a *dikē emporikē*, the
summons ($\pi\rho\acute{o}\sigma\kappa\lambda\eta\sigma\iota\varsigma$) could be served on him during
the sailing-season. He would then be free to conduct his

[118] See Chapter 2 below.

[119] εἰ γὰρ μὴ δι᾽ ὑμῶν ἔρημος ἐγίγνεθ᾽ ἡ δίκη, ἅμ᾽ ἂν αὐτὸν προσεκαλοῦ καὶ κατηγγύας πρὸς τὸν πολέμαρχον, καὶ εἰ μὲν κατέστησέ σοι
τοὺς ἐγγυητάς, μένειν ἠναγκάζετ᾽ ἄν, ἢ σὺ παρ᾽ ὧν λήψει δίκην ἑτοίμους
εἶχες. εἰ δὲ μὴ κατέστησεν, εἰς τὸ οἴκημ᾽ ἂν ᾔει (Dem. 32.29). See
below, "Rigor," p. 74.

[120] Thus Paoli's remark is not valid: "il commerciante convenuto dovesse ugualmente rassegnarsi o a farsi condannare in
contumacia o a non partire" (*SPA*, p. 179), if the trials were held
in the winter.

trade during the summer, but would have to appear at the earliest opportunity for presentation of a *lēxis* in the month of Boēdromion. If he normally resided in Athens, as was likely, he could then appear without difficulty; if not, he would have to remain for the hearing, but could leave Athens when the litigation was concluded.[121] If the foreigner failed to appear at the hearing, he would then be liable to personal constraint through the polemarch. A merchant so summoned conceivably could avoid trial if he never returned to Athens—but this would necessitate surrender of his livelihood (commerce at Athens) in order to avoid Athenian jurisdiction. In most cases this would in itself constitute severe punishment. If however he returned to Attica in the summer for a commercial undertaking he would then be subject to personal constraint. Even then however it is unlikely that he would have to remain in prison (failing bail) until the following winter. It is the *lēxis* that is *emmēnos* in the winter months. Once the *lēxis* had been introduced in the winter, the trial might legally have taken place in the summer. This would of course be exceptional. We do not know for certain that such trials did take place—but the mere possibility shows the range and scope of opportunity for meaningful regulation of trade agreements by commercial courts hearing suits whose *lēxeis* must be introduced in the winter.

In all likelihood, since the *dikai emporikai* dealt with contractual matters, a number of disputes would arise during the winter when contracts were being checked or made, when merchant and creditor had opportunity to take stock of the past year's, or to plan for next year's, business activity. Hence a number of *lēxeis* would be

[121] In the Peiraeus inns and hotels were numerous. Amit, p. 83. Cf. Xen., *Poroi*, 3.12.

ready for presentation each month during the winter season, and the courts would operate on a recurring pattern during the months from Boēdromion to Mounichion. The process was altogether workable, consistent with its purpose, and compact in its detail. This piece of legal history need not be rewritten. It can stand precisely as recorded at Dem. 33.23.

SUPRANATIONALITY

Another departure of the *dikai emporikai* from the otherwise prevailing civil procedure lay in the admission of individuals to litigation without regard to nationality.

Accordingly at Dem. 21.176 we learn of an Athenian commercial trial involving two foreigners, Evander of Thespiai and Menippos of Karia. Foreigners appear as litigants in full standing in Dem. 32 (Massiliots), 33 (Byzantines), 35 (Phaselites). In the speeches at Dem. 34 and 56, the individuals involved include both metics and non-metic foreigners.[122] This supranational aspect of the commercial courts has long been recognized,[123] but there has been little exploration of the background against which and the milieu in which Athens came to separate her commercial (i.e. commercial maritime) from her civil pro-

[122] For a more detailed analysis of the persons involved in *dikai emporikai* and their personal status, see below, "Non-Existence of a 'Commercial Class,'" p. 114.

[123] See H. F. Hitzig, SZ, 28 (1907), p. 228: "Zur Zeit des Demosthenes macht es für die Gerichtsorganisation keinen Unterschied, ob die Parteien in den *dikai emporikai* Bürger oder Fremde sind; die Gerichtsvorstandschaft haben in einem und im anderen Fall die Thesmotheten." Cf. Paoli, SDA, pp. 88 ff.

cedure, departing from the otherwise inflexible dictum that, special international agreements excepted, admission to the court of a *polis* required membership in that *polis*.[124]

One view would make Athens' disregard of nationality in the fourth century B.C. a pioneering step in the development of legal institutions probably attained by Athens alone, since evidence indicates that even in Hellenistic times certain cities in Asia Minor were entering into special bilateral arrangements, συμβολαί, providing for the admission of each other's citizens to the local courts.[125] At the other extreme it has been contended that even in the fifth century various states in the Hellenic world "did not entirely deny access to their courts to foreigners belonging to states which had not entered into συμβολαί with them."[126]

Both beliefs are predicated on insufficient evidence. The existence of συμβολαί has no necessary relationship to the existence or non-existence of commercial maritime courts freely open to international litigation. The greatest profusion of extant συμβολαί dates precisely

---

[124] Aristotle, *Politics*, 1275a: πολίτης δ' ἁπλῶς οὐδενὶ τῶν ἄλλων ὁρίζεται μᾶλλον ἢ τῷ μετέχειν κρίσεως καὶ ἀρχῆς. For κρίσις as right to litigate rather than power of judge, see Paoli, *SDA*, pp. 283 ff. The status of metics at Athens is both exceptional and doubtful— how exceptional in juridical procedure the *Ath. Pol.* makes clear, καὶ τἄλλ' ὅσα τοῖς πολίταις ὁ ἄρχων, ταῦτα τοῖς μετοίκοις ὁ πολέμαρχος (58.3). Debate continues on the metic's need of a προστάτης in normal litigation: cf. Paoli, *SDA*, p. 89, n. 1; Lipsius, *AR*, p. 622, p. 791, n. 10; Harrison, *Family and Property*, pp. 190-192; Clerc, *Les Métèques*, pp. 260 ff.

[125] Gernet, *REG* 1938, pp. 14-15.

[126] G. E. M. de Ste. Croix, *Classical Quarterly*, 11 (1961), p. 111.

from the period in which the supranational courts were in operation (mid-fourth century) and specifically from the supposedly sole state possessing supranational maritime courts, Athens.[127] Aristotle in the *Ath. Pol.* does not judge the two institutions incompatible: he assigns to the *thesmothetai* jurisdiction over both the *dikai* ἀπὸ συμβόλων (59.6) and the *dikai emporikai* (59.5).

A general *forum concursus* principle of admitting plaintiffs to local courts without reference to treaty arrangements and without requirement of local citizenship is not established by the single evidence suggesting it, the statement at Dem. 7.13 that the Athenians, before the establishment of regularly recurring *dikai emporikai*, had brought suits under Macedonian law, and the Macedonians, under Athenian law.[128] The truth of the text is too insecurely attested to establish even a limited *forum concursus* between Macedonians and Athenians in the fifth century B.C.[129]

[127] A. G. Woodhead, "Greek Inscriptions," *Hesperia*, 26 (1957), pp. 221-233. These inscriptions (*SEG* XVII. 17-20) together with *IG* II².179 (Naxos) constitute a corpus of mid-fourth-century Athenian decrees on συμβολαί arrangements. The only other Attic inscription known to contain similar provisions is the Phaselis decree—for its fifth-century date, see below, Chapter 3, n. 60, p. 183.

[128] ἀλλ' ἡμεῖς τε τοῖς ἐκεῖ νομίμοις ἐκεῖνοί τε τοῖς παρ' ἡμῖν τὰς δίκας ἐλάμβανον.

[129] Even de Ste. Croix qualifies his "direct evidence" by the condition "If the speaker can be trusted. . . ." However he believes the passage under any condition only confirms "what we would have surmised anyway." (*Classical Quarterly*, 11 (1961), p. 111.) Gomme believes the citation wholly lacking in historical validity: "we may doubt the truth of a passage which includes the statement ὑφ' ἡμῖν γὰρ ἦν ἡ Μακεδονία καὶ φόρους ἡμῖν ἔφερον." (*Commentary on Thucydides*, I, Oxford, 1944, p. 238.) The pas-

For the fourth century, however, a limited *forum concursus* in maritime disputes is revealed by a dual investigation of the overall nature of private international law (whose dominant component today as in Hellenic times is commercial maritime law) and of the commercial procedure prevailing in Hellenic states during the fourth century B.C. Both areas, taken together or analyzed separately, strongly suggest that Athens either deviated from her otherwise prevailing "closed" litigation in the face of an "open" maritime procedure universally recognized and sanctioned by custom, or that the Athenian innovation of supranational commercial courts was immediately and widely adopted in the Aegean.

Nature of Commercial Maritime Law

The procedural separation of "commercial" and "civil" law has long been recognized in modern juristic thinking.[130] Admiralty procedure in the United States of America for example contrasts with normal civil procedure most spectacularly in its simplicity—there is no jury, witnesses need not be present, the hearing is rigorously restricted to the issue at question.[131] In fact, the U.S. Supreme Court, in an important modern case, cited Admiralty Law's "traditions of simplicity and practicality" in refusing to extend the complex common

---

sage is treated in detail by A. R. W. Harrison, *Classical Quarterly*, 10 (1960), pp. 248 ff.

[130] For an historical summary of scholarly opinion, see M. Rotondi, "L'autonomia del codice di commercio nei lavori della Commissione reale per la riforma dei codici," *Studi dedicati alla memoria di P. P. Zanzucchi*, Milan, 1927.

[131] Cf. W. McFee, *The Law of the Sea*, London, 1951, pp. 13-14.

law of trespassary classifications to an accident suffered aboard ship in a U.S. harbor by a "social invitee."[132] This modern separation has often been ascribed to a simple historical development, the division of the two procedures during the Middle Ages and the consequent continuation of the dichotomy in subsequent Western systems.[133] In contrast, the variation has been ascribed by others to the inherent nature of commerce: "business demands" will necessitate in any mature legal system a variation in procedure from that found in the "civil" area.[134] Support for both positions can be won from the Athenian *dikai emporikai,* so different from the typical Attic *dikē* and even significantly at variance with other Attic commercial case categories.[135]

The peculiar procedural characteristics of emporic cases developed in a legal system that had attained considerable sophistication in its commercial maritime regulations. *Prima facie,* this suggests an inherent cause of variation contingent on a certain degree of maturity

[132] Kermarec v. Compagnie Generale, 378 U.S. 625 (Sup. Ct. 1958).

[133] For typical views, see Finzi, "Verso un nuovo diritto del commercio," *Archivio di Studi corporativi,* 4 (1933), fasc. 2, p. 9; T. Ascarelli, "La funzione del diritto speciale e le transformazioni del diritto commerciale," *Rivista del Diritto commerciale e del Diritto generale delle obbligazioni,* 33 (1934), #1 & #3, p. 1, pp. 2 ff.

[134] See U. E. Paoli, *Atti, Associazione Italiana di Diritto Marittimo,* 1 (1934), pp. 165 ff.

[135] The further question of the difference in procedure in *maritime* commerce as contrasted with other commercial categories has not been fully developed in the long discussion of procedural commercial law. The central factor here lies in the ambivalent position of maritime law, inherently a constituent of "international" law but no less implicitly connected with commercial law.

of the economic system and a sophistication in the legal system—perhaps these two developments are interdependent. Against this view stands the fact of an actual historical connection between Greek law and modern commercial maritime law.[136] Perhaps those seeing a simple historical connection have isolated a true link— they simply have not gone back far enough in their quest for a historical source. The wider question of historical vs. inherent origin of a separate commercial procedure remains unresolved.[137]

Two other characteristics of modern private maritime law shed useful light on the origin of the supranational status of the Athenian *dikai emporikai*: the great importance of "custom" in shaping maritime procedure, and the high influence of the great maritime powers in formally legitimatizing that custom. These two factors, together with the autonomy of the commercial from the civil procedure, are of virtually the same significance in an analysis of fourth-century as well as modern maritime commerce.

The importance of "custom"[138] in shaping all facets of

[136] See above, pp. 4-6.

[137] The two procedures are not of course entirely independent. For a possible connection (i.e. the concept of πίστις or *fides*) between the civil and commercial procedure in the fourth century, see L. Gernet, "Droit commercial et droit civil en Grèce," *Revue historique de droit français et étranger*, 29 (1951), p. 457.

[138] For general discussions of "custom" in private international law, see W. W. Bishop, Jr., *International Law*, Boston, 1971, pp. 26-33; H. W. Briggs, *The Law of Nations*, New York, 1953, p. 46; I. Spyropoulos, *Théorie générale du droit international*, Paris, 1930, pp. 83-114; Finch, "Les sources modernes du droit international," *Recueil*, 53 (1935), pp. 581 ff.; A. Alvarez, *Exposé de motifs et déclarations des grands principes du droit international moderne*, 1936, articles 5-9.

international intercourse has received its classic expression from Chief Justice John Marshall of the United States Supreme Court: "the usage of nations becomes law and that which is an established rule of practice is a rule of law."[139]

In transforming that custom into recognized legal procedure acceptable to all nations or at least sanctioned by most, the actions of the great maritime powers are of vital importance.[140] In the modern world, so predominant has been the influence of Great Britain and the United States that "no novel principle of international maritime law can be considered as of universal application unless accepted by these two countries."[141] For most of the fourth century B.C. the *polis* of the Athenians could claim a similarly predominant position in determining international principles.[142]

Athens' Great Interest in Regulating Commerce

The overwhelming commercial power of Athens[143] was accompanied by an exceptional interest in the regulation of private international law, if not exclusively in her own narrow interest, at least not against her interest.[144] The economic conditions under which Greek

[139] United States v. Percheman, 7 Peters 51 (U.S. Sup. Ct. 1833).

[140] C. J. Columbos, *International Law of the Sea*, 6th ed., London, 1967, p. 10.

[141] *Ibid.*

[142] For most of this period the Athenian navy was also preeminent. See Amit, pp. 24-26. During the struggle with Philip of Macedon, Demosthenes was able to boast that Athens possessed more ships than ever before. Dem. 9.40.

[143] See above, pp. 6-8.

[144] In this she followed Aristotle's dictum that one duty of the state is to pay proper heed to commerce: (It is necessary to know)

civilization functioned demanded such attention to trade. No state was self-sufficient,[145] and so trade was certain to be of great importance.[146] The ideal of self-sufficiency had always to be tempered by a practical dependence upon soil outside the political control of even the strongest Hellenic military or commercial power.[147]

ἔτι δὲ περὶ τροφῆς πόση δαπάνη ἱκανὴ τῇ πόλει καὶ ποία, ἡ αὐτοῦ τε γιγνομένη καὶ εἰσαγώγιμος, καὶ τίνων τ' ἐξαγωγῆς δέονται καὶ τίνων εἰσαγωγῆς, ἵνα πρὸς τούτους καὶ συνθῆκαι καὶ συμβολαὶ γίγνωνται . . . (Aristotle, Rhet., 1360a).

[145] Ἔτι δὲ τὴν χώραν οὐκ αὐτάρκη κεκτημένων ἑκάστων, ἀλλὰ τὰ μὲν ἐλλείπουσαν, τὰ δὲ πλείω τῶν ἱκανῶν φέρουσαν, καὶ πολλῆς ἀπορίας οὔσης τὰ μὲν ὅπου χρὴ διαθέσθαι, τὰ δ' ὁπόθεν εἰσαγαγέσθαι. . . . (Isocrates 4.42). The Old Oligarch (2.12) says virtually the same thing: οὐδ' ἔστι τῇ αὐτῇ ξύλα καὶ λίνον, ἀλλ' ὅπου λίνον ἐστί πλεῖστον, λεία χώρα καὶ ἄξυλος· οὐδὲ χαλκὸς καὶ σίδηρος ἐκ τῆς αὐτῆς πόλεως οὐδὲ τἆλλα δύο ἢ τρία μιᾷ πόλει, ἀλλὰ τὸ μὲν τῇ, τὸ δὲ τῇ.

[146] There is no need to continue the old Meyer-Bücher disagreement on the significance of trade in the Hellenic world, least of all the dispute concerning the applicability of modern concepts to ancient commerce. The discussion came to a head with the series of publications by Hasebroek in the 1920's and early 1930's (following ground broken by Bolkestein), and was resolved by the overwhelming decisiveness of the criticism evoked by Hasebroek's theses. A middle ground now seems generally accepted: care must be exercised in employing modern terminology in the description of ancient economic phenomena, but the essential significance of trade in the ancient world cannot be doubted. See in particular Gomme, Essays, pp. 42-67. For a summary of varied views prior to the 1940's, see Rostovtzeff, SEHHW, III, pp. 1327-1328, n. 25. Cf. Amit, p. 57, n. 3.

[147] The philosophical idea of autarkeia expressed in the works of Aristotle and Plato was more than an intellectual concept— Greek policy was probably motivated by it in some degree, at least in the so-called "commercial" states. See M. Wheeler, "Self-Sufficiency and the Greek City," Journal of the History of Ideas, 16 (1955), pp. 416-420. But no state attained true self-suffi-

Under such conditions, the Athenian state not surprisingly took a substantial interest in commerce. The operation of the fifth-century Empire, as we have seen,[148] provided her with an abundant variety of material goods from all parts of the Aegean and beyond. Even at this time, the Methone decrees show the importance of imported grain to the Athenian economy.[149] It was this food supply that in the troubled fourth century demanded from Athens a continuing concern of the highest priority.

Because of her food requirements, Athens had always been favorably disposed toward her overseas merchants. Such a motivation could be appealed to in litigation—thus the speaker at Lysias 22.17 warns the jurors of the "impossibility" of acquitting defendants who had confessed to conspiring against the maritime traders—such an acquittal would appear to be a blow against the importers.[150] Such motivation substantially affected Athenian political and legal measures in the fourth century. A wise political policy mixing potential naval pressure with personal honors for benefactors of the Demos ($\epsilon \vec{v} \epsilon \rho \gamma \acute{\epsilon} \tau \eta s$) helped insure sources

---

ciency. Athens even at her apex depended heavily on grain imported from areas outside her empire. Lacedaemon probably came closest to satisfying her own spartan needs, but even she depended upon imported foodstuffs. The attempt to sever the trade routes between Sparta and her overseas grain suppliers figures prominently in the strategy of the Peloponnesian War. For imports of grain to Lacedaemon, see Thucydides 4.53.3; to the Peloponnesus generally see Thucydides 3.36.4; Herodotus 7.147.

[148] Above, p. 6.

[149] *ATL*, II, D 3-6. See below, Chapter 2, n. 14, p. 102.

[150] ἐνθυμεῖσθαι δὲ χρὴ ὅτι ἀδύνατον ὑμῖν ἐστιν ἀποψηφίσασθαι. εἰ γὰρ ἀπογνώσεσθε ὁμολογούντων αὐτῶν ἐπὶ τοὺς ἐμπόρους συνίστασθαι, δόξεθ᾽ ὑμεῖς ἐπιβουλεύειν τοῖς εἰσπλέουσιν.

of supply. The actual delivery of this supply was regulated by legal provision.

For example, there was a prohibition on importation of grain by residents of Attica for markets other than the Attic.[151] Even foreign nationals could not re-export more than one-third of the grain that they processed through the Peiraeus. This grain trade was supervised by two groups of officials, the σιτοφύλακες and the ἐμπορίου ἐπιμεληταί. The latter were charged with seeing that at least two-thirds of the grain imported by merchants through the Athenian grain emporium was brought up to the city (τοῦ σίτου τοῦ καταπλέοντος εἰς τὸ σιτικὸν ἐμπόριον τὰ δύο μέρη τοὺς ἐμπόρους ἀναγκάζειν εἰς τὸ ἄστυ κομίζειν) (Ath. Pol. 51.4).[152] The sitophylakes had a more general supervision of grain. Their tasks however were important[153]—for negligence or dishonesty they could be subject to capital punishment.[154]

Hence the supervision of the grain supply at Athens alone specifically refutes Bolkestein's contention that "the State occupied itself little with trade."[155] To the contrary, state protection and regulation of trade was inevitable, at least at Athens.[156]

[151] Cf. Dem. 34.37: τῶν δὲ νόμων τὰ ἔσχατα ἐπιτίμια προτεθηκότων, εἴ τις οἰκῶν 'Αθήνησιν ἄλλοσέ ποι σιτηγήσειεν ἢ εἰς τὸ 'Αττικὸν ἐμπόριον. Dem. 35.51: (ΝΟΜΟΣ) 'Αργύριον δὲ μὴ ἐξεῖναι ἐκδοῦναι 'Αθηναίων καὶ τῶν μετοίκων τῶν 'Αθήνησι μετοικούντων μηδενί, μηδὲ ὧν οὗτοι κύριοί εἰσιν, εἰς ναῦν ἥτις ἂν μὴ μέλλη ἄξειν σῖτον 'Αθήναζε. . . . Also see Lykurgos, Against Leokrates, 27.

[152] Cf. Harpocration and Suidas, s.v. ἐπιμεληταὶ ἐμπορίου.

[153] For the nature of their duties, see Ath. Pol. 51.3.

[154] Lysias 22.16; Harpocration, s.v. σιτοφύλακες.

[155] Economic Life in Greece's Golden Age, revised edition, Leiden, 1958, p. 137.

[156] Cf. Beauchet IV, p. 82; Amit, p. 132. There remains however some question as to the exact strictness of the Attic regulation of the grain trade. We possess scholia to Dem. 24.136:

Autonomy of Commercial Procedure

With commerce so vital to Athens, with the state interest in trade accordingly high, the autonomy of commercial procedure at Athens is understandable. But the evidence of practice elsewhere indicates that in Syracuse, Rhodes, and Byzantion, among others, nationals of foreign states could also litigate freely in the local commercial courts.

At Dem. 32.18 we hear of international access ἐπὶ τὴν ἀρχὴν τὴν τῶν Συρακοσίων [to the magistracy of the Syracusans].[157] Similarly there is the possibility of recourse by non-Rhodian merchants to the commercial courts in Rhodes: εἰ μὲν οὖν, ὦ ἄνδρες 'Αθηναῖοι, ἐν τῷ 'Ροδίων δικαστηρίῳ ἐκρινόμεθα . . . (Dem. 56.47).

Υ: οὗτοι οὖν δίκας ἐδίδοσαν. νόμος γὰρ ἦν ἀπείργων μὴ ἀλλαχοῦ σιτηγεῖν εἰ μὴ εἰς 'Αθήνας. More specifically scholia A.V.: ἐξηγοῦνται περὶ ἐμπόρων τινῶν 'Αθηναίων, ὅτι ἥλωσαν σιτηγοῦντες εἰς ἄλλον λιμένα παρὰ τὸν τῶν 'Αθηναίων νόμον. νόμος δὲ ἦν παρὰ 'Αθηναίοις τιμωρεῖσθαι τὸν 'Αθηναῖον ναύκληρον σιτηγοῦντα ἀλλαχοῦ, ἐπειδὴ λεπτόγεως ἦν ἡ 'Αττική. Beauchet (IV, p. 83) goes too far in concluding from these scholia that "l'exportation des céréales était formellement prohibée." The scholia seem also, just as the texts, to refer only to those resident in Attica (τὸν 'Αθηναῖον ναύκληρον). A formal prohibition on all exportation of home-grown foodstuffs would be theoretically uncalled for. The prevailing price in Athens was based on foreign growing costs plus high transport rates plus profits for middlemen and original producers. This would almost inevitably assure high profits at Athens for domestic foods not subject to transport fees. Profits would be especially high in times of special need, as the price tended to rise, even in the face of legal restrictions.

[157] The importance of the passage was recognized by P. S. Phōtiadēs, "'Αττικὸν ξίκαιον" in 'Αθηνᾶ, 36 (1924), pp. 111-112: "(δεῖται) μακρᾶς καὶ κατὰ λεπτὸν ἐξετάσεως." But the evidence it offers for supranational procedure at Syracuse has been continually overlooked.

In a more general context, it is suggested that commercial mercantile cases might be admitted to various δικαστήρια [courts of justice] under certain conditions. The speaker at Dem. 34.43 asks: ἀλλ' εἰς ποῖον δικαστήριον εἰσέλθωμεν, ἄνδρες δικασταί, εἰ μὴ πρὸς ὑμᾶς, οὗπερ τὸ συμβόλαιον ἐποιησάμεθα; [But to what court should we go, jurors, if not to you since here in Athens we made the agreement?] Since at 34.44 reference is made to τὸ 'Αθηναίων δικαστήριον [the Athenian court], not to the emporic court, it is clear that the tribunals under discussion are those of various cities, not the varied courts of a single *polis*.

Elsewhere in our sources an Athenian takes charge of business matters at Byzantion, even entering into litigation with Kalchēdonians: ᾤχετ' εἰς Βυζάντιον πλέων [ὁ Στέφανος] ἡνίκ' ἐκεῖνοι τὰ πλοῖα τὰ τούτου [Φορμίωνος] κατέσχον, τὴν δὲ δίκην ἔλεγεν τὴν πρὸς τοὺς Καλχηδονίους . . . (Dem. 45.64).

In another case an Athenian, a guardian of children, has the opportunity to litigate in Bosporos.[158] No wonder then that one ancient commentator tells us that a foreign merchant could litigate wherever he wished: ἐξῆν γὰρ τοῖς ξένοις ἐμπόροις ὅπου ἐβούλοντο ποιεῖσθαι τὰς δίκας (Scholion to Dem. 21.176).

Customary Supranationality in Commercial Procedure

The possibility of international access to the commercial courts of various states in the fourth century *ipso facto* denies the uniqueness of the Athenian supranational procedure. It suggests strongly that throughout maritime Greece commercial cases were open to merchants of varied citizenship.

---

[158] ἦν μὲν γὰρ τὸ χρέως ἐν Βοσπόρῳ, ἀφίκετο δ' οὐδεπώποτ' εἰς τὸν τόπον τοῦτον ὁ Δημάρετος· πῶς οὖν εἰσέπραξεν; (Dem. 38.11).

Such a situation holds no surprise: the very existence, the very substance of maritime commerce is international. The solution of its problems, legal or otherwise, quite naturally demands international action, international access, international cooperation. "Being in its very nature an international enterprise, shipping tends more and more to favor an international solution of its problems . . . a universally accepted code of sea laws may well anticipate by many years the proposals for the modification of the idea of sovereignty."[159]

This basic tendency toward internationalism reveals itself no less in the Hellenic world. International sea-projects were not unknown, nor were they restricted to military undertakings.[160]

This internationalism, combined with the exigencies of sea transportation, clarifies the conditions under which even in the fifth century *forum concursus* might have existed in commercial litigation even among states lacking special provision (συμβολαί) for the settlement of disputes arising between their respective nationals.[161] The resolution of the dispute as to destination of the ship—Syracuse or Athens—in Dem. 32 (§9 and §14) illustrates how in practice officials of the various states (this time Kephallēnia) were compelled to take a quasi-juridical role in commercial disputes involving foreign commercials. From here to supranational access to the courts of the Greek states is a short distance.

Another factor arguing for similarity of procedure in the various Greek states is the underlying similarity of

[159] W. McFee, *The Law of the Sea*, London, 1951, p. 22.

[160] Cf. the commercial project mentioned at Dem. 58.53: Μοιροκλῆς τοίνυν, ὁ τὸ ψήφισμα γράψας κατὰ τῶν τοὺς ἐμπόρους ἀδικούντων καὶ πείσας οὐ μόνον ὑμᾶς ἀλλὰ καὶ τοὺς συμμάχους φυλακήν τινα τῶν κακουργούντων ποιήσασθαι. . . .

[161] Cf. Dem. 7.13, above, p. 61.

all Greek commercial law,[162] including the commercial maritime.[163] This is illustrated by a group of Amorgian inscriptions (*IG* XII.7.66-70) dated about 300 B.C. dealing with money lent to the *polis* of Arkesinē on Amorgos, where the similarity to Athenian practice is striking.[164]

[162] Similarity of positive law does not, however, justify facile assumptions of relationship among dissimilar institutions having somewhat similar names. See above, on *triakostaiai dikai*, p. 40.

[163] This common usage was certainly not limited to commercial matters, as Isocrates 19.12-15 demonstrates in dealing with a will (cf. E. Weiss, SZ, 33 (1912), pp. 215 ff.). Vinogradoff well summarizes the situation in his article on "Greek Law" in *Hastings' Encyclopedia of Religion and Ethics* (1914), Vol. VII: "Although the Greek world was made up of a great number of commonwealths, each possessing independent law of its own, and although every allowance must be made for local peculiarities, the leading conceptions of Greek law as a whole may still be considered as a unity." And speaking of commercial law, the same writer says, ". . . towards the end of the fourth century, one may speak of a private international law of Greece, which, though not codified, was governed in most important respects by similar if not identical principles. . . ." (P. Vinogradoff, *Collected Papers*, II, Oxford, 1928, p. 263, as reprinted from "Historical Types of International Law," *Bibliotheca Visseriana dissertationum jus internationale illustrantium*, 1923). This does not, of course, justify cavalier utilization of the laws of one *polis* as proof for a specific practice in another. Cf. J. Triantaphyllopoulos, Ἀρχαῖα Ἑλληνικὰ δίκαια, Ἀθῆναι, 1968, pp. 1-2.

[164] E.g. the κυρία-clause, the hypothec on property at home and abroad, the existence of σύμβολα-arrangements concurrently between Arkesinē and Naxos, in reference to which *IG* XII.7.67, l. 48, provides ". . . κατὰ τὸ σύμβολον τὸ Ναξ[ίων κ]αὶ Ἀρκεσινέων." In the same inscription at lines 76 ff., the *kyria*-clause is given precedence over the *symbolon*:

(77) <ὡ>μολόγησαν Ἀρκ[εσιν]εῖς μηδὲν εἶναι κυριώτερον μήτε νόμον μήτε ψ[ή]

(78) [φ]ισμα μήτε δ[όγμ]α [μή]τε στρατηγὸν μήτε ἀρχὴν ἄλλα κρινοῦ

72

This common legal tradition was joined to similar economic motivation. As we have seen, no state in the Hellenic world was truly self-sufficient. A large number were strongly interested on a governmental level in the provision of an adequate food supply. For example, the letters of Antigonos concerning Teos and Lebedos in the late fourth century strikingly confirm governmental activity outside Athens in providing grain for citizens.[165] Antigonos' refusal to permit to the cities independent food storage undoubtedly arose from politico-military motivation. But the interest of the various cities in so possessing food supplies, despite Antigonos' final reluctant concession to the Lebedeans, suggests that this independent food storage represented not a post-Alexandrian departure, but a continuation of the Hellenic concern for self-sufficiency as a prelude and precondition to *autonomia*.[166]

---

(79) [σ]αν ἢ τὰ ἐν τ[ῆ συγγ]ραφῆ γεγ[ρ]αμμ[ένα] μήτε ἄλλο μηθὲν μήτε τέχ-
(80) νη μήτε πα[ρε]υρέσει μηδεμιᾷ, ἀλλ' εἶναι τὴν συγγραφὴν κυρίαν

The similarity in terminology to the provisions of the *syngraphē* in Dem. 35 is obvious: κυριώτερον δὲ περὶ τούτων ἄλλο μηδὲν εἶναι τῆς συγγραφῆς (§13). Finley's statement is correct: "The close link between Athenian law and Amorgian has been frequently noted. . . . Students have seen in this parallel strong proof of the existence, by the end of the fourth-century B.C., of a more or less universal commercial law in the Greek world." M. I. Finley, *Studies in Land and Credit in Ancient Athens 500-200 B.C.*, New Brunswick, 1951, p. 198, n. 17.

[165] Says Antigonos: οὐ[κ ἐβουλόμεθα μηδεμίαι πό]λει δίδοσθαι τὰ σιτηγήσια μηδ[ὲ σίτοι γίνεσθαι παράθε[σιν, οὐκ ἐῶντες τὰς π]όλεις εἰς ταῦτα ἀναλίσκειν χρήματα συχνὰ οὐκ ἀναγκαῖα [ὄντα κ. τ. λ. . . . (Dittenberger, *Syll.*³ #344, ll. 81 ff.).

[166] I cannot agree with Bickerman that *autonomia* exists not *iure naturali*, φύσει, but only *iure gentium*, νόμῳ. See E. J. Bickerman, "Autonomia—Sur un passage de Thucydide," *RIDA* (3rd

Supranationality then was an attribute of the Athenian *dikai emporikai*. But it seems likely that this supranationality arose from the conditions of Greek trade, from the existence of an autonomous commercial procedure based on the particular demands of trade, from a natural necessity for maritime courts open to individuals of various nations. Athens, as we shall see, established specified conditions for this supranational access, based on the principle of admissibility in disputes arising from written contracts providing for the Attic market. Here lay her genius, in manipulating a common Hellenic heritage or innovation in the interest of her own trade.[167] The principle of supranationality itself seems to have been achieved by a number, perhaps all, of the Hellenic states. It cannot be said that Athens alone accomplished it, or with any likelihood that Athens originated it. It cannot be denied that Athens used it wisely.

RIGOR

In one respect at least, supranational access to the commercial courts led to a related "rigor" in procedure, viz. the possibility of pre- and post-trial incarceration of individual defendants. In Athenian private suits of the fifth and fourth centuries judgment could not be executed against the person of an individual defendant —only his property could be the object of judicial retribution. Not so in the *dikai emporikai*. Here the individual stood in reserve. Any deficiency in property was

---

Ser. 5) (1958), pp. 313-344. Whatever the difference between ἐλευθερία and αὐτονομία, the introduction of Roman legal concepts here clarifies nothing.

[167] See below Chapter 2.

to be paid with the body. This unusual rigor, found in private commercial maritime cases alone, is not difficult to explain.

Post-Judgment Incarceration

Prior to the reforms of Solon, individuals were subject to arrest for failure to pay debts.[168] The course of ancient legal history here runs smoothly parallel. Just as the Roman law moved from the same harshness of prosecution against individual bodies[169] to a virtually absolute requirement of penalization in money terms in private procedure,[170] as Hebrew law moved from the primitive and physical "lex talionis"[171] to the Talmudic doctrine of retribution in money terms,[172] so Athenian law moved from personal physical responsibility for obligations

---

[168] χρέα λαμβάνοντες ἐπὶ τοῖς σώμασιν ἀγώγιμοι τοῖς δανείζουσιν ἦσαν, οἱ μὲν αὐτοῦ δουλεύοντες, οἱ δ' ἐπὶ τὴν ξένην πιπρασκόμενοι (Plutarch, *Solon*, 13.2).

[169] Cf. of course the Twelve Tables, III.2 (Bruns, *Fontes*), "Post deinde manus iniectio esto etc."

[170] The Roman law, however, in abolishing *manus iniectio* only formally followed the Athenian legal development. Although A. Watson suggests that by 200 B.C. sale of a judgment debtor *trans Tiberim* was already obsolete (*Roman Private Law Around 200 B.C.*, Edinburgh, 1971, p. 44), evidence exists that in fact personal seizure still abided and that it continued in use throughout the classical period. See W. W. Buckland, *A Text-Book of Roman Law from Augustus to Justinian*, Cambridge, 1921, pp. 636-638; O. Lenel, *Das Edictum Perpetuum*, 3rd ed., Leipzig, 1927, pp. 395 ff.

[171] *Exodus* XXI.22-25: "Thou shalt give life for life, eye for eye, tooth for tooth, burning for burning, wound for wound, stripe for stripe."

[172] The Mishna, "Bava Kamma," 83b ff. Cf. G. Horowitz, *The Spirit of Jewish Law*, New York, 1953, pp. 593-595; David Daube, *Studies in Biblical Law*, Ch. III, "Lex Talionis," Cambridge, 1947.

into the reformed air of Solonian legislation prohibiting loans secured by the borrower's person.[173] But just as Athenian law (so far as we know) had never been as harsh in its action against the individual offender as the early Roman or original Hebrew, so the reform came easier and went further. Nonetheless certain exceptional cases remain in which action against the individual's person, in the form of incarceration, was ordained.

The commercial courts constitute the only such "private" case category. The fact and the motive of this exception are clarified by Dem. 33.1: Τοῖς μὲν ἐμπόροις, ὦ ἄνδρες δικασταὶ, καὶ τοῖς ναυκλήροις κελεύει ὁ νόμος εἶναι τὰς δίκας πρὸς τοὺς θεσμοθέτας . . . καὶ τοῖς ἀδικοῦσιν δεσμὸν ἔταξεν τοὐπιτίμιον, ἕως ἂν ἐκτείσωσιν ὅ τι ἂν αὐτῶν καταγνωσθῇ, ἵνα μηδεὶς ἀδικῇ μηδένα τῶν ἐμπόρων εἰκῇ. [The law orders that actions for maritime traders and ship owners shall be before the *thesmothetai* . . . and for wrongdoers it has established imprisonment as the penalty, until they should pay the judgment against them, so that no one lightly should wrong any of the maritime traders.] Even for the plaintiff imprisonment was possible, for if he failed to capture a minimum share of the ballots he was liable to pay one-sixth the sum in litigation,[174] the so-called *epōbelia* (ἐπωβελία).[175] Inability to pay the *epōbelia* actually led to imprisonment, no less

---

[173] Σόλων τόν τε δῆμον ἠλευθέρωσε καὶ ἐν τῷ π[α]ρόντι καὶ εἰς τὸ μέλλον, κωλύσας δ[ανε]ίζειν ἐπὶ τοῖς σώμασιν (*Ath. Pol.* 6.1). Cf. Plutarch, *Solon*, 15.2.

[174] Dem. 35.46-47: ἀλλὰ τί κελεύεις, ὦ Λάκριτε; μὴ ἱκανὸν εἶναι ἡμᾶς ἀποστερεῖσθαι ἃ ἐδανείσαμεν χρήματα ὑμῖν, ἀλλὰ καὶ εἰς τὸ δεσμωτήριον παραδοθῆναι ὑφ' ὑμῶν προσοφλόντας τὰ ἐπιτίμια, ἐὰν μὴ ἐκτίνωμεν; (47) καὶ πῶς οὐκ ἂν δεινὸν εἴη καὶ σχέτλιον καὶ αἰσχρὸν . . . εἰ οἱ δανείσαντες ἐν τῷ ἐμπορίῳ τῷ ὑμετέρῳ . . . ἀπάγοιντο εἰς τὸ δεσμωτήριον; . . .

[175] On which, see below.

than inability to pay other damages assessed by the court.[176]

Unlike the pre-Solonian form of involuntary bondage to one's creditor for failure to meet debts, conviction in a commercial maritime case and subsequent inability or refusal to pay the penalty assessed led to public incarceration (εἰς τὸ οἴκημα). Nonetheless enforcement of judgment still devolved on the plaintiff.[177] If he were unable to lead his convicted opponent to jail immediately, he might attempt arrest at a later time.[178] The state's role was only to give its sanction to the arrest and to provide the prison. Here as in all cases[179] individual responsibility in ancient Athens remained high.[180]

There were in fact other case categories in which im-

[176] Dem. 56.4: δῆλον ὡς ζημιώσων ἡμᾶς τῇ ἐπωβελίᾳ καὶ καταθησόμενος εἰς τὸ οἴκημα πρὸς τῷ ἀποστερεῖν τὰ χρήματα. "οἴκημα" was the Athenian euphemism for δεσμωτήριον. Cf. Plutarch's interesting note (Solon, 15.2-3): "Ἃ δ᾽ οὖν οἱ νεώτεροι τοὺς ᾽Αθηναίους λέγουσι τὰς τῶν πραγμάτων δυσχερείας ὀνόμασι χρηστοῖς καὶ φιλανθρώποις ἐπικαλύπτοντας ἀστείως ὑποκορίζεσθαι, τὰς μὲν πόρνας ἑταίρας . . . οἴκημα δὲ τὸ δεσμωτήριον καλοῦντας.

[177] On enforcement of judgment in Athenian law, see the good discussion by Lipsius, "Vollziehung des Urteils," AR, pp. 942-952; also, Weiss, pp. 451 ff.; Bo.-Sm. II, pp. 271-287; Harrison, Procedure, pp. 185-190.

[178] [ὁ Εὔανδρος] δίκην ἐμπορικὴν καταδικασάμενος τοῦ Μενίππου, οὐκ ἔχων πρότερον λαβεῖν αὐτόν, ὡς ἔφη, τοῖς μυστηρίοις ἐπιδημοῦντος ἐπελάβετο (Dem. 21.176).

[179] Bo.-Sm. II, p. 271: "When the verdict of a court required a defeated litigant to pay anything to the plaintiff in the way of damages or debt, it was the business of the successful litigant to execute the judgment."

[180] It would not have been so in the ideal state sketched by Plato in the Laws. There the state officials would have had prime responsibility for the execution of judgment in private suits (958A-E), a responsibility later accorded general acceptance in Western law.

prisonment might be utilized following judgment, for example cases involving those who were delinquent in their debts to the state.[181] None of these cases, however, involved litigation between private adversaries, but rather might be classified as public cases (ἀγῶνες δημόσιαι).

Incarceration, for example, could follow upon a criminal conviction for theft (Lysias 6.21) or for violation of the tax laws (Dem. 24.144). Imprisonment might be utilized in connection with a debt to the state arising from the provisions of a specific law or decree.[182] In all these cases imprisonment is utilized as an *added* punishment, not as a means of enforcing a judgment.

In certain other public cases imprisonment was utilized after a failure to pay the damages adjudged. Such cases included the γραφὴ ὕβρεως [indictment for "outrage"] (Dem. 21.47) and εἰσαγγελία ["denunciation"] (cf. Dem. 24.63). Again, an attempt to serve as a juror after official adjudgment as a state debtor carried with it personal servitude until the debt was paid, together with any penalty voted by the court.[183] Unlike the *dikai emporikai*, these cases do not therefore constitute an exception to the general rule that execution of judgment in private actions in fourth-century Athens was undertaken by an individual against the property of his opponent, never against the person.

---

[181] Cf. Beauchet, "De la contrainte par corps," IV, pp. 450-460.

[182] Cf. the *nomos* quoted at Dem. 24.71: καὶ εἴ τινι τῶν ὀφειλόντων τῷ δημοσίῳ προστετίμηται κατὰ νόμον ἢ κατὰ ψήφισμα δεσμοῦ ἢ τὸ λοιπὸν προστιμηθῇ, εἶναι αὐτῷ ἢ ἄλλῳ ὑπὲρ ἐκείνου ἐγγυητὰς καταστῆσαι. There is no question here of "surety for pre-trial bail," for previous conviction is assumed.

[183] ἐὰν δὲ ἀργυρίου τιμηθῇ, δεῖ αὐτὸν δεδέσ[θαι], ἕως ἂν ἐκτείσῃ τό τε πρότερον ὄφλημα ἐφ᾽ ᾧ ἐνεδείχθη, καὶ ὅ τι ἂν αὐτῷ προστιμήσῃ τ[ὸ δικ]αστήριον (*Ath. Pol.* 63.3).

Indeed, although employed outside the *dikai empori-kai*, imprisonment was not as extensively utilized at Athens as in many modern systems. Ancient sources do seem to present, on rapid perusal, evidence of imprisonment at Athens much more widespread than that of maritime traders and state debtors. This literary appearance has given long life to a myth of "extensive imprisonment" at Athens.

Part of the fantasy arises from the Athenian practice of holding in custody persons awaiting execution or individuals accused of flagrant crimes.[184] Since history deals often with the spectacular, cases such as that of Socrates or Miltiades come readily to mind, and Athenian prisons are as vivid in the minds of the chance reader of classical literature as they were in the speeches of individuals involved in commercial cases. This proves nothing about the extent of their use.[185]

---

[184] Cf. Xen., *Hellenica*, 1.7.2-3 (generals accused after Arginusai); Plutarch, *Phocion*, 36; Antiphon 5.69.

[185] Meier in 1819 sought to utilize Antiphon 5.63 to establish the extensive employment of imprisonment as a punishment at Athens. *Historiae iuris attici de bonis damnatorum et fiscalium debitorum duo libri*, Berlin, 1819, pp. 27-28. Harrison in 1971 follows Meier (*Procedure*, p. 177). The Antiphon passage, however, is not general in implication and apparently refers to the extraordinary case of public debt considered above. And in the 19th century after Meier, this was repeatedly seen. Cf. Gilbert (English translation), p. 414; G. F. Schömann, *Griechische Alterthümer*, 4th ed., Berlin, 1897, I, p. 533; J. J. Thonissen, *Le droit pénal de la république athénienne*, Brussels, 1876, p. 114; Beauchet IV, p. 453. T. Reinach in *DS*, s.v. *emporikai dikai*, referred to 19th-century scholarship in concluding, "C'est sans raison qu'on a prétendu que toute la différence entre les affaires commerciales et ordinaires consistait en l'absence d'un délai accordé au débiteur condamné, avant qu'il fût contraignable par corps." Nonetheless the old view was revived by I. Barkan,

Pre-Trial Bail for Defendants

The unusual rigor of the *dikai emporikai* procedure regarding bail (ἐγγύη) for accused individuals arises not from any special legal procedure, but from the heavy participation of foreigners in the commercial cases. Possibly foreigners were required generally to furnish monetary security to guarantee their presence at trial.[186] The citizen had no such obligation. But since the supranational nature of the *dikai emporikai* was unique among the Attic courts, a requirement of pre-trial bail for "foreigners" (ξένοι) meant that a substantial proportion of litigants in the *dikai emporikai* were subject to a procedural "rigor" not encountered by litigants in other courts.

The only other cases in which non-resident foreigners might appear before Athenian tribunals would be *dikai ἀπὸ συμβόλων* [treaty cases]. In such cases the provisions agreed on in the international *symbolon* would be likely to specify conditions of trial for the citizens of the respective states in the courts of the other state. The only

---

Cl. Phil., 31 (1936), p. 341 (and accepted by Bo.-Sm. II, pp. 275-276), who concluded: "When the evidence is weighed, it seems indisputable that imprisonment was a penalty per se in Athens and was probably used even more frequently than the sources indicate." But all of his specific examples of "general uses" are either exceptional or based on questionable interpretations. A good short survey of incarceration in ancient Athens is offered by Thalheim, *RE*, s.v. δεσμωτήριον.

[186] E. Caillemer thought that "(the provision of bail) était, de droit commun, obligatoire pour les étrangers. . . . L'étranger, assigné à comparaître devant un tribunal, était tenu de fournir immédiatement des cautions (ἐγγυητάς) qui garantissaient sa comparution au jour indiqué. S'il n'en trouvait pas, les magistrats . . . le contraignaient à aller en prison (εἰς τὸ οἴκημα)." *DS*, s.v. *Eggye*, p. 493.

other foreigners involved in litigation would be the resident metics, and the great bulk of their business would be heard not in the regular state courts but before the special tribunal of the *polemarch*.

Bail too would be arranged before the *polemarch*. This would be true apparently whether the case was a normal one involving metics and heard before the *polemarch*'s court or a *dikē emporikē* to be heard before the magistrate responsible for the *dikai emporikai*. Thus at Dem. 32.29, a case arising out of a commercial contract providing for the Attic mart (*dikē emporikē*) is spoken of in the following terms: εἰ γὰρ μὴ δι' ὑμῶν ἔρημος ἐγίγνεθ' ἡ δίκη, ἅμ' ἂν αὐτὸν προσεκαλοῦ καὶ κατηγγύας πρὸς τὸν πολέμαρχον, καὶ εἰ μὲν κατέστησέ σοι τοὺς ἐγγυητάς, μένειν ἠναγκάζετ' ἄν, ἢ σὺ παρ' ὧν λήψει δίκην ἑτοίμους εἶχες, εἰ δὲ μὴ κατέστησεν, εἰς τὸ οἴκημ' ἂν ᾔει. [For if you were not responsible for the suit being undefended, you would have summoned him and at the same time made him furnish security before the *polemarch*, and if he had provided sureties to you, he would have been forced to remain, or you would have had men at hand from whom to take compensation, but if he had not furnished sureties, he would have gone to jail.] Similar evidence concerning the establishment of bail (or the Roman *cautio iudicio sistendi causa*) is furnished by Lysias 13.23, Isocrates 17.12, and Dem. 25.60.

It is a passage from Antiphon's famous speech on the "Murder of Herodēs" (5.17) that has nourished in scholars the belief that a universal requirement of bail for foreigners was a meaningful factor in the Athenian juridical structure. There Antiphon's client says: Ἔτι δὲ μάλ' ἐδέθην, ὦ ἄνδρες, παρανομώτατα ἁπάντων ἀνθρώπων. ἐθέλοντος γάρ μου ἐγγυητὰς τρεῖς καθιστάναι κατὰ τὸν νόμον, οὕτως οὗτοι διεπράξαντο ὥστε τοῦτο μὴ ἐγγενέσθαι

81

μοι ποιῆσαι. τῶν δὲ ἄλλων ξένων ὅστις πώποτε ἠθέλησε καταστῆσαι ἐγγυητάς, οὐδεὶς πώποτε ἐδέθη. καίτοι οἱ ἐπιμεληταὶ
τῶν κακούργων τῷ αὐτῷ χρῶνται νόμῳ τούτῳ. [Indeed I
was imprisoned most illegally of all men. For although I wished to provide three sureties in accord
with the law, these men so contrived that it was
not possible for me to do so. But of the other foreigners
whoever wished to provide sureties, not one ever was
imprisoned. Indeed the epimelētai tōn kakourgōn use
this same law.][187] At the time the statement was made
(probably between 417 and 414),[188] the bail provision
for "foreign" defendants was no doubt quite important,
but in a criminal, not a civil, context. The Athenian Empire still held wide juridical sway over her subject
states.[189] Numerous citizens from "allied" (subject)
states were coming to Athens for trial. Their right or
lack of right to the posting of pre-trial bail would under
such circumstances be extremely important, not only to
them (as the speaker makes clear that in fact it was)
but to the proper functioning of Attic juridical procedure.

In the fourth century the political environment was
far different, and the legal implications of such bonds
quite changed. Now the dikai emporikai substantially
were alone in handling cases where foreigners appeared

[187] The identity of these fifth-century officials termed ἐπιμεληταὶ τῶν κακούργων is obscure. Possibly they were the Eleven,
mentioned in the same speech at §70.

[188] Cf. L. Gernet, Antiphon, Paris, 1923, p. 197. Blass concurs.

[189] Cf. Old Oligarch, 1.16: Δοκεῖ δὲ ὁ δῆμος ὁ 'Αθηναίων καὶ
ἐν τῷδε κακῶς βουλεύεσθαι, ὅτι τοὺς συμμάχους ἀναγκάζουσι πλεῖν
ἐπὶ δίκας 'Αθήναζε. These trials included, broadly speaking, political and criminal cases. G. E. M. de Ste. Croix, "Notes on
Jurisdiction in the Athenian Empire," Classical Quarterly, 11
(1961), pp. 95 ff.

as parties under supranational access. Those defendants coming before the commercial courts, unless citizens, would therefore be subjected to a rigor not prevailing in the procedure of the other civil courts. The rigor derived however not from any innovation in commercial procedure as against civil, but was carried over from the civil and left isolated in the commercial courts when foreigners no longer could appear before other Athenian tribunals. It was this deviation of the commercial from the civil procedure in allowing supranational access that made meaningful the rigor of required pre-trial bail in the *dikai emporikai* for foreign defendants.

This required *cautio iudicio sistendi causa* makes clear again the commercial advantage inherent in monthly introduction of *lēxeis* during the winter months.[190] Even cases subject to an expeditious procedure demanded some time allowance between introduction and adjudication. If individuals were to be incarcerated upon failing bail, this bondage would more profitably fall upon them during the winter than in the "working season." The *emmēnoi* ("monthly") procedure as outlined above made it possible to proceed against an individual upon his summer appearance for trade, if the *lēxis* had been introduced during the winter, but only if he had refused appearance and trial during the winter. Again the maturity of the Attic commercial maritime law grows clear.

Epōbelia, Phasis, and The Attack on Sycophancy

Another manifestation of rigorous procedure in the commercial courts arose from the state's desire to protect individual merchants from that form of intimidation or blackmail known to the Athenians as "syco-

190 See above, pp. 36 ff.

phancy." The *epōbelia* (ἐπωβελία) and the *phasis* (φάσις), together with restrictive legislation against sycophants, had a strong impact on the functioning of the *dikai emporikai.*

The *epōbelia* in particular tended to discourage irresponsible litigation in the commercial field.[191] A fine amounting to one-sixth the sum in litigation,[192] it was awarded on the failure of a party to receive one-fifth of the total votes. Greater detail on its functioning is beyond our present knowledge, for the ancient sources are incomplete and even contradictory.[193]

In public suits a fine equivalent in character to the *epōbelia* generally prevailed: a prosecutor's failure to capture one-fifth the ballots carried a penalty of 1,000 drachmai and partial ἀτιμία [deprivation of civic rights].[194]

[191] A full study of the *epōbelia* with reference to ancient sources was made as early as A. Boeckh—see *Die Staatshaushaltung der Athener*, 3rd ed., 1886, pp. 416 ff. (English translation of second edition, pp. 457 ff.). On the *epōbelia* in general, cf. Thalheim, *RE*, s.v. *epōbelia*; *MSL*, pp. 949 ff.; Lipsius, *AR*, pp. 937 ff.; C. Lécrivain, *DS*, s.v. *epōbelia*; Lofberg, *Sycophancy in Athens*, pp. 87-89; Paoli, *SPA*, p. 114; Bo.-Sm. II, pp. 80, 87, 89; Wolff, pp. 87 ff.

[192] Pollux 8.39: ἦν τὸ ἕκτον τοῦ τιμήματος, ὃ ὤφειλεν ὁ αἱρεθείς. It was so named because ὀβολὸς ἦν τὸ ἕκτον τῆς δραχμῆς. Cf. Harpocration, s.v. *epōbelia*.

[193] Paoli, *SPA*, p. 114. A. Boeckh had said almost a century earlier (*Public Economy*², p. 474): About the *epōbelia*, "the questions still remain undetermined, in what actions, by whom, under what circumstances, with what connected, and to whom was it paid."

[194] Cf. Andocides 1.33; 4.18; Dem. 21.47; 22.21; 23.80; 24.3; 24.7; 58.6; Plato, *Apology*, 36B. This risk, of course, was not run in public suits brought in accordance with governmental mandate.

84

It is in the private suits however that confused sources lead to confused modern scholarship. For example, the Scholiast to Plato, *Laws*, 921D, commenting on the word *epōbelia* as it appears in Platonic trade regulation, reports: ἐπιτίμιόν τι, τοῦτ᾽ ἔστι τοῖς διώκουσι χρηματικήν τινα δίκην, ἐὰν μὴ ἕλωσιν [some penalty for unsuccessful prosecutors of a "monetary suit"]. From this, it has been concluded, in all probability incorrectly,[195] that so-called δίκαι χρηματικαί ["monetary suits"] were subject to *epōbelia*. Since damage suits were expressed in monetary terms, these *dikai* χρηματικαί ["monetary suits"] might encompass all private suits, and hence all Athenian *dikai* would be subject to *epōbelia*. Nothing in the extant corpus of Attic orations justifies such a conclusion. No known category of Attic cases gives insight into the nature of *dikai* χρηματικαί. It seems likely that the Scholiast here is describing specific suits (known to him but unknown to us) by a non-technical phrase, satisfactory for literary interpretation but meaningless for juristic exegesis.

Similar considerations hold for the other suits where the *epōbelia* may have been at stake. It is possible that the δίκη ἐπιτροπῆς [guardianship suit] carried this rigor (Dem. 27.67) and perhaps also the δίκη συνθηκῶν παραβάσεως [violation of agreement] (Aeschines 1.163). But there can be no certainty about either of these case categories.

Only in the "special pleas"[196]—ἀντιγραφή, παραγραφή, διαμαρτυρία—do clarity and a virtual certainty appear. In all of these cases the penalty of one-sixth loomed. For example, the literary sources make clear that in the

[195] Cf. C. Lécrivain, *DS*, s.v. *epōbelia*.
[196] Lécrivain terms the special pleas the "domaine principal" of the *epōbelia* (*DS*, s.v. *epōbelia*).

paragraphē, "special plea against jurisdiction," both the prosecutor and the defendant are subject to *epōbelia*.[197] The same is probable in the *antigraphē* and *diamarturia*. But in the other case categories it seems likely that only the prosecutor was open to payment of the *epōbelia*.[198] Such a restricted application would be in line with the *epōbelia*'s goal of dealing with sycophancy (see below); its extension to both prosecutor and defendant in the *paragraphē* would be consistent with the greater rigor of the *dikai emporikai*.

Paragraphic hearings occurred most often in the commercial courts.[199] The strict rules of admissibility to these hearings called forth this phenomenon.[200] This circumstance explains why ancient and medieval authorities connected the existence of the *epōbelia* with the protection of commercial interests, and especially the protection of merchants from intimidation or blackmail through the threat of court action by the sycophants. The parallel exposure of the defendant in the *paragraphē* to the *epōbelia* would militate against reckless invocation of the special plea.

Thus Suidas reports (following in this case the general text of the lexicographical stream he shares with

[197] Cf. Paoli, *SPA*, p. 172.

[198] Pollux (8.39, 48) does, to be sure, maintain that both defendant and plaintiff were subject to the *epōbelia* (ὁ αἱρεθείς [39], ὁ δὲ μὴ μεταλαβὼν τὸ πέμπτον μέρος τῶν ψήφων [48]). Harpocration however (s.v. *epōbelia*) defines it as "ἐπιτίμιον . . . ὅπερ ἐδίδοσαν οἱ διώκοντες τοῖς φεύγουσιν, εἰ μὴ ἕλοιεν."

[199] Even allowing for the role played by chance in determining the content of surviving literary works, one is struck by the predominance of *dikai emporikai* among the paragraphic speeches examined by Wolff in his analysis of "Der Paragrapheprozess," pp. 17-86.

[200] See below, Chapter 2.

Photios the Lexicographer): πολλῶν εἰς χρήματα συκοφαντούντων τοὺς ἐπιεικεῖς καὶ ἀπράγμονας τῶν πολιτῶν καὶ
μάλιστα τοῦτο πράττειν διαβαλλομένων τῶν περὶ τὸ ἐμπόριον
συμβαλλόντων ἐπὶ ναυτικοῖς τόκοις, Ἀθηναῖοι ζημίαν ἔταξαν
κατὰ τῶν ἐγκαλούντων ὀβολὸν ἐκτίνειν, εἰ μὴ καθ' ὧν ἐνεκά-
λουν, τούτους ἕλοιεν. ταύτην τὴν ζημίαν ἐπωβελίαν ὠνόμασαν.
[Since many sycophants for financial gain were attacking the decent and law-abiding citizens, and individuals
making contracts for trade at nautical interest rates
were complaining that they suffered this most, the
Athenians established a fine of one-sixth against prosecutors if they did not convict those whom they prosecuted. This fine they named the *epōbelia*.] Suidas thus
limits the *epōbelia* to a penalty against the prosecutor;
but in the protection of the *emporoi* it was the paragraphic *epōbelia* (applicable to prosecutor and de-
fender alike) that played the major role.[201]
It must be emphasized that while the wider purpose
of the *epōbelia* was to deal with false prosecutions, its
specific effect was to prevent (or at least to punish)
sycophantic litigation in the commercial courts.[202] Here
again in the *dikai emporikai* an effort intended to aid the
conduct of commerce had the immediate effect of introducing a greater rigor into the procedural circumstances
of the commercial courts. As with detention and incar-

[201] Although Suidas implies that the *epōbelia* was payable upon
simple failure to convict (εἰ μὴ . . . τούτους ἕλοιεν), other sources
make clear the requirement of one-fifth. Cf. Pollux *re phasis*:
ὁ δὲ μὴ μεταλαβὼν τὸ πέμπτον μέρος τῶν ψήφων τὴν ἐπωβελίαν
προσωφλίσκανεν (8.48).
[202] Cf. Lécrivain's words in *DS*, s.v. *epōbelia*, "D'une part
cette amende est la peine des plaideurs téméraires ou malveil-
lants; d'autre part elle est destinée à protéger quelques intérêts
particulièrement chers aux Athéniens, particulièrement les intérêts commerciaux."

ceration, the operation of the *epōbelia*, while not unique to the commercial courts, nonetheless differentiates in rigor the commercial from the ordinary civil procedure. Another rigor operating in the interest of those engaged in mercantile operations was the availability of the *phasis* (φάσις),[203] or prosecution by denunciation, as a means of instituting litigation in commercial maritime matters. Such prosecutions could be brought by any interested citizen, even those having no connection with the matter. These denunciations were limited to prosecutions of an economic and financial nature: protection of the mines, trade, tax revenue, public property, orphans, and the prevention of sycophancy.[204]

The *phasis* was available accordingly in commercial maritime matters, but the emporic procedure itself (*dikai emporikai*), with its advantage of speed, supranationality, and rigor, could be employed only where the legally established condition (litigation arising from a written contract concerning the Attic market) could be met.[205] Still the possibility remained open in the appropriate cases for parties unconnected with the maritime commercial world to commence litigation,[206] al-

[203] On the *phasis* see Lipsius, *AR*, pp. 309-316, and more recently, R. Bogaert, "A propos de la phasis," *RIDA* (3rd Ser. 9) (1962), pp. 157-167.

[204] Pollux (8.47): φάσις δὲ ἦν τὸ φαίνειν τοὺς περὶ τὰ μέταλλα ἀδικοῦντας, ἢ περὶ τὸ ἐμπόριον κακουργοῦντας ἢ περὶ τὰ τέλη, ἢ τῶν δημοσίων τι νενοσφισμένους, ἢ συκοφαντοῦντας, ἢ περὶ τοὺς ὀρφανοὺς ἐξαμαρτάνοντας.

[205] Use of the *phasis* in regard to commercial matters not qualifying for the *dikai emporikai* is indicated in the hypothesis to Dem. 58: κατὰ τῶν ἑτέρωσέ ποι καὶ μὴ Ἀθήναζε σεσιτηγηκότων ἐμπόρων ἢ ναυκλήρων Ἀθηναίων φάσεις ἦσαν δεδομέναι.

[206] This consideration refutes from yet another aspect the contention of those who maintain that commercial cases were esta-

though any damages assessed went only to the injured party.[207]

At Athens the battle against sycophancy was fought bitterly in a variety of areas.[208] The general practice of allowing prosecutors to share in damages assessed served to spur not only denunciations beneficial to the people and the state but selfish exploitation. The very threat of prosecution might be profitable. The actual prosecution, even without personal financial gain for the plaintiff, might effectively punish a personal but innocent enemy.

To all of this the commercial world was particularly susceptible. Because time was of the essence during the sailing season and because the merchants comprised a large foreign element, the mercantile class constituted a rich temptation to malicious elements. The protection of her commerce demanded that Athens protect her commercials. The rigor in judicial procedure was a partial answer to this danger. But the very *phasis* that might protect commerce from actual operational evil lent itself to sycophantic exploitation by facilitating prosecution by those basely motivated.

Hence the *phasis* was so constituted that it operated in both directions, that is, it could be used itself against those falsely employing it. As Pollux put it at 8.47, one

blished *ratione personarum* rather than *ratione rerum*. See Chapter 2.

[207] Pollux, 8.48: καὶ τὸ μὲν τιμηθὲν ἐγίνετο τῶν ἀδικουμένων, εἰ καὶ ἄλλος ὑπὲρ αὐτῶν φήνειεν. In other types of cases, the individual bringing the *phasis* did share the damages with the victim. Plato, *Laws*, 928BC (orphans). Harrison's argument to the contrary (*Procedure*, p. 220) is not persuasive.

[208] The standard study remains Lofberg, *Sycophancy in Athens.* Cf. Bo.-Sm. II, pp. 39-75.

of its purposes was τὸ φαίνειν . . . συκοφαντοῦντας [prosecution of sycophants]. Such an employment could easily protect merchants in turn from base uses of the *phasis* by facilitating prosecutions against false prosecutors.[209]

Such a weapon would be consistent with the picture painted by Suidas:[210] πολλῶν εἰς χρήματα συκοφαντούντων τοὺς ἐπιεικεῖς καὶ ἀπράγμονας . . . μάλιστα . . . τῶν περὶ τὸ ἐμπόριον συμβαλλόντων. It would fall under the ἄλλοις ["other things"] mentioned by the speaker at Dem. 58:10: ὅτι δ᾽ οὐ ταῖς χιλίαις[211] μόνον ἔνοχός ἐστιν, ἀλλὰ καὶ ἀπαγωγῇ καὶ τοῖς ἄλλοις, ὅσα κελεύει πάσχειν ὁ νόμος οὑτοσὶ τὸν συκοφαντοῦντα τοὺς ἐμπόρους καὶ τοὺς ναυκλήρους, ῥᾳδίως ἐξ αὐτοῦ τοῦ νόμου γνώσεσθε. [That not to a 1,000 *drachmai* fine alone is he liable, but even to summary arrest and to the other things, which the law orders against the man sycophanting the sea traders and ship owners, you will know easily from this law.] Hence the dual nature of the laws on access to the commercial courts and for prosecution of commercial cases: alleviation of certain procedural requirements balanced by a rigor in certain particulars, here exemplified by a wide freedom of prosecution restrained by special mercantile protection from sycophancy.

This tidy picture is rejected by some authorities. The open employment of the *phasis* against those who unfairly prosecuted merchants has been denied in particular because of the alleged unreliability of the lexicographer Pollux. Thus Lofberg charges: "According to

[209] See Lipsius, *AR*, p. 314. [210] Above, pp. 86-87.

[211] This refers to the 1,000-drachmai fine incurred by a prosecutor's dropping a suit once instituted, another theoretical check on litigations poorly based. Cf. §6 of the present speech; Dem. 21.47; 21.103.

90

Pollux, one of the uses of the *phasis* was to prosecute sycophants. There is reason for doubting this, since no authority of greater reliability mentions such a use . . . the statement is confused . . . the *phasis* which is a favorite method of attack open to sycophants is said to be a method of attacking them."[212]

Such a judgment is unfortunate, for it reveals a false evaluation of Pollux' position in our tradition and of Pollux' own sources.[213] The value of Pollux lies not in his position as a commentator living in the second century A.D., but in his reliance for Attic legal history upon sources long-since lost. Thus for us Pollux is not a commentator of Hadrianic time but a filter for information from the Hellenic period itself.[214] That the filter was a fool is a proposition long entertained but by now substantially refuted.[215]

A statement based upon Pollux is *prima facie* to be accepted—only ancient evidence to the contrary or overwhelming considerations of historical or literary criticism can offset a soundly attested lexicographical tradition.

There is only one positive objection to Pollux' insistence that the *phasis* was available not only for syco-

[212] *Sycophancy in Athens,* p. 92. Bo.-Sm. concur in this criticism (II, p. 71).

[213] A similar undervaluation of Pollux' testimony has created confusion in ascertaining the chronology of the *dikai emporikai.* See below, Chapter 3, pp. 191-195.

[214] By most happy accident we now have a text of the *Ath. Pol.* of Aristotle and can appreciate Pollux' intimate acquaintance with the information offered by that work and available in the fourth century B.C. but in the case of the other ancient monographs not later, save through the lexicographers.

[215] Cf. below, Chapter 3, pp. 191-195.

phants but also against them, namely "that Isocrates (15.314) did not add it in his list of processes against sycophants."[216]

In fact the Isocrates passage may very well include the *phasis* against sycophants. The orator says (at paragraphs 313.314 in the standard pagination): περὶ δὲ τῶν συκοφαντῶν χαλεπωτέρους ἢ περὶ τῶν ἄλλων κακουργιῶν τοὺς νόμους ἔθεσαν. τοῖς μὲν γὰρ μεγίστοις τῶν ἀδικημάτων ἐν ἑνὶ τῶν δικαστηρίων τὴν κρίσιν ἐποίησαν, κατὰ δὲ τούτων γραφὰς μὲν πρὸς τοὺς θεσμοθέτας, εἰσαγγελίας δ' εἰς τὴν βουλήν, προβολὰς δ' ἐν τῷ δήμῳ. [They enacted harsher laws against the sycophants than against other wrongdoers. They provided for trial in a single court for the greatest crimes, but against the sycophants, *graphai* before the *thesmothetes*, *eisaggeliai* to the *Boulē*, *probolai* to the *Dēmos*.] Since it is not known to which magistrate the *phasis* was presented (Pollux mentions only ὁ ἄρχων), it is by no means unlikely that Isocrates, pressed to specify to which *graphai* he had reference,[217] would have enumerated, among others, *phaseis*. In fact any wide enumeration of individual *graphai* would have been inconsistent with a passage whose point is rhetorical and not substantial.[218] It is however useful evidence on sycophancy, and its testimony does not contradict that of Pollux' source. Pollux rather augments Isocrates. And from this agreement there emerges useful information about a procedure allied to the rigor of the *dikai emporikai.*

[216] Bo.-Sm. II, p. 71; Harrison, *Procedure*, p. 219.

[217] Isocrates had no great distaste for specifics. Cf. *Panegyricus*, 4.11: καίτοι τινὲς ἐπιτιμῶσι τῶν λόγων τοῖς ὑπὲρ τοὺς ἰδιώτας ἔχουσι καὶ λίαν ἀπηκριβωμένοις. . . .

[218] Norlin comments in the "Loeb" *Isocrates*, Cambridge, 1928: "This was, however, true of so many crimes that the point of Isocrates is rather rhetorical."

Special Judges

Our texts suggest that specially chosen "judges" sat in the commercial courts. The presence of voting dicasts selected from those conversant with commercial matters is implied strongly by two separate passages in Dem. 35. At §43 the speaker, after proposing a number of absurdities for his opponent to justify, challenges: τούτων ὅ τι βούλεται πεισάτω ὑμᾶς. καὶ ἔγωγε καὶ αὐτὸς συγχωρῶ σοφώτατον εἶναι τοῦτον, ἐὰν ὑμᾶς πείσῃ τοὺς περὶ τῶν συμβολαίων τῶν ἐμπορικῶν δικάζοντας. [Let him prove to you whichever of these propositions he desires. I'll admit myself that this fellow is quite clever, if he should persuade you the men judging emporic contracts.] Again at §46 the suggestion is echoed that a certain super-sophistication would be required to deceive *these* judges of the commercial courts. The orator sarcastically queries: ἀλλ' οὕτως βδελυρός τίς ἐστι καὶ ὑπερβάλλων ἅπαντας ἀνθρώπους τῷ πονηρὸς εἶναι, ὥστ' ἐπιχειρεῖ πείθειν ὑμᾶς ψηφίσασθαι μὴ εἰσαγώγιμον εἶναι τὴν ἐμπορικὴν δίκην ταύτην, δικαζόντων ὑμῶν νυνὶ τὰς ἐμπορικὰς δίκας. [But is he so base and so far surpassing in evil all men, that he seeks to persuade you to vote that this *dikē emporike* is not admissible, with you now judging the *dikai emporikai*?]

Athens would not be alone in allowing judgments in emporic cases to be rendered by dicasts who differed fundamentally from those of the other courts. Maritime law in American jurisdiction knows no popular juries— decisions are made by expert judges knowledgeable of commercial affairs.[219] America's faith in the jury (a com-

---

[219] For the use of an expert as adviser to an American federal judge, by consent of the parties in highly technical cases, see, *e.g.*, United States v. Morgan, 118 F. Supp. 621, 650 (S.D.N.Y. 1953).

mon-law inheritance now abolished for civil cases in virtually every other common-law jurisdiction, including its English motherland) is no less than the trust of the ancient Athenians in "popular justice."[220] But American admiralty law, no less than Athenian, allows special solutions to the special problems of maritime commerce.

Some scholars have been reluctant to recognize this special position of marine law. The chief objection to "commercially experienced" judges is that this exception for the *dikai emporikai* modifies the overall structure of Attic justice.[221]

But the permission of exceptions to the normal procedure for the *dikai emporikai* seems almost to have been the rule in ancient Athens. The selection of judges from among those commercially active in the Peiraeus conforms to the practice of choosing emporic arbitrators from the same group.[222] Thus it is not surprising

---

[220] The seventh amendment to the Constitution of the United States of America guarantees "the right of trial by jury" in "suits at common law." No such right adheres in equity or maritime procedure. This special maritime position has allowed the admiralty courts to develop the principle of "divided fault," strongly at variance with the spirit of the common law. Whereas in the courts of the Commonwealth of Pennsylvania, for example, partial negligence denies a plaintiff the right to any and all compensation, the admiralty tribunals separate degrees of fault and allocate divided damages (see *The North Star*, 106 U.S. 17, 20 [1882]). The wisdom of the jury system for *civil* suits has often been questioned. See Benjamin Kaplan, "Trial by Jury," *Talks on American Law*, New York, 1961, pp. 50 ff.

[221] Gernet, *Budé Demosthenes*, comment on 35.43; Lipsius, *AR*, p. 143, n. 31. Thalheim however believed "die Richter für solche Prozesse mit Rücksicht auf ihr Verständnis für Handelssachen bestellt worden zu sein." *RE*, s.v. ἐμπορικαὶ δίκαι.

[222] . . . περὶ δὲ τῶν ἀντιλεγομένων [ὡς] ἑτοίμων ὄντων κριθῆναι, εἴτε βούλοιντο ἐφ᾽ ἑνὸς εἴτε κἂν πλείοσι τῶν ἐκ τοῦ ἐμπορίου . . . (Dem. 56.16).

94

that the judges themselves could be expected to recognize a "group of rascals" from the Peiraeus, as at Dem. 32.10,[223] a feat within the reasonable power only of judges acquainted with the harbor.

It seems likely then that the decisions rendered by the *dikai emporikai* were made by those conversant with the commercial world. When jury duty beckoned in the winter, many merchants would be available. Why should they not sit on the courts deciding problems that they understood? It appears that they did. In so doing they enabled Athenian commercial procedure once again to deviate from the civil and added another peculiarity to the procedural characteristics of the *dikai emporikai*.

[223] ἔστιν ἐργαστήριον μοχθηρῶν ἀνθρώπων συνεστηκότων ἐν τῷ Πειραιεῖ· οὓς οὐδ' ὑμεῖς ἀγνοήσετ' ἰδόντες.

2

JURISDICTION OF THE
DIKAI EMPORIKAI

Scope of the Commercial Courts

The positive law of Athens is, for us, more or less probable uncertainty. Definition of terms, discussion of conditions, analysis of procedure, all must be attempted with too much doubt and perhaps insufficient hesitation to restore an Athenian legal situation that may never have existed.[1]

Thus in the study of the scope of the *dikai emporikai*, there has been scholarly concern for the precise determinant of admissibility to these courts, *ratione personarum* or *rei*, but too little attention to the extent to which the Athenians themselves made such legal differentiations. In a system where equity was integral, and the εὐθεῖα of the question all important, where not only jurists and law schools[2] but even lawyers[3] in our

[1] Cf. U. E. Paoli, *Civiltà Moderna*, 4 (1932), pp. 210-227, reprinted *SPA*, pp. 3-19, esp. section 8, "il diritto attico positivo è per noi un diritto supposto." Pringsheim, *GLS*, p. 5, notes that "The fragments of Greek law which have come down to us show a deep understanding of fundamental principles, the first comparative law known to us and the conception of institutions which were imitated elsewhere, even in Rome." But there is preserved no Code, no Pandects, no Gaian textbook. What we seek to find, we cannot be certain ever was.

[2] A. H. M. Jones, *The Greek City*, Oxford, 1940, pp. 224, 253.

[3] See Jones, *Legal Theory*, pp. 128 ff.; R. J. Bonner, *Lawyers and Litigants in Ancient Athens*, Chicago, 1927, esp. pp. V. 1,

96

sense did not exist, to what extent can legal scholarship be justified in seeking the fine distinctions apparent in other legal systems at other times?

Of the five speeches normally cited as emporic,[4] it is vital to note that all but one are arguments against the admissibility of a suit [παραγραφικοὶ λόγοι]. In the *Pros Zēnothemin* (32), in the *Pros Apatourion* (33), in

---

135. Different aspects of the work of the present legal profession and their handling in ancient Athens are studied by G. M. Calhoun, *Athenian Clubs in Politics and Litigation*, Austin, 1913; E. Drerup, *Aus einer Advokatenrepublik*, Paderborn, 1916; Lofberg, *Sycophancy in Athens*; M. Lavency, *Aspects de la logographie judiciaire attique*, Louvain, 1964, esp. pp. 96-109. For a survey of varied views on the workings of the system, with a favorable estimate, see Bo.-Sm. II, pp. 288-306.

[4] Clerc, *Les Métèques*, p. 95; Lipsius, *AR*, p. 631; Hasebroek, *Trade and Politics*, p. 170; Paoli, *SDA*, p. 9, n. 1; F. Pringsheim, *Der Kauf mit fremdem Geld*, Leipzig, 1916, who treats 32, 34, 35, 56, at pp. 4-27 (Griechische Quellen I: Seedarlehnen). More legally oriented than the traditional Schäfer and Blass is L. Gernet in his Budé edition of Demosthenes (4 Vols., 1954-60). See, for 32, T. Thalheim, "Der Prozess Demons gegen Zenothemis," *Hermes*, 23 (1888), pp. 202-210; L. Mitteis, *SZ*, 23 (1902), pp. 288 ff., E. Rabel, *SZ*, 36 (1915), pp. 340-390; P. Vinogradoff, *Revue d'histoire du droit*, 3 (1922), pp. 63 ff., and *Outlines of Historical Jurisprudence*, II, Oxford, 1922, pp. 222, 227; P. S. Phōtiadēs, 'Αθηνᾶ, 36 (1924), pp. 109 ff.; M. Clerc, *Massalia, histoire de Marseille dans l'antiquité*, I, Marseille, 1927, pp. 301-306; Ziebarth, *Beiträge*, pp. 50-51; Meyer-Laurin, pp. 5 ff. On 33 see Wolff's analysis, pp. 25-35, with reference to earlier work. Dem. 34 has been studied by T. Thalheim, "Der prozess des Chrysippos gegen Phormion," *Philologische Abhandlungen für Martin Hertz*, 1888, pp. 58-68, and by E. Ziebarth, *Eine Handelsrede aus der Zeit des Dem.*, Heidelberg, 1936. For 35 see T. Thalheim, "Der Prozess des Androkles gegen Lakritos und seine Urkunden," *Hermes*, 23 (1888), pp. 333-345; Wolff, pp. 74-81. On 56, see Gernet, *Budé Demosthenes*, III, pp. 131-135, and Meyer-Laurin, pp. 12-14.

the *Pros Phormiōna* (34), in the *Pros Lakriton* (35), the question at issue is precisely the admissibility of the particular case as a *dikē emporikē*. What is more, the question is not being debated before jurists in a Faculty of Law nor even before the highly trained judges of a common-law appeals court but before Athenian citizens, at best before members of the Athenian commercial class.[5] Additionally, some of the other speeches in the Attic oratorical corpus may in fact, unperceived today, have been heard originally under emporic proceedings, while one or more presently included in the emporic category may not originally have been such.[6] The possibility of conflict of laws in the legislation of fourth-century Athens should never be, but often has been, disregarded. And even the possibility of interpolations in the extant texts is always with us.[7]

[5] For specially qualified judges from the commercial classes, see above, pp. 93-95.

[6] An actual reference to νόμοι ἐμπορικοί is made only at Dem. 35.3. Among the five *dikai emporikai*, modern scholarship believes itself to have discovered the additional categories of δίκη ἐξούλης, δίκη βλάβης and δίκη χρέως. Cf. Lipsius, *AR*, p. 644, n. 28, p. 657, esp. n. 77, p. 669, n. 119; Hasebroek, *Trade and Politics*, p. 169; Harrell, *Public Arbitration*, pp. 37-38; above, Chapter 1, n. 17, p. 9.

[7] The authenticity of the documents contained in the Demosthenic corpus has often been attacked. J. E. Kirchner had a generally high opinion of their worth (*De litis instrumentis quae exstant in Demosthenis quae fertur in Lacritum et priore adversus Stephanum orationibus*, Halle, 1883). H. T. Schucht considered them of no value: *De documentis oratoribus atticis insertis et de litis instrumentis prioris adversus Stephanum orationis Demosthenicae*, Jena, 1892. A reaction to Schucht, but not a totally convincing one, was offered by E. Drerup, "Ueber die bei den attischen Redern eingelegten Urkunden," in *Neue Jahrb. für Klassische Philologie*, Supplem., 24 (1898), pp. 221-366. In

These factors are cause, however, not for despair, but for care. From the emporic cases can be won a reasonable working definition of their fundamental nature, and from the problems involved in their jurisdiction important conclusions may be derived. But the approach must be twofold: (1) an awareness that the positive law that is to be recaptured is that of a living, controversial, non-academic juridical world, (2) a treatment of the texts stressing analytic handling of *all* the materials available, not subjective decisions as to which of the extant passages shall be excised and which accepted. As the scholarly history of the topic shows, various conclusions are possible on various evidence. The total evidence provides, I believe, a single interpretation of the jurisdictional nature of the *dikai emporikai.*

The *dikai emporikai,* offering substantial procedural advantages, encompassed only commercial maritime cases involving a written contract providing for trade to or from the port of Athens. The scope of these trials was widely debated in the courts themselves. The procedural advantages were balanced by strict requirements for admissibility. Hence a prominent defense was the *paragraphē,* here when granted (in effect) always final and never interlocutory, heard apart from and before the trial proper (εὐθυδικία), pleading that the suit was not actionable as a *dikē emporikē* because the plain-

---

recent years their value has been widely accepted. Thus Gernet: "Il convient d'admettre l'authenticité de presque tous les documents des plaidoyers civils, dont quelques-uns sont de première valeur" (1954, *Budé Demosthenes*, I, p. 22). A similar trend toward acceptance of the authenticity of the letters of Demosthenes is heralded by J. A. Goldstein, *The Letters of Demosthenes*, New York, 1968.

tiff's charges did not meet the state's requirements for introduction of a commercial maritime action.

DEFINITION OF THE DIKAI EMPORIKAI

The clearest and most definitive statement on the nature of the emporic suit is offered by the speaker in Dem. 32.1: οἱ νόμοι κελεύουσιν, ὦ ἄνδρες δικασταί, τὰς δίκας εἶναι τοῖς ναυκλήροις καὶ τοῖς ἐμπόροις τῶν Ἀθήναζε καὶ τῶν Ἀθήνηθεν συμβολαίων, καὶ περὶ ὧν ἂν ὦσι συγγραφαί. ἐὰν δέ τις παρὰ ταῦτα δικάζηται, μὴ εἰσαγώγιμον εἶναι τὴν δίκην.[8]

Here all the essential factors in the definition of *dikai emporikai* are present: the cases are *commercial maritime* (τοῖς ναυκλήροις καὶ τοῖς ἐμπόροις) *limited to contracts from Athens or to Athens* (τῶν Ἀθήναζε . . συμβολαίων) *which are written* (περὶ . . . συγγραφαί).[9]

[8] The primacy of this citation has been recognized by polemicists of varied opinions on the general scope of the *dikai emporikai*. Reinach, *DS*, s.v. *emporikai dikai*, "la meilleure définition . . ."; Lipsius, *AR*, p. 631, "am glaubwürdigsten"; Paoli, *SDA*, p. 102, "più esatta e più completa"; Gernet, *REG* 1938, p. 22, "la plus proche du texte authentique."

[9] Not only the importance of the passage but the difficulty of interpreting it have often been noted, the latter especially in regard to the words περὶ ὧν ἂν ὦσι συγγραφαί. A century and a half ago, it was proposed to disregard the requirement περὶ ὧν κ.τ.λ. (A. W. Heffter, *Die athenäische Gerichtsverfassung. Ein Beytrag zur Geschichte des Rechts, Insbesondere zur Entwickelung der Idee der Geschwornengerichte in alter Zeit*. Cologne, 1822, p. 400). The evidential value of the phrase was supposedly nil. More constructively, A. Phillipi, *Neue Jahrb. für Klassische Philologie*, 95 (1867), p. 592, held that περὶ ὧν must be taken in a limiting sense, "und bezüglich der Punkte, über die ein Vertrag vorhanden ist." But to limit the case category to particular points from a larger oral agreement encompassed in a more definitive written contract is without support in the sources. This interpre-

Two basic interpretations of the definition have been advanced, the conjunctive and the disjunctive.[10] Disjunctively the passage is understood as stating that two types of agreements are actionable as bases for *dikai emporikai*, contracts of any nature provided they be to or from Athens, and written agreements no matter where the destination or origin of the goods: "les deux membres de phrase—τῶν συμβολαίων . . . d'une parte, περὶ ὧν . . . de l'autre—se rapportent à deux espèces différentes."[11] The conjunctive approach however is correct, I believe, and establishes both the written contract as well as the agreement for the movement of goods from Athens or to Athens[12] as requirements in all *dikai emporikai*.

The double qualification demanded for admissibility is strongly confirmed by Dem. 32.22: καὶ μὴν οὐδὲ τοῦτ' ἐμέλλομεν ὑμῶν καταγνώσεσθαι, ὡς εἰσαγώγιμον ψηφιεῖσθε τούτῳ τὴν δίκην περὶ τούτων τῶν χρημάτων, ἅ κατὰ πολλοὺς τρόπους οὗτος ἔπραττεν ὅπως μὴ εἰσαγώγιμα δεῦρ' ἔσται, πρῶτον μὲν ὅτ' αὐτὰ καταλιπεῖν τοὺς ναύτας ἔπειθεν, εἶθ' ὅτ'

---

tation is contradicted by Dem. 35.27 and convincingly refuted by Beauchet IV, pp. 94-95. Lipsius, *AR*, p. 632, definitively recognized the importance of the passage, although he failed to see that it was not contradicted by other sources (pp. 631-633). The passage is dealt with parenthetically by T. Thalheim, *Hermes*, 23 (1888), p. 210, and Wolff, pp. 142-143, n. 11.

[10] The disjunctive was proposed first by H. Hitzig, *SZ*, 28 (1907), p. 227; incidentally by J. Partsch, *Griechisches Bürgschaftsrecht*, Leipzig, 1909, p. 153; later by Gernet, *REG* 1938, p. 23. The conjunctive by Beauchet IV, pp. 94 ff.; Lipsius, *AR*, p. 632; Paoli, *SDA*, p. 126.

[11] Gernet, *REG* 1938, p. 23.

[12] That the goods had to be delivered to or removed from the specified legal harbor of the Peiraeus is suggested by Dem. 25.28.

ἐν Κεφαλληνίᾳ μὴ δεῦρο πλεῖν τὴν ναῦν ἔπραττεν. [We certainly had no intention to insult you by expecting you to vote that this suit is admissible in regard to these goods which in varied ways he sought to prevent being admitted here, first when he tried to persuade the sailors to abandon them, then when in Kephallēnia he tried to prevent the ship from sailing here.]

The same sentiment is immediately repeated in paragraph 23: ἃ μὴ καταπλεῖν ὅλως οὗτος δεῦρ' ἔπραττεν, ταῦτ' εἰσαγώγιμα τούτῳ ψηφίσαισθε; Such statements would be meaningless if a written contract alone were required, and actual delivery to or removal from Athens, or agreement for such transportation, of no importance. The speaker's contention that he who attempted to block introduction of the goods into Athens has no right to introduce a commercial case into Athenian courts must be posited on some connection between actionability of cases and agreements for delivery to Athens ('Αθήναζε) or from Athens ('Αθήνηθεν). The importance of the geographical requirement was seen by Libanios in his analysis of the speech, where he cites the law limiting emporic cases to "contracts to and from Athens":[13] ὁ δὲ παραγράφεται μὴ εἰσαγώγιμον εἶναι τὴν δίκην, νόμον παρεχόμενος τὸν διδόντα τοῖς ἐμπόροις τὰς δίκας εἶναι περὶ τῶν 'Αθήναζε καὶ τῶν 'Αθήνηθεν συμβολαίων: Ζηνοθέμιδι δέ φησι μηδὲν συμβόλαιον εἶναι πρὸς αὐτόν.

The insistence on the Attic emporion goes beyond legalism. Throughout the fifth and fourth centuries the provision of food from abroad was of vital importance to Athens.[14] It seems certain that the greater part of

[13] Gernet, Budé Demosthenes, translates less literally but exactly, "pour obligations contractées dans le commerce de ou vers Athènes." See below, note 19.

[14] Dem. 20.31: πλείστῳ τῶν πάντων ἀνθρώπων ἡμεῖς ἐπεισάκτῳ

total Athenian trade was concerned with the importation of grain.[15] In Dem. 35, the requirements of the Attic mart for loans on foodstuffs and for admissibility into court of any cases thus arising are juxtaposed in the text of the speech against Lakritos and in the citation of the law concerning loans for importation of food. The speaker (§50) tells the dicasts: ἴστε . . . τὸν νόμον ὡς χαλεπός ἐστιν, ἐάν τις Ἀθηναίων ἄλλοσέ ποι σιτηγήσῃ ἢ Ἀθήναζε, ἢ χρήματα δανείσῃ εἰς ἄλλο τι ἐμπόριον ἢ τὸ Ἀθηναίων, οἷαι ζημίαι περὶ τούτων εἰσίν, ὡς μεγάλαι καὶ δειναί. [You know . . . the law, how harsh it is if any of the Athenians should transport grain anywhere else than to Athens, or should lend money for some other mart than that of Athens, how severe and how dreadful the penalties are for this.] At §51 the law as cited concludes: καὶ δίκη αὐτῷ μὴ ἔστω περὶ τοῦ ἀργυρίου, ὃ ἂν ἐκδῷ ἄλλοσέ ποι ἢ Ἀθήναζε, μηδὲ ἀρχὴ εἰσαγέτω περὶ τούτου μηδεμία. [There shall be no right to bring an action for

---

σίτῳ χρώμεθα. The Methone decrees are typical of the fifth-century situation, at least after the Persian Wars. The best overall treatment of grain (in the Greek world) is that of F. Heichelheim, "Sitos," in *RE*, Supplement VI (1935), cc. 819-892, with abundant bibliography and citation. Still of value, for Athens, is L. Gernet, "L'Approvisionnement d'Athènes en blé au Ve et au IVe siècles," *Mélanges d'Histoire Ancienne*, 1909 (Université de Paris), pp. 273-391. Much data is easily accessible in Knorringa, *Emporos*.

15 Lacking statistics—see A. H. M. Jones' remarks on this factor in *Ancient Economic History*, London, 1948, pp. 1 ff.—it is difficult for us to make precise determinations. But it is significant that the term *emporos* was especially used to indicate "corndealer" (Knorringa, *Emporos*, p. 47. Cf. p. 16). Criticizing Knorringa's use of terms, M. I. Finklestein still more generally holds that "food products, and particularly grain and wine, were the principal objects of ancient trade" (*Cl. Phil.*, 30 (1935), p. 334).

the money which an individual lends other than (for voyages) to Athens, and no magistrate shall introduce (to the court) any such suit.] The statement in the law, if a later addition to the text, is gratuitous. It does not complement the text directly, nor is it required by the speech itself, although it does strengthen the point being made by the speaker. Unlike the other emporic speeches, Dem. 35 otherwise offers no argument on the content of the *nomoi emporikoi*. The citation agrees with the conjunctive interpretation of 32.1 and is in all probability sound.[16] If cases arising from nautical loans for grain not imported to Athens were not actionable in any court for citizens or metics of Athens, it is extremely unlikely that the special process of the emporic court at Athens was thrown open to all those everywhere who troubled to write their contracts. Such a provision would have been absolutely senseless especially since the nautical contract was already by tradition and form a written one. Thus, in effect, the major part of Athenian trade, commerce in grain, operated under the conjunctive conditions of 32.1, even without special legislation: using the written contract as a matter of course, the merchants could give legal effect at Athens to these contracts only by stipulating delivery to Athens.[17]

The suggestion has been made that the conjunctive interpretation of 32.1 is not grammatically viable.[18] To the contrary, the precise rendering of this passage of-

[16] On the validity of the document, see Calhoun, *Cl. Phil.*, 13 (1918), p. 175, n. 10; Blass, III.1, p. 562, n. 4.

[17] For the universal use of writing in maritime agreements of this period, see below, pp. 129-136.

[18] Most recently by Gernet, *REG* 1938, p. 23, n. 4. On the presence of ἄν cf. Wolff, p. 143, n. 11.

fers a valuable insight for defining the case category *dikai emporikai*. The word συμβόλαιον denotes in a broad sense "agreement"; the word συγγραφαί by the fourth century in commercial maritime matters had come to have the specific connotation "written agreement." The speaker is thus saying that trials are actionable τοῖς ναυκλήροις καὶ τοῖς ἐμπόροις [to ship owners and sea traders], (1) on agreements from and to Athens, and (2) "about which" (περὶ ὧν) [agreements] there are συγγραφαί ["written arrangements," "written agreements"]. It is the old problem of Euler's Circles: a wider class encompassing a smaller. When mentioned in the context of maritime commerce all *syngraphai* are *symbolaia*, but not all *symbolaia* are *syngraphai*.[19]

Similarly to be solved is the more general problem involved in utilizing the various definitions of *dikai emporikai* to produce a unified concept.[20] Unity is the result if we consider the description of *dikai emporikai* in 32.1 not as "la meilleure définition" in the sense that it

---

[19] In this context the translation of συμβόλαιον as "obligation," possibly non-contractual, seems to me impossible. To speak of "obligations from Athens or to Athens," in a non-contractual sense, is unintelligible. Gernet's translation, "obligations contractées dans le commerce de ou vers Athènes," is not literal, but still not incompatible with the interpretation of *symbolaion* as involving contractual and not tortious relationships. In agreement with Gernet (*Budé Demosthenes*, p. 112) in attaching a wider meaning than "contract" to *symbolaion* in this passage are Meyer-Laurin, p. 9, and Wolff, p. 143. But, in my opinion, it is only in the period of the Roman law that *symbolaion* was on occasion contrasted with "contracts in writing." Cf. The Tebtunis Papyri, 397.17 (late second century A.D.).

[20] The chronological element is without influence here. There is no indication that, once established as *emmēnoi* (after 355), the area of action in the commercial maritime courts was appreciably changed.

offers grounds for rejecting as interpolation other statements about this case category, but as the best definition in that it is more rigorous and more exact. Examined in this light, the other definitions and all the emporic speeches show that they meet (or the plaintiff alleges they meet) the conditions set forth at 32.1 for emporic cases—agreements in writing connected with the Athenian mart.

Thus in the speech *Pros Zēnothemin* (32) itself, there is a written agreement (§16; cf. hypothesis, §2, ἐπειδὴ γὰρ ἐγέγραπτ᾽ ἐν τῷ συμβολαίῳ) contracted from Athens to Athens (§14). Similarly in *Pros Apatourion* (33), an original loan was made for the voyage to Athens: the speaker says that immediately upon arrival in Athens (κατέπλευσαν δεῦρο, §5) they were required to pay the creditors. Although we do not know specifically here whether the original loan was premised on written or unwritten contract, it is important to note that all later agreements mentioned in this case are in writing (loan to meet Apatourios' creditors, §12; the arbitration agreements, §15).

In the *Pros Phormiōna* (34), both the *paragraphē* and Chrysippos' answer to it are concerned with the existence or non-existence, the actionability or non-actionability, of a written agreement from Athens to Athens. The defendants allegedly claim that they have violated no provision written in the contract. Here too throughout the speech when agreements are mentioned they are in writing.[21]

The *Pros Lakriton* (35) is no exception. In fact, here the *syngraphē* has actually been preserved for us (§10-§13).[22] The written contract (συγγραφή) in maritime

---

[21] Cf. §6: συγγραφὴν ἐθέμην παρὰ Κίττῳ τῷ τραπεζίτῃ.

[22] Its validity is beyond doubt. Aside from the general discus-

commercial dealings is alluded to as commonplace: (§1) ἐπειδὰν δὲ λάβωσιν καὶ συγγραφὴν συγγράψωνται ναυτικήν. There is a provision covering transportation from or to Athens: χρήματα δανείσας . . . κατὰ τοὺς ἐμπορικοὺς νόμους, εἰς τὸν Πόντον καὶ πάλιν Ἀθήναζε (§3).

Finally *Kata Dionysodōrou* (56) is precisely the same situation: a written contract for transportation of goods to Athens. The references here are numerous and clear beyond quibbling: εἰς ἕτερον ἐμπόριον οὐδὲν ἀλλ᾽ ἢ εἰς Ἀθήνας . . . καὶ συγγραφὴν ἐγράψαντο (§6).[23]

The various definitions contained in these speeches, when seen in context, further necessitate strict limitation on the scope of the *dikai emporikai* to cases arising from written contract for delivery of goods to or from Athens: Dem. 33.1: τοῖς μὲν ἐμπόροις, ὦ ἄνδρες δικασταί, καὶ τοῖς ναυκλήροις κελεύει ὁ νόμος εἶναι τὰς δίκας πρὸς τοὺς θεσμοθέτας, ἐάν τι ἀδικῶνται ἐν τῷ ἐμπορίῳ ἢ ἐνθένδε ποι πλέοντες ἢ ἑτέρωθεν δεῦρο. [The law orders that actions for maritime traders and ship owners shall be before the *thesmothetes*, if they should be wronged in any way in the market, either sailing from here to any place, or from elsewhere here.] Quoted in this form, the citation has been the basis of the "wider" interpretation. The phrase ἐάν τι ἀδικῶνται ἐν τῷ ἐμπορίῳ ["if they should be

---

sions referred to in n. 7 of this chapter, see specifically T. Thalheim, *Hermes*, 23 (1888), p. 341; E. Drerup, *Neue Jahrb. für Klassische Philologie*, Supplem., 24 (1898), pp. 315 ff.; Lipsius, *AR*, p. 685, n. 32; Gernet, *REG* 1938, p. 39. Even its detractors admit its importance. Thus Ashburner, p. ccxii, claims that the document does not refer to the events described in the speech, but adds that "the model was evidently a good one, and may be taken to represent the law not later than the third century B.C."

[23] Additionally, compare 56.3, 56.9, 56.10, etc., especially 56.36: . . . . Ἀθήνηθεν εἰς Αἴγυπτον.

wronged in any way in the market"] has been seized upon as an excuse for ignoring Dem. 32.1, as a disproof of 32.1, as a complementary extension of the jurisdictional area of the *dikai emporikai* beyond the scope defined by Dem. 32.

On the basis of this passage many scholars have concluded that the *dikai emporikai* were not after all limited only to contractual disputes, but encompassed any wrong done *emporoi* or *nauklēroi* in connection with voyages to or from Athens.[24] In turn those scholars who did not welcome a citation apparently contradictory to 32.1 have found it easy or necessary to ignore or bracket the passage.[25]

In fact not only the opening passage but the speech itself has been cited as clear proof that *dikai emporikai* have no necessary connection with litigation arising from commercial contracts—for it has been argued that

[24] As seen by Beauchet, "Il y aurait donc lieu à une *dikē emporikē*, lorsque, par exemple, dans le cours du voyage, un des intéressés dans le navire a disposé indûment des marchandises chargées sur le navire, lorsqu'il s'élève des difficultés à l'occasion des droits de douane, lorsqu'une personne élève des prétentions illégitimes sur les marchandises débarquées ou lorsqu'un négociant est illégalement entravé dans sa liberté commerciale." Beauchet IV, p. 91. The citation splits scholarship into partisans of *dikai emporikai* requirements *lato sensu* (Beauchet IV, p. 92; Hitzig, *SZ*, 28 (1907), p. 225; Paoli, *SDA*, p. 105; Gernet, *REG* 1938, p. 16) and believers in *dikai emporikai* provisions *stricto sensu* (Reinach, *DS*, s.v. *dikai emporikai*; Clerc, *Les Métèques*, p. 94; Lipsius, *AR*, pp. 631 ff.; Hasebroek, *Trade and Politics*, pp. 169-170).

[25] Lipsius, *AR*, pp. 631-632: "Die weitere Ausdehnung, die man den Handelsklagen auf alle Rechtsstreite hat geben wollen, die sich auf Handelsangelegenheiten bezogen, findet in dem offenbar ungenauen Gesetzzitat der Rede gegen Apaturios keine Stütze."

the case really concerns arbitration agreements.[26] However those who have so contended have failed to note two important factors: (1) the case itself may not belong in the category *dikai emporikai*. This like all the others (except 56) is a hearing where the basic point in litigation is precisely its admissibility as a *dikē emporikē*. We have the speech (παραγραφικὸς λόγος) of the party contending that it is not. To assume that this particular action is "commercial" is unsafe, especially when the speech is pleading that "the action is not 'commercial.'" It is the definition of the category that must determine the essential nature of the *dikai emporikai*. (2) Apatourios may nonetheless be in the right, and the case may truly fall under Athenian emporic jurisdiction. If so, the cause of its being admissible can easily and, I believe, necessarily derive from an original contract 'Aθήναζε, which would have activated the entire complicated commercial and legal epilogue.[27] This

[26] This view has been especially virulent. See E. Platner in 1824, *Der Process und die Klagen bei den Attikern*, Darmstadt, I, p. 292. See Beauchet IV, p. 91, "Il ne s'agissait point ici d'une convention commerciale proprement dite, d'un *symbolaion*." See Gernet, *Budé Demosthenes*, 1954, p. 131: "Il est curieux que, dans les discussions qu'il y a eu au sujet du domaine d'application des *dikai emporikai* on n'ait pas songé au cas du Contre Apatourios. . . . L'action est 'commerciale,' simplement parce qu' Apatourios, négociant maritime, poursuivait l'exécution d'une obligation sur le fondement d'un acte écrit—l'acte du compromis."

[27] Paoli, himself an advocate of the *lato sensu* interpretation, has incidentally noted this possibility: "Nell'orazione *contro Apaturio* . . . nel racconto degli antefatti si fa menzione di una serie di prestiti, fra i quali, secondo ogni verosimiglianza, un prestito marittimo . . ." (*SDA*, p. 9). The creditors could have proceeded against Apatourios' ship under an agreement such as

would have been the contract creating the original debt that Parmenōn and the unnamed pleader assumed when Apatourios and Parmenōn sailed to Athens (κατέπλευσαν δεῦρο). At the conclusion of a commercial journey Apatourios may well have come to Athens— otherwise his behavior in arriving at the Athenian port is inexplicable, since creditors were waiting to attach his vessel. If however he was bringing with him goods that failed to satisfy his debt and if as a result his ship had become liable for the deficit, his arrival in Athens and his consequent difficulties would be rationally explicable.

As for the definition offered in the first paragraph of the oration, read in context it is a virtual duplication of the requirements mentioned in 32.1, for the speaker goes on to add: καὶ τοῖς ἀδικοῦσιν δεσμὸν ἔταξεν τοὐπιτίμιον, ἕως ἂν ἐκτείσωσιν ὅ τι ἂν αὐτῶν καταγνωσθῇ, ἵνα μηδεὶς ἀδικῇ μηδένα τῶν ἐμπόρων εἰκῇ. τοῖς δὲ περὶ τῶν μὴ γενομένων συμβολαίων εἰς κρίσιν καθισταμένοις ἐπὶ τὴν παραγραφὴν καταφεύγειν ἔδωκεν ὁ νόμος, ἵνα μηδεὶς συκοφαντῆται, ἀλλ' αὐτοῖς τοῖς τῇ ἀληθείᾳ ἀδικουμένοις τῶν ἐμπόρων καὶ τῶν ναυκλήρων αἱ δίκαι ὦσιν. [and for the wrongdoers it has established imprisonment as the penalty, until they should pay the judgment against them, so that no one lightly should wrong any of the maritime traders. But to traders brought into court about contracts which never existed, the law allows a special plea, so that no one should be "sycophanted," but trials should be confined to those of the merchants and owners truly

---

that contracted by the brothers of Lakritos in the *syngraphē* quoted in 35: καὶ ἐάν τι ἐλλείπῃ τοῦ ἀργυρίου . . . ἔστω ἡ πρᾶξις τοῖς δανείσασι καὶ ἐκ τῶν τούτων ἁπάντων, καὶ ἐγγείων καὶ ναυτικῶν . . . (12).

110

wronged.] The speaker may mention ἐάν τι ἀδικῶνται ["if they should be wronged in any way"], but in the very next breath he defines the basis of taking exception to the introduction of *dikai emporikai*, the non-existence of a contractual relationship, [τοῖς δὲ περὶ τῶν μὴ γενομένων συμβολαίων εἰς κρίσιν καθισταμένοις.]. In other words, for the introduction of a case in the category *dikai emporikai*, it is maintained that a contract is required—otherwise the *paragraphē* is available. This is no variant definition. It is identical in all particulars with 32.1, except that it does not expressly mention the need for a *written* contract. But the requirement of Athens as port, the limitation to commercial maritime matters (with virtually the same terminology [τοῖς ἐμπόροις καὶ τοῖς ναυκλήροις]), the requirement of contract—these are the same.

Another important citation of the scope of *dikai emporikai* is offered at 34.3-4:[28] οὗτοι οὐ τὸ παράπαν συμβόλαιον ἐξαρνοῦνται μὴ γενέσθαι ἐν τῷ ἐμπορίῳ τῷ ὑμετέρῳ, ἀλλ᾽ οὐκέτι εἶναί φασι πρὸς αὐτοὺς οὐδὲν συμβόλαιον · πεποιηκέναι γὰρ οὐδὲν ἔξω τῶν ἐν τῇ συγγραφῇ γεγραμμένων. οἱ μὲν οὖν νόμοι . . . οὐχ οὕτως λέγουσιν, ἀλλ᾽ ὑπὲρ μὲν τῶν μὴ γενομένων ὅλως συμβολαίων Ἀθήνησι μηδ᾽ εἰς τὸ Ἀθηναίων ἐμπόριον παραγράφεσθαι δεδώκασιν. . . . [These men do not absolutely deny the existence of a contract on your market, but claim rather that it no longer affects them, for they have violated no provision in the contract. However the laws . . . do not employ such language, but they permit a plea against jurisdiction (*paragraphē*) on the grounds of there being no contract at all at Athens or to the Athenians' market.] The same

---

[28] A passage cited by Beauchet (IV, p. 92, n. 2) but generally ignored.

111

elements appear here. The contract must be in writing (γεγραμμένων). The reference to ἐν τῷ ἐμπορίῳ τῷ ὑμετέρῳ is immediately clarified by the explicit 'Αθήνησι μηδ' εἰς τὸ 'Αθηναίων ἐμπόριον.

In the same speech, at paragraph 42, reference is made to "the law . . . ordering dikai emporikai for contracts made at Athens and to the Athenian market, and not only for those made at Athens, but even [for] whichever should be made for the purpose of the voyage to Athens." [ὁ νόμος . . . κελεύων τὰς δίκας εἶναι τὰς ἐμπορικὰς τῶν συμβολαίων τῶν 'Αθήνησιν καὶ εἰς τὸ 'Αθηναίων ἐμπόριον, καὶ οὐ μόνον τῶν 'Αθήνησιν, ἀλλὰ καὶ ὅσα ἂν γένηται ἕνεκα τοῦ πλοῦ τοῦ 'Αθήναζε.] The similarity in terminology to 32.1 has been often noted, but the final clause has been judged pure interpolation, i.e. from καὶ οὐ μόνον on.[29] It seems however that the passage simply is stating that Athens need not be the site of contract in disputes actionable as dikai emporikai—the principle forum contractūs does not here hold.[30] Contracts wherever made, provided they are for (ἕνεκα) Athens, will be actionable. It is natural that ὅσα have an antecedent, and the only possible one here is symbolaia. The sentence may be poorly phrased, but it is consistent.

A final footnote to the general discussion is offered at 56.2: πιστεύοντες . . . ὑμῖν, ὦ ἄνδρες δικασταί, καὶ τοῖς νόμοις τοῖς ὑμετέροις, οἳ κελεύουσιν, ὅσα ἄν τις ἑκὼν ἕτερος

[29] Cf. MSL, p. 636, n. 411; A. Fränkel, De condicione, iure, iurisdictione sociorum Atheniensium, Rostock, 1878, p. 67; Reinach, DS, s.v. emporikai dikai, n. 2. But Beauchet properly judges (IV, p. 92): "Il n'y a point, en effet, de raison décisive pour rejeter comme interpolée dans le plaidoyer de Phormion la phrase."

[30] Cf. the contract at Dem. 32.4, signed at Syracuse but leading to an emporic hearing at Athens.

ἑτέρῳ ὁμολογήσῃ, κύρια εἶναι. [Trusting to you, o jurors, and your laws which order that whatever an individual willingly agrees with another shall be binding.] Inevitably there have been those who would see here a contradiction to the requirement of a written agreement for admissibility to the commercial maritime courts at Athens. But again the context of the citation is entirely at variance with any interpretation linking the reference to a pure consensual contract (*contractus consensu*). In the preceding sentence the written nature of the ὁμολογία [agreement] has been made clear: λαβὼν γὰρ ἀργύριον φανερὸν καὶ ὁμολογούμενον ἐν γραμματειδίῳ δυοῖν χαλκοῖν ἐωνημένῳ καὶ βυβλιδίῳ μικρῷ πάνυ τὴν ὁμολογίαν καταλέλοιπε τοῦ ποιήσειν τὰ δίκαια. The following paragraph contains a specific reference to written contract: ἀλλά μοι δοκεῖ οὔτε τῶν νόμων οὔτε συγγραφῆς οὐδεμιᾶς ὄφελος[31] εἶναι οὐδέν, ἂν. . . .

In short, from the references to *dikai emporikai* in the salient orations it becomes clear that it is necessary to examine citations in context. No dictionary definitions

[31] The existence of consensual contract has been generally acknowledged by students of Greek law, on the basis of a number of passages from the orators and Plato (Dem. 42.12; 44.7; 47.77; 48.11; the present passage; Isocrates 18.24; Hyperides Ath. 13, Ath. 15; Deinarchos 3.4; Plato, *Symposium*, 196C; *Crito*, 52E; *Laws*, 220D. Cf. Beauchet; Lipsius, *AR*; P. Vinogradoff, *Outlines of Historical Jurisprudence*, II, Oxford, 1922, p. 238; G. Ferrari, *Atti del R. Istituto di scienze, lettere e arti*, 59 (1910), p. 1198, and *Byzantinische Zeitschrift*, 20 (1911), p. 538; L. Mitteis and U. Wilcken, *Grundzüge und Chrestomathie der Papyruskunde*, Leipzig, 1912, II, 2, "Chrestomathie," p. 73, n. 1. But Pringsheim may be right in his conclusion (*GLS*, p. 47), "Greek law never recognized informal agreements, it did not know consensual contracts." Cf. his discussion at pp. 14-57. Less detailed is Jones, *Legal Theory*, pp. 216-235.

are being given by these orators, but chance descriptions. To extrapolate a lexicographical citation is the task of those who desire to know what grounds specifically and juridically were required for admissibility of cases to *dikai emporikai* in fourth-century Athens. From all the references in the orators and from the actual dispute involved in all the emporic cases, two elements remain uncontradicted constants: the necessity of a written contract for admissibility to the *dikai emporikai*; the requirement that the written contract provide for transportation of goods to or from Athens.

But vital questions still remain unanswered. Within the restrictions of contractual nature and contractual purpose, was admissibility further restricted only to members of a clearly constituted commercial class? That is, were the cases actionable not only *ratione rerum* but also or rather *ratione personarum*? How prevalent was the written contract, and what was the significance of its requirement in the *dikai emporikai*? To what purpose was the *paragraphē* employed in these cases? Was a special plea against admissibility of the dispute to *dikai emporikai* an effective defense in a commercial dispute?

Non-Existence of a "Commercial Class"

From late antiquity to the present there have been those who believed that the *dikai emporikai* at Athens were concerned with or limited to members of a "commercial class."[32] It is indeed possible, though unlikely,

[32] The medieval "commenda" relationship in which "creditor" and "borrower" were replaced by financier and merchant sharing proportionately in profits may have been a source of confusion. For the "commenda," cf. Ashburner, pp. ccxxxvii-ccxl.

that *dikai emporikai*, in their embryonic form under the *nautodikai*, were actionable *ratione personarum*.[33] But there is no evidence that at any time under the *eisagōgeis* or the *thesmothetai* the *dikai emporikai* were limited to members of the "commercial class."

Theoretically it is conceivable that commercial maritime cases, even within the strict limitations of contract and import-export site (Ἀθήνηθεν ἢ Ἀθήναζε), were further limited to members of a recognized commercial class (τοῖς ναυκλήροις καὶ τοῖς ἐμπόροις).[34] But an examination of the evidence indicates the great implausi-

[33] If so, the theoretical defects sketched below would have occurred, and their manifestation would have necessitated reform in the courts. Cf. Lysias 17.5 and the discussion of that passage below, p. 179. That text is the probable explanation of the definitions offered by Pollux and the *Lexica Segueriana*. Thus Pollux 8.63: ἐμπορικαὶ δὲ δίκαι ἔμμηνοι αἱ τῶν ἐμπόρων ἢ τῶν περὶ τὸ ἐμπόριον. *Lexica Segueriana*, p. 237, "ὄνομα δίκης, ἢν πρὸς τοὺς ἐμπόρους περὶ ὁτουδὴ λαγχάνουσιν. ἦσαν δὲ αὗται ἔμμηνοι ὑπὲρ τοῦ μὴ τρίβεσθαι αὐτοὺς δικαζομένους καὶ ἀργεῖν τῆς ἀγορᾶς." The definitions are clearly not systematic—neither are they chronologically differentiating. Just as they fail to note the period when *dikai emporikai* were not *emmēnoi*, so the *Lexica Segueriana* fails to make clear the period when they were not decided *ratione personarum*. Modern scholars following Lysias especially have come to the same probably erroneous conclusions. E. Platner, *Der Prozess und die Klagen bei den Attikern*, I, Darmstadt, 1824, pp. 290 ff. (esp. 291) relying on Pollux' definition together with Dem. 33.1, saw emporic cases as being of extremely wide scope; G. Perrott, *Essais sur le droit public et privé de la république athénienne*, Paris, 1867, p. 311, n. 1, following Lysias 17.5 in particular, believed that the *basic* determinant of *dikai emporikai* was *personal*.

[34] The special selection of judges (see above, pp. 93-95) implies no "commercial class." Those inexperienced in commercial affairs would simply have been debarred from service on the *dikai emporikai*.

115

bility of such an assumption, for (1) such a commercial class did *not* in reality exist, and (2) such a commercial class could not in fourth-century Athens *juridically* exist —the difficulty of determining personal status would so proscribe.

In fact the litigants involved in *dikai emporikai* are of the most varied types—citizens, metics, foreigners,[35] individuals engaged in trade, individuals engaged in finance, possibly even slaves. Although in particular cases it is often difficult (or better, never really possible) to determine precisely the exact status of a specific individual, even a rapid perusal of the speeches dealing with emporic matters demonstrates the great variability of participants.[36]

In *Pros Zēnothemin* (32) a citizen and a foreigner are involved: Dēmon, allegedly a kinsman of Demosthenes,[37] and Zēnothemis, a Massaliōtēs. *Pros Apatourion* (33) probably is of the same sort: the nameless pleader appears by his arguments to be an Athenian, while Parmenōn and Apatourios are from Byzantion.[38]

[35] The conduct of trade by foreigners was common in the ancient world: Hellenistic Rhodes forms an apparent exception. See L. Casson, *Transactions of the American Philological Association*, 85 (1954), p. 172.

[36] We will not here attempt to define individual statuses. This is impossible because (1) we do not know precisely what determined particular classes juridically in Athens—it remains a burning scholarly question; (2) we have no precise knowledge of the individuals involved in these cases. The crux of the problem is the identification and isolation of metics—the classic statement on the difficulty remains Clerc, *Les Métèques*, pp. 10-14, 295-297.

[37] Cf. §23, τὰ τῶν πολιτῶν, and §31, ἐμοὶ δ᾽ ἐστὶ . . . Δημοσθένης οἰκεῖος γένει. See Davies, pp. 116-117, who identifies the speaker "beyond any doubt" as Δήμων (II) Δημομέλους Παιανιεύς.

[38] For the speaker's civil status there is really no substantial

The status of the individuals in *Pros Phormiōna* (34) is highly disputed: Chrysippos is certainly a non-citizen; Lampis, if not a slave, is perhaps a metic; Phormiōn may be an out-and-out foreigner, or he may indeed be an isotelēs.[39] The speech *Pros Lakriton* (35) offers similar problems. Probably we again have a case involving citizen and foreigner. In the contract, cited at paragraphs 10-13, Androklēs is termed Σφήττιος, hence a citizen. Nausikratēs is a Καρύστιος, i.e. from Karystos on Euboea. The original nationality of Artemōn and Lakritos is Phaselite, and it further appears from the opening paragraph of the speech, in which the Phaselites as a group are denounced, that the defendants in this case were considered if not juridically, at least popularly, Phaselites. Legally the vital passage is §16, αὐτὸς [Λάκριτος] γὰρ ἔφη ποιήσειν μοι τὰ δίκαια ἄπαντα

---

evidence. Schäfer III.2, p. 297, thinks him a metic. Cf. Blass III.1, p. 572; Paoli, *SDA*, p. 89. Apatourios resides normally at Byzantion (§5).

[39] Lipsius, *AR*, p. 792 sensibly observed, "Bei der . . . Rede gegen Phormion, lässt sich nicht entscheiden ob die Parteien Metoiken waren." Schäfer (III.2, p. 300, n. 4) and Blass (III.1, p. 577, n. 1) consider Chrysippos and his brother to be metics. To the contrary, Paoli, *SDA*, pp. 92-93. But probably Paoli makes too much of the verb ἐπιδημοῦντες in positing its use as an absolute requirement for identifying metics. As Clerc long before observed, "des étrangers établis pour un séjour de courte durée, étaient . . . enrôlés parmi les métèques" (*Les Métèques*, p. 295). The vital passage is §1, where the brothers are identified as εἰς τὸ ὑμέτερον ἐμπόριον εἰσαφικνούμενοι. Lampis' status as a metic depends on §37, οἰκῶν μὲν Ἀθήνησιν, οὔσης δ' αὐτῷ γυναικὸς ἐνθάδε καὶ παίδων. Schäfer identifies Phormiōn as an *isotelēs* from §12, and Paoli cites him as a foreigner, contrasting §12 (ἐπειδὴ τοίνυν . . . ἐπεδήμησεν Φορμίων οὑτοσὶ σεσωσμένος 'εφ' ἑτέρας νεώς) to §50 (θανάτῳ ζημιώσαντες εἰσαγγελθέντα ἐν τῷ δήμῳ, καὶ ταῦτα πολίτην ὑμέτερον ὄντα καὶ πατρὸς ἐστρατηγηκότος).

117

καὶ ἐπιδημήσειν ᾿Αθήνησιν. . . . [For Lakritos said that he would do all justice by me and would stay at Athens. . . .] If Lakritos made this promise because he normally did not reside at Athens, he was not a metic; if he was able to say this because he normally resided at Athens, he was.

In the speech *Kata Dionysodōrou* (56) Dareios and Pamphilos appear to be Athenian metics (§14), while Dionysodōros and Parmeniskos are totally foreign (§7).[40]

Thus the *dikai emporikai* involved a wide variety of nationalities. This is of course to be expected, since there were clearly a large number of metic-foreigners among the *emporoi*. Aeschines (1.40) accordingly speaks of τῶν ἐμπόρων ἢ τῶν ἄλλων ξένων [the *emporoi* or the other foreigners]. Xenophon in the *Poroi* (3.12) stresses the advisability of building καταγώγια ["inns"] at Athens for the *nauklēroi* and *emporoi*, which indicates that substantial numbers of traders did not own permanent housing in Attica. Similarly Hesychios identifies the *emporoi* with the metics [ἔμπορος:μέτοικος]. Lysias (22.17) refers to *emporoi* as τοῖς εἰσπλέουσιν [lit. "those sailing in"]. The honorary decrees show clearly a heavy foreign influence: *IG* II².283 and 360 (Cyprus), 342 (Tyre), 401 (Kyzikos), 407 (Miletos?), 408 (Herakleia), *SEG* III.92 (Chios).[41]

With such a variety of individuals involved in commerce[42] and more particularly in *dikai emporikai*, the

[40] Cf. Blass III.1, p. 583.

[41] Cf. L. Casson, *Transactions of the American Philological Association*, 85 (1954), p. 169. That the fifth-century situation was somewhat analogous to that of the fourth is indicated by the Old Oligarch's allusion to foreigners among the *emporoi* (1.12).

[42] The personal status of individuals involved in Attic trade is

basis for individual participation in these cases becomes important. It is not very useful to posit a tradesman's right, *quā* tradesman, to litigate, without determining who constitutes a "tradesman."[43]

The prevailing belief is that the commercial world in ancient Athens was well defined, somewhat like an "exchange."[44] Correspondingly, entrance to the *dikai emporikai* allegedly would be limited to those whose membership card in this clearly defined world of commerce was valid.[45]

---

discussed by Hasebroek, *Trade and Politics*, pp. 1-44, esp. pp. 13-15 and 22; Paoli, *SDA*, pp. 88-96, pp. 99-109; Knorringa, *Emporos*, pp. 79-80; Amit, pp. 54-57. Hasebroek's overall belief in the insignificance of trade in classical Greece and in the meanness of the traders has been often attacked and substantially refuted, particularly by Gomme, "Traders and Manufacturers," *Essays*, pp. 42-67. Still Hasebroek's work is abundant in reference to the literary sources.

[43] Paoli, *SDA*, p. 105: "ogni commerciante, purchè tale, aveva capacità di stare in giudizio."

[44] "*L'emporion* lui-même a pu être comparé, d'un certain point de vue, à une Bourse." Gernet, *REG* 1938, p. 21, n. 2. Cf. J. Hasebroek, *Hermes*, 58 (1923), p. 418.

[45] Two different problems tend at this point to become confused, the matters with which *dikai emporikai* were concerned, and the persons to whom juridical rights in these courts were granted. From the belief that there was a "World of Emporoi," the notion arises that those in this charmed circle were able to bring all their problems to the emporic courts without limitation. Thus Gernet does not demur to Beauchet's statement (IV, p. 95) that "c'est la nature même de l'affaire qui détermine son caractère de *dikē emporikē*," but immediately adds (*REG* 1938, p. 20) "on ne peut guère croire que des *naukleroi* ou *emporoi* occasionnels fussent exclus du bénéfice de la loi." Similarly Paoli, believing that members of the commercial class as such were admitted to the *dikai emporikai*, asks, "perchè escludere che i tribunali em-

Such a commercial world did not exist. Evidence that it did is slight, and the obstacles to recognizing such a group either practically or definitively are insurmountable. We find no evidence anywhere in the sources of anything resembling the medieval *commenda*, which formed a legally recognized unit with specific membership. In fact, in a legal world where there was no recognition of the legal existence of private associations, apart from the personalities of their individual members,[46] there could be no recognition of unincorporated, loosely connected individuals as a legal class.[47]

Any individual taking part in commerce was, for fourth-century Athens, a "commercial person." Individuals importing goods for their own purposes, individuals normally engaged in other pursuits but at the moment transporting materials for themselves or for others, *emporoi* earning their living from maritime trade—all were legally in the same position in approaching the *dikai emporikai*. Furnishing in writing the legal contract providing for the movement of goods from or to Athens, they were admitted to the commercial maritime courts at Athens.

---

porici si pronunziassero anche in materia non contrattuale?" (*SDA*, p. 102). The reason "perchè" is of course that all our evidence limits the commercial maritime courts to contractual matters—there is no reason nor need to assign to them a wider sphere.

[46] See Jones, *Legal Theory*, pp. 152-166. *Digest* 47.22.4 (law concerning associations, attributed by Gaius to Solon) is consistent with a collective, rather than corporate, existence of these groups.

[47] Beauchet saw this clearly (IV, p. 95) and noted it in cursory fashion, "A Athènes, en effet, la loi ne reconnaît point à certains individus la qualité de commerçant avec les conséquences juridiques que comporte cette qualité dans le droit moderne."

Commercial courts with jurisdiction over international trade were necessarily "international" in admission of individuals. It was the contract, not the person, that counted. This is why, perhaps, even slaves could testify and participate in these trials.[48] Similarly metics participate neither as metics nor as commercials. Their personal capacity is of no significance.[49]

If one were however to posit the existence of a "com-

[48] Thus Zēnothemis is at 32.4 termed an ὑπηρέτης. Lampis is at 34.5 the οἰκέτης of Diōn, at 34.10 παῖς of Diōn: αὐτὸς μὲν ἀπεσώθη ἐν τῷ λέμβῳ μετὰ τῶν ἄλλων παίδων τῶν Δίωνος, ἀπώλεσε δὲ πλέον ἢ τριάκοντα σώματα ἐλεύθερα χωρὶς τῶν ἄλλων. It is not absolutely certain that either one is a slave: cf. Schäfer III.2, pp. 305 ff., "früher Dions Sklave"; Blass III.1, p. 577; Lipsius, *AR*, p. 797, n. 28; Beauchet II, p. 461; J. Partsch, *Griechisches Bürgschaftsrecht*, Leipzig, 1909, p. 136. Also it must be noted that Lampis, for whom slavery is more likely or at least better testified a possibility than for Zēnothemis, did not in fact testify at the trial. The question of procedural capacity of slaves is tantalizingly unclear in Lysias 23, where the speaker seems to be arguing that his case is admissible *because* his opponent is not a Plataian but a slave. In the case of Lampis, Paoli (*SDA*, p. 107) concludes that he would have been able to testify, "pur essendo schiavo, perchè nei processi commerciali si prescinde dallo stato personale del commerciante." But it seems more reasonable to assume that if slaves, lacking all legal personality, could testify at these trials, it was not because, being *commercianti*, they met the personal requirements, but because *there were no personal requirements*.

[49] If the personal status of metics was of significance in the *dikai emporikai*, a difficult problem of conflict of jurisdiction would necessarily have resulted. *Ath. Pol.* 58.2: δίκαι δὲ λαγχάνονται πρὸς αὐτὸν (the Polemarch) ἴδιαι μὲν αἵ τε τοῖς μετοίκοις καὶ τοῖς ἰσοτελέσι καὶ τοῖς προξένοις γιγνόμεναι. *Ath. Pol.* 58.3: ὅσα τοῖς πολίταις ὁ ἄρχων, ταῦτα τοῖς μετοίκοις ὁ πολέμαρχος. Again Paoli incorrectly concludes (*SDA*, p. 92): The metics "stanno in giudizio non già come meteci, ma come commercianti, altrimenti adirebbero il Polemarco e non i Tesmoteti." But again the personal status of the metics is not germane.

mercial class," the practical difficulties in identifying it would be great. Many individuals mentioned in commercial sources participated in a number of activities, often of little relationship, often outside the commercial world. Thus we find a farmer from Pantikapaion engaged in trade: τινὶ γεωργῷ παρεκομίζετο ἐν τῷ πλοίῳ ἐκ Παντικαπαίου εἰς Θεοδοσίαν (Dem. 35.32). The son of Sōpaios, wealthy Bosporan landowner, was sent to Athens, partly for trade, partly for education.[50]

Thus the classical world is not comparable to the medieval period, when maritime commerce encompassed a partnership of financial backer and actual trader; as we have noted, the man providing the capital and the man handling the goods at that time shared equally or proportionately in profit and loss.[51] The classical situation was far different; the relationship between *nauklēroi* and *emporoi* on the one hand and their financial supporters on the other was simply one of credit and repayment, although the particular terms of the maritime loan (no repayment unless ship or cargo serving as security survived the voyage) did give the two parties in a specific transaction a certain community of interest.[52] Still they were not a single class, and in reality this would have presented great barriers to a single juridical treatment. The commercial banking class, quite amorphous, switching its investments at will

[50] Isocrates 17.3-4, 42. Cf. Hasebroek, *Hermes*, 55 (1920), p. 151; *Trade and Politics*, p. 13.

[51] See Knorringa, *Emporos*, p. 92, n. 4; Paoli, *SDA*, pp. 56-57.

[52] Cf. G. M. Calhoun, *J. Econ. and Bus. Hist.*, 2 (1930), pp. 581-582, and Paoli, *SDA*, p. 55, "i contraenti sono tuttavia legati dal vincolo di un interesse commune." In Hellenistic and Roman times liability was allocated by contractual agreement. See C. H. Brecht, *Zur Haftung der Schiffer im antiken Recht*, Munich, 1962.

from one field to another,[53] having in its ranks both part-time and full-time creditors, had no necessary connection with *emporoi* or *nauklēroi*. And it must be remembered that the trials preserved to us invariably pit a commercial creditor against a maritime operator, no matter what the specific inciting factor in a particular case. For the courts, then, to define and to delimit a "commercial" class, of necessity not limited solely to those of the name *nauklēroi* or *emporoi*,[54] would in practice have proven either impossible or absolutely arbitrary.

Even those who engaged in maritime commerce seldom did so exclusively. Knorringa notes that "prob-

[53] See R. J Hopper, "Attic Silver Mines in the Fourth Century B.C.," *Annual of the British School at Athens*, 48 (1953), pp. 249-254. On the role of Athenian banks as providers of credit, see Bogart, pp. 367-375.

[54] The terms *nauklēros* and *emporos* themselves seem certainly to have been used in no definitely consistent fashion in antiquity. See M. I. Finkelstein, " Ἔμπορος, ναύκληρος and κάπηλος," *Cl. Phil.*, 30 (1935), pp. 320-336, who demonstrates that these nouns were "used in one way and in other cases differently." The difficulties of modern scholarship in attempting to define *nauklēros* and *emporos* demonstrate how involved would have been the task of the judges in the *dikai emporikai* in deciding who was and who was not, by definition, a commercial. Cf. J. Hasebroek, "Die Betriebsformen des griechischen Handels im IV. Jahrh.," *Hermes*, 58 (1923), pp. 393-425; Knorringa, *Emporos*, esp. pp. 46-47, 51-52, 96-98, and 113-118; U. E. Paoli, "Grossi e piccoli commercianti nelle liriche di Orazio," *Rivista di Filologia*, 52 (1924), pp. 45-63, and in *SDA*, pp. 23-24. It may be noted that in the medieval period the same fuzziness of definition prevailed. As Ashburner (p. cxxxv) points out, "No category is clearly defined. Whatever class you belong to, you are constantly found performing the functions of another class." In the Rhodian Sea Law itself, for example, *nauklēros* is employed in no less than four differing fashions.

ably almost all *emporoi* in Athens were occasional moneylenders."[55] Thus Antipatros of Kition (Dem. 35.32) defies modern definition—he may have been an *emporos*, or he may have been a *trapezitēs* ("banker"). Nikoboulos, together with Evergos, lent money on a silver mine at Laurion. But immediately after this, he departs for the Pontic area on business (Dem. 37.6). Conversely Phormiōn the *trapezitēs* owned ships (Dem. 45.64).[56]

In short, the interrelation of interests would have made it impossible to delimit the class,[57] and arbitrary to define the individual.[58]

[55] *Emporos*, p. 91.

[56] On the background and familial relationships of Phormiōn see the excellent treatment in Davies, s.v. Πασίων (I) 'Αχαρνεύς, esp. pp. 435-437.

[57] Paoli's suggestion for defining members of the commercial class, based on no ancient evidence, suggests the difficulties an approach *ratione personarum* would have encountered: "Nella maggior parte dei casi la qualità di commerciante doveva risultare indirettamente dalla natura dell'atto in rapporto al quale era sorta la controversia; si sarà dunque giudicato della commercialità dell'atto ricorrendo al comune concetto di commercio di cui mancava—nè se ne sentiva la necessità—una precisa definizione giuridica. . ." (*SDA*, p. 100). In fact the working definition of commercial persons might have been "those who were signatories to a contract providing for transportation of goods to or from Athens." Any other definition, even a popular one of no legal significance, meets the practical difficulty of connecting in the public mind members of two different groups: financial and maritime. The connection is a difficult one. Hasebroek, *Trade and Politics*, p. 10, simply makes the statement, "Those who owned capital did not take part in commerce."

[58] The situation has not changed. So inherently difficult is the separation of the "merchant" from the "non-merchant" that "les législations commerciales modernes arrivent à peine à marquer la

It is true that references to occupation are made in the *dikai emporikai*, but there is no indication that these allusions relate to a legal class. Thus the speaker at Dem. 33.4 alludes to having spent much time in "maritime affairs" and to familiarity with "most of those sailing the sea." [ἐγὼ γὰρ, ὦ ἄνδρες δικασταί, πολὺν ἤδη χρόνον ἐπὶ τῆς ἐργασίας ὢν τῆς κατὰ θάλατταν, μέχρι μέν τινος αὐτὸς ἐκινδύνευον, οὔπω δὲ ἔτη ἐστὶν ἑπτὰ ἀφ᾽ οὗ τὸ μὲν πλεῖν καταλέλυκα, μέτρια δ᾽ ἔχων τούτοις πειρῶμαι ναυτικοῖς ἐργάζεσθαι· διὰ δὲ τὸ ἀφῖχθαι πολλαχόσε καὶ διὰ τὸ εἶναί μοι τὰς διατριβὰς περὶ τὸ ἐμπόριον γνωρίμως ἔχω τοῖς πλείστοις τῶν πλεόντων τὴν θάλατταν.] The reference is to a profession, not to a juridical grouping. This the speaker in Dem. 35.49 makes clear: ἐγὼ δ᾽ εἰμὶ ἔμπορος, καὶ σὺ ἀδελφὸς καὶ κληρονόμος ἑνὸς τῶν ἐμπόρων. [I am an *emporos*, and you are the brother and heir of an *emporos*.] If the world of *emporia* were composed of a single legal class, and only this group were admitted to the *dikai emporikai*, then the speaker, by stressing his opponent's relation to an *emporos* and admitting implicitly therefore that Lakritos was not himself such, would be arguing against his own contention that the case is admissible.[59]

---

ligne qui sépare le commerçant du non-commerçant." P. Huvelin, *DS*, s.v. Mercator, p. 1731.

[59] Paoli must have had this passage in mind when he wrote: "Vediamo nell'orazione *contro Lacrito* che il convenuto ha eccepito, fra l'altro, di non esser commerciante, declinando così il fòro al quale è stato citato" (*SDA*, p. 101). But Paoli gives no reference, and mention of such a defense does not in fact appear in the speech. Cf. the analysis by Libanios: Ἀνδροκλῆς . . . δύο προβαλλόμενος δίκαια, ὅτι τε παρόντος Λακρίτου καὶ ἀναδεξαμένου τὸ ἀργύριον ἐδάνεισε τῷ Ἀρτέμωνι, καὶ ὅτι κληρονόμος ἐστὶ τῶν Ἀρτέμωνος Λάκριτος. ὁ δὲ τῆς μὲν κληρονομίας ἀφίστασθαί φησι, παρα-

In fact, disregard of juridical personality is strongly indicated at §45, where the speaker asks, "Have not the same laws been written for all of us and the same rights in the *dikai emporikai?*"[60]

The answer is yes. These laws provided for admissibility to the *dikai emporikai* only of cases arising from contracts in writing providing for the Athens market, independent of questions of personality. Other disputes arising among maritime traders and ship owners would be handled under other existing jurisdictions. Those who were citizens or legally recognized metics could look for the defense of their rights to the *epōnymos archon* and the *polemarch.* Of those who did not so qualify many would have rights of litigation secured under *symbolaia* and could approach the δίκαι ἀπὸ συμβόλων.[61]

Additionally there were the ἐπιμεληταὶ ἐμπορίου, the administrative officials of the harbor, who certainly

---

γράφεται δὲ τὴν δίκην, λέγων μηδὲν ἑαυτῷ πρὸς ᾿Ανδροκλέα συμβόλαιον εἶναι μηδὲ συγγραφὴν μηδεμίαν. πάντως δὲ καὶ τὸ ἀναδεδέχθαι ἔξαρνος γίνεται·οὐδὲ γὰρ ἂν τοῦθ᾽ ὁμολογῶν ἠγνωμόνει πρὸς τὴν ἔκτισιν.

[60] οὐχ ἅπασιν ἡμῖν οἱ αὐτοὶ νόμοι γεγραμμένοι εἰσὶν καὶ τὸ αὐτὸ δίκαιον περὶ τῶν ἐμπορικῶν δικῶν;

[61] G. E. M. de Ste. Croix, *Classical Quarterly*, 11 (1961), p. 96, shows that "δίκαι ἀπὸ συμβόλων arising out of what we call torts or crimes are likely to have formed a class at least as important and as numerous as those arising out of contract." Cf. his Appendix A, *ibid.*, pp. 108-110. His conclusion (p. 109): "Of anything that might be called 'commercial' suits, there is no sign." This is precisely what we should expect. Although de Ste. Croix' basic concern is the Athenian Empire, in exploring the nature of the δίκαι ἀπὸ συμβόλων, he is working entirely with sources from the "second quarter of the fourth century." At that time "commercial cases" were of course handled in the *dikai emporikai.*

possessed both limited juridical and police power: ἐμπορίου δ' ἐπιμελητὰς δέκα κληροῦσιν. τούτοις δὲ προστέτακται τῶν τ' ἐμπορίων ἐπιμελεῖσθαι . . . (*Ath. Pol.* 51.4). Similarly the law cited at Dem. 35.51 speaks of these officials as recipients of the *phasis*.[62] In fact, in the text of another speech of Demosthenes (58), we learn of the actual deposit of a *phasis* with the secretary of the *epimelētai emporiou*.[63]

Thus there was no compelling need for members of the merchant group, *quā* merchants, to be specially protected. Hence the scope of the *dikai emporikai* naturally would run parallel to that of the *dikai metallikai*, which clearly were concerned with the action involved, not with the person.[64]

Nor were the *dikai emporikai* unimportant because thus limited to contractual obligations in writing. True, a creditor speaks, but there must have been substantial basis for the famous assertion at Dem. 34.51 that, in the absence of those lending money on sea voyages, not a ship would sail: οὔτε ναῦν οὔτε ναύκληρον οὔτ' ἐπιβάτην ἔστ' ἀναχθῆναι, τὸ τῶν δανειζόντων μέρος ἂν ἀφαιρεθῇ. It is clear that these loans provided the financial basis for commerce—all our evidence for commercial maritime activities in the Athenian market consistently shows this. Further it appears probable that the maritime loan (*nauticum foenus*) represented, in part at

[62] "τὴν φάσιν καὶ τὴν ἀπογραφὴν τοῦ ἀργυρίου πρὸς τοὺς ἐπιμελητάς."

[63] See §8: ταύτην τὴν φάσιν . . . ἔλαβεν δὲ ὁ γραμματεὺς ὁ τῶν τοῦ ἐμπορίου ἐπιμελητῶν, Εὐθύφημος . . . οὗτος εἴασε διαγραφῆναι καλούντων αὐτὸν εἰς τὴν ἀνάκρισιν τῶν ἀρχόντων. ὅτι δὲ ταῦτ' ἀληθῆ λέγω, πρῶτον μὲν κάλε: ὃς ἐγραμμάτευε τῇ ἀρχῇ, Εὐθύφημον. In these cases "φάσις" is apparently not employed in the technical sense.

[64] Dem. 37.35-38 proves this at length: οὗτος σαφῶς ὁ νόμος διείρηκεν ὧν εἶναι δίκας προσήκει μεταλλικάς κ. τ. λ.

least, an early form of insurance.[65] The risk was assumed by the creditor—if the ship or the cargo serving as security did not survive the voyage, the loan need not be repaid. Only if the creditor were financing a considerable number of voyages would there be any rationale for the transfer of risk from borrower to lender— the principle of insurance is simple: the risk that is in one case a great uncertainty becomes, over a sufficiently large number of cases, a virtual certainty. Thus only where many loans were made could it be reasonably foretold approximately how many would be annulled through loss of cargo or ship. A large volume would be required for any sensible operation of such a principle.

[65] Cf. Ziebarth, *Beiträge*, p. 52; Knorringa, *Emporos*, p. 92, "loan combined with assurance"; Calhoun, *J. Econ. and Bus. Hist.*, 2 (1930), pp. 579-584. For early views, see H. J. Sieveking, *Das Seedarlehen des Altertums*, Leipzig, 1893, p. 10. No other devices to transfer risk from one party to another were known in the ancient world. (The text of the English edition of Poulsen's *Delphi* is in error when it speaks of "high insurances" (p. 148) in explaining the great expense involved in the construction of the mid-fourth-century temple of Apollo at that site.) The origins of modern insurance have been variously sought. Generalizations such as that of Cafiero ("il mondo greco-romano non conoscesse le assicurazioni," *Atti Associazione Italiana di Diritto Marittimo*, Vol. I (13), 1934, p. 73) overlook the true nature of *nauticum foenus*. G. Valeri, *Rivista di diritto commerciale*, 26 (1928), pp. 616 ff., is opposed to seeing any relationship between *nauticum foenus* and insurance, but not persuasively so. See F. Edler de Roover, "Early Examples of Marine Insurance," *Journal of Economic History*, 5 (1945), pp. 172-200; P. Civiletti, "Origini dell' Assicurazione," *Atti Associazione Italiana di Diritto Marittimo*, Vol. I (13), 1934, pp. 115-137. For bibliography, cf. E. Besta, *Le obbligazioni nella storia del diritto italiano*, pp. 379-380. Also, R. Doehaerd, "Chiffres d'assurance à Gênes en 1427-28," *Revue Belge de Philologie et d'Histoire*, 27 (1949), pp. 736-756.

The creditor who could sustain the total loss of a loan could certainly sustain a considerable amount of business.[66]

THE REQUIREMENT OF WRITTEN CONTRACT

The requirement of a written contract would not impede the smooth workings of the emporic courts nor upset the practices of commerce. "Writing" was of importance comparatively early in Greek legal history, and the written contract was in general use in maritime trade at Athens in the fourth century.[67]

The normal instrument of Athenian commerce in the fourth century was the συγγραφή, often in the Demosthenic corpus referred to in the plural. In popular terminology the contract could be, and was, cited under a number of terms: συγγραφή, συγγραφαί, συνθῆκαι, συμβόλαια, συμβόλαιον. Whichever term is used, in the emporic courts a written agreement is *sub iudice*.[68] The

[66] We hear of creditors active in the market over a considerable period of time—cf. Dem. 34.2. At a later date Zeno the Philosopher is said to have made bottomry loans amounting to over 1,000 talents. As the source of our information on Zeno's mercantile operations is Diog. Laertios 7.13, the statement is not unimpeachable.

[67] On the general importance of the written form in Greek law, see L. Mitteis, *Reichsrecht und Volksrecht in den östlichen Provinzen des römischen Kaiserreichs*, Leipzig, 1891, p. 514, and F. Pringsheim, *Der Kauf mit fremdem Geld*, Leipzig, 1916, pp. 99, 114.

[68] Sometimes in the fourth century, in casual references, no differentiation is made among contracts of different sorts. This does not mean that then or later there were not legal differences, more or less subtle, among the various written forms. Thus ὑπόμνημα is unquestionably simply an entry on bankers' books (cf. Dem. 49.5; Bogaert, p. 381, n. 454). As for the other terms,

129

prevailing use of written forms in commercial agreements and the naturalness of the references to writing are the important factors in ascertaining the reasonableness of a provision requiring the presentation of *syngraphai* for action in *dikai emporikai*. The vexing question of the specific legal concept of the *syngraphai* is

---

the reasons for confusion are clear: *syngraphē* was so thoroughly connected with the concept of "written" form that it was applied carelessly to various other contracts, while *synthēkai* or *symbolaia* were so implicitly "contractual," that all contracts could be thus characterized. The precise legal differentiations however are difficult to isolate. Paoli has suggested in reference to *synthēkai* and *syngraphē* that:

1) the *syngraphē* is limited to contracts of loan, while the *synthēkai* can include contracts of loan as well as other agreements of a wide nature.

2) the *syngraphē* is executory; the *synthēkai* as a rule is not. No action can be based on it alone.

3) the *syngraphē* is *necessary* to the taking of action; the *synthēkai* is necessary as proof of an agreement. (See Paoli, *SDA*, pp. 123-124.)

These categories, especially the second, are probably too rigid, and M. I. Finley is certainly correct in saying that "a proper study of these terms, based on an analysis of every known use, would be invaluable" (*Land and Credit*, New Brunswick, 1952, p. 217, n. 73). Pending such a detailed investigation, the inadequate literature on the subject remains: (for the *syngraphē*) Beauchet IV, pp. 69-82; R. Dareste, "Sur la *syngraphē* en droit grec et en droit romain," *Bulletin de correspondance héllenique*, 8 (1884), pp. 362-374; Paoli, *SDA*, ch. VI, "La syngraphe," pp. 121-137; Schwahn, s.v. *syngraphai*, *RE*, cols. 1369-1376, and Kunkel, *RE*, s.v. *syngraphē*, cols. 1376-1387 (including the Roman period and giving bibliography to 1931); Jones, *Legal Theory*, pp. 219-221; F. Meulemans and M. Verschueren, "De sungraphè in de 4de eeuwo," *RIDA*, 3rd Ser., 10 (1963), pp. 163-173; for the *synthēkai* and its differentiation from the *syngraphē*, Schulthess, Synthēkē, *RE*, Suppl. VI (1935), cols. 1158-68.

130

not here relevant—long discussions on the Roman legal category into which classical Greek contracts should be placed are better left to late classical Roman jurists or modern scholars concerned with the assignments of contracts *re, verbis, litteris* or *consensu.*[69]

In the *emporikoi logoi* there are clear illustrations of the use of varying terms to describe the same written agreement. Thus at Dem. 32.5 συγγραφαί exist for Zēnothemis and Hēgestratos; at 32.7 the same agreement is referred to as τὰ συμβόλαια. Similarly *syngraphē* and *synthēkai* are shown to be terms applied to the identical contract: ΜΑΡΤΥΡΙΑ: Ἀρχενομίδης . . . μαρτυρεῖ συνθήκας παρ᾽ ἑαυτῷ καταθέσθαι Ἀνδροκλέα Σφήττιον . . . καὶ εἶναι παρ᾽ ἑαυτῷ ἔτι κειμένην τὴν συγγραφήν (35.14).

Most important for the definition of jurisdiction in emporic cases is the clear evidence for the relationship of *syngraphai* to *symbolaia*. The two terms are equated at Dem. 34.31: τὴν γὰρ συγγραφὴν ἀνελόμενος ἀπήλλαξο ἂν τοῦ συμβολαίου. But immediately thereafter appears a clear parallel to the wording of the definition at 32.1 (τῶν . . . συμβολαίων, καὶ περὶ ὧν ἂν ὦσι συγγραφαί) : οἶδε μὲν πρὸς σὲ δύο συγγραφὰς ἐποιήσαντο ὑπὲρ τοῦ συμβολαίου (34.32). Similarly τὰ ὁμολογηθέντα is used in the sense of τὰ συμβόλαια and implicit there is the concept of συγγραφαί: τὰ δὲ παρ᾽ ἀμφοτέρων ὁμολογηθέντα τῶν συντιθεμένων, καὶ περὶ ὧν συγγραφαὶ κεῖται ναυτικαί, τέλος ἔχειν ἅπαντες νομίζουσιν, καὶ χρῆσθαι προσήκει τοῖς γεγραμμένοις (Dem. 35.27). And Androklēs, after much discus-

---

[69] Cf. L. Mitteis, *Reichsrecht und Volksrecht in den östlichen Provinzen des römischen Kaiserreichs*, Leipzig, 1891, pp. 459 ff.; L. Mitteis and U. Wilcken, *Grundzüge und Chrestomathie der Papyruskunde*, Leipzig, 1912, II.1, pp. 116 ff.; F. Meulemans and M. Verschueren, "De sungraphè in de 4de eeuwo," *RIDA*, 3rd Ser. 10 (1963), pp. 165-173.

sion of συγγραφαί in the same speech, refers in contractual context to συμβόλαια: ἀλλὰ ποῦ χρὴ λαβεῖν δίκην, ὦ ἄνδρες δικασταί, περὶ τῶν ἐμπορικῶν συμβολαίων; (47).

In short, the *syngraphai* was the normal means of commercial agreement. Thus the written nature of the contract need not be specified by a speaker unless relevant to the particular point involved. There even existed a prescribed or traditional form for the *syngraphai*: οὐσῶν δὲ τῶν συγγραφῶν, ὥσπερ εἰώθασιν ἅπασαι . . . (Dem. 32.5). No less ingenuous are the references to *syngraphai* at Dem. 33.36, 35.1, 56.1, and earlier in time at Lysias 30.17.

The absence of written receipts attesting to payments of money in the fourth century has seemed to some remarkable.[70] The inference even has been made that those engaged in trade were "for the most part illiterate and uneducated."[71] That receipts were not used does not however necessarily prove the illiteracy of those who might have employed them, any more than the lack of printing proves the basic illiteracy of the ancient world, Dr. Johnson's dictum notwithstanding. Simple and convenient devices are often obvious only after their discovery.

Furthermore the prevalent element of good faith and the prevailing importance of witnessing as a prime form of attestation together would have inhibited the general development of writing for purposes of proof.[72]

[70] Cf. J. Hasebroek, "Die Betriebsformen des griechischen Handels im IV. Jahrh.," *Hermes*, 58 (1923), pp. 393 ff. Receipts were widely used in the Hellenistic period, as the papyri testify. But classical Greece knew nothing of them. See Dem. 33.12; 34.30; 48.46.

[71] Hasebroek, *Trade and Politics*, p. 21.

[72] Concerning the "legally indispensable witnesses," see Pringsheim, *GLS*, pp. 18 ff.

The doctrine has generally prevailed that the Greeks, and especially the Athenians, were a particularly litigious people—*Graeca fides* has become a synonym for dishonest dealing. There is, in fact, no sound reason to suppose the Greeks abnormally litigious or especially dishonest[73]—spectacular cases, by their nature exceptional and preserved perhaps for their scandalous notoriety, and prejudiced statements from Romans (such as Juvenal) about Orientals and Greeks of a later time, have created the myth. To the contrary there is abundant opportunity to see from the sources that, in the Greek business world, good faith and fair dealing, not litigation, were the lubricants of commerce. The creditor trusted not to laws and formal contracts, but to the borrower's reliability: οὔτε τῶν νόμων οὔτε συγγραφῆς οὐδεμιᾶς ὄφελος εἶναι οὐδέν, ἂν ὁ λαμβάνων τὰ χρήματα μὴ πάνυ δίκαιος ᾖ τὸν τρόπον (56.2).

Philosophically, moreover, there loomed a barrier to the introduction of the receipt in the Greek concept of sale as a ready-money affair.[74] The ownership of the goods presumed the payment of the price.

Under these conditions, the widespread use of writing in maritime loans is noteworthy. Nor is it simply that our sources covering cases presented as *dikai emporikai* give a false picture of the predominance of written contract, resulting from the exclusion of all other commercial disputes aside from those for which written agreements existed.

A priori, the general use of writing in maritime agreements would seem likely. A contract such as Dem. 35.

[73] Cf. Gernet, *REG* 1938, pp. 30-31; Paoli, *SDA*, p. 86; Jones, *Legal Theory*, p. 232.

[74] Pringsheim, *GLS*, pp. 190-196, esp. pp. 190-191, "The popular feeling in Athens was that without the receipt of the price sale is out of the question."

133

10-13 shows the intellectual complexity of fourth-century commercial dealings. Jones is right that "by this time maritime loans had become the subject-matter of agreements of such length and complication that any other method of evidencing them than writing would have been hopelessly inadequate."[75] The contract had to be in writing so that later disagreements might be referred to it: πάντες ἄνθρωποι, ὅταν πρὸς ἀλλήλους ποιῶνται συγγραφάς, τούτου ἕνεκα σημηνάμενοι, τίθενται παρ' οἷς ἂν πιστεύσωσιν, ἵνα, ἐάν τι ἀντιλέγωσιν, ᾗ αὐτοῖς ἐπανελθοῦσιν ἐπὶ τὰ γράμματα, ἐντεῦθεν τὸν ἔλεγχον ποιήσασθαι περὶ τοῦ ἀμφισβητουμένου (Dem. 33.36).

Hence the requirement of written contract for introduction of *dikai emporikai* was entirely consistent with the sophisticated nature of maritime commerce in the fourth century B.C. In fact, the heavy reliance of later Greek law upon the written form[76] can be traced to the nautical loan; this pioneering trait, written documentation, became an essential feature of Hellenistic and later Greek law, and provided powerful contrast to the characteristic oral stipulation of the Roman law.[77]

[75] *Legal Theory*, p. 219.

[76] The written contract survived in the eastern provinces of the Roman Empire despite its inconsistency with the principles of classical Roman law. Justinian's *litterarum obligatio* (Inst. 3.21) "has no connexion with the classical litteral contract" (See F. Schulz, *Classical Roman Law*, Oxford, 1951, p. 506) and may represent the final incorporation of the Greek written concept into the transmitted Roman system.

[77] Cf. Pringsheim, who observes that "it became more and more advisable and usual, especially as commercial life developed, to combine both, the legally indispensable witnesses and the expedient documentation. This is the first step of the triumphal career of the written document through the Greek and Hellenistic world" (*GLS*, p. 44). Similarly M. I. Finley: "It was

134

JURISDICTION OF DIKAI EMPORIKAI

The fourth century was the focal point of this development, for it was then that the *syngraphē* developed from its original meaning of "something written down" to its specialized contractual context. The development of the term συγγραφή is illustrated by the parallel development of the term συγγραφεύς, originally referring to a writer of prose, as opposed to poetry.[78] Its specific connotation differs with specific context. A συγγραφεύς generally referred to is simply a writer in general.[79] Specifically referred to, as in the fifth-century historians, he is a specific type of writer, as a writer of history.[80] Additionally there was the term συγγραφής, denoting commissioners assigned to draw up measures.[81] But between these classical Greek usages and the terminology in Hellenistic and post-Hellenistic times there is vast difference. Thus in the first-century A.D. συγγραφεύς can refer specifically to the party in a contract (cf. *BGU* 636.23). This does not mean that terminology was necessarily so limited, and indeed in modern Greek the word συγγραφεύς denotes the author of a work in prose.

The development of the term *syngrapheus* was paralleled by the specialization in meaning of the *syngraphē* itself. At Thucydides 1.97 it is still "that which is written down" and in *IG* I².76.47 it is the draft decree drawn up by the συγγραφής. But gradually the term came to have

in the commercial field, more narrowly in the speculative world of maritime loans, that the written contract became more or less universal" (*Land and Credit*, New Brunswick, 1952, p. 22).

[78] Cf. Plato, *Phaedrus*, 235C; 278E (λόγων); Isocrates 15.35.
[79] Aristophanes, *Acharnians*, 1150; Plato, *Phaedrus*, 272B.
[80] Cf. Herodotus 1.93; Thucydides 1.1.
[81] Thus Thucydides 8.67; *IG* I².22.3; Philochoros, *FGH* (Jacoby) 136; Isocrates 7.58.

the meaning of "contract," probably derived from its use in reference to building regulations, which necessarily involved contractual relationships between the state and those engaged in the construction.[82] But it is in maritime commerce that *syngraphē* was first extensively used to denote written contract, and it is from this context that its meaning finally broadened, and from this beginning that the written form itself took on contractual significance.[83]

THE PARAGRAPHĒ: ITS IMPORTANCE IN THE EMPORIC COURTS

Like the emporic court itself, the *paragraphē* makes its first definite appearance shortly after the restoration of the democracy in 403.[84] And, like the emporic courts,

[82] Cf. Gernet, *REG* 1938, p. 28.

[83] Cf. Paoli, *SDA*, pp. 121 ff.

[84] Information on the nature and use of this special plea in bar of action is found chiefly in the παραγραφικοὶ λόγοι of the Demosthenic corpus: speeches 32 through 38. Important historical evidence on the development of the institution is offered by Isocrates 18 (Pros Kallimachon) and Lysias 23 (Kata Pankleōnos). On the background and interpretation of the nonemporic paragraphic speeches, see the classic commentaries of Schäfer and Blass, and for the legal problems, Gernet's *Budé Demosthenes*. The *paragraphē* has been much studied, most recently and effectively by Wolff. For the *dikai emporikai* such vexing problems as the relationship of magisterial power to special pleas and the connection of arbitration and *paragraphai* are fortunately peripheral. Other than Wolff, the most important studies, with abundant reference to other relevant materials, include *MSL*, pp. 852 ff.; Lipsius, *AR*, pp. 846 ff., especially pp. 846-847; Wilamowitz, *A & A*, II, pp. 368-369; Glotz, *DS*, s.v. *paragraphē*, pp. 323-325; G. M. Calhoun's series of articles, "Διαμαρτυρία, Παραγραφή and the law of Archinus," *Cl. Phil.*, 13

the *paragraphē* has a history, testifying anew to the
refinement and development of Attic legal institutions
during the formulative fourth century.
The *paragraphē*, as a separate pleading to forestall
court action, seems not to have existed before the over-
throw of the Thirty. Thus the speaker in the "Herodēs
Murder" case (Antiphon 5.8-18; cf. 85-96), within his
speech, pleads against the jurisdiction of the trial court
but makes no special plea and raises no specific legal
doctrine. This is a special type of negative evidence, for
the situation described would have demanded a *paragraphē*, had such a concept then existed.[85]

(1918), pp. 169-185. "Παραγραφή and Arbitration," *Cl. Phil.*,
14 (1919), pp. 20-28; "Athenian Magistrates and Special Pleas,"
Cl. Phil., 14 (1919), pp. 338-350; U.E. Paoli, "L'inscindibilità
del processo in diritto attico," in *SPA*, pp. 75-174; Bo.-Sm. II,
"Special Pleas," pp. 75-96; F. Lämmli, *Das attische Prozess-
verfahren in seiner Wirkung auf die Gerichtsrede*, Paderborn,
1938, pp. 146-165; W. Hellebrand, *RE*, s.v. *paragraphē*, cols.
1169-1181; A. Biscardi, *Novissimo Digesto Italiano*, s.v. "Giu-
dizi paragrafici"; E. Schönbauer, *Anzeiger der Akademie der
Wissenschaften*, 1964, pp. 203 ff. Hellebrand in particular offers
extensive annotation covering earlier research. Hellebrand's
bibliography is updated by Wolff, p. 10. On the connection of
paragraphē and *prothesmia*, Charles' treatment is interesting:
Statutes of Limitations, pp. 62-63.
[85] Thus Wilamowitz, *A &A*, II, p. 369; Lipsius *AR*, p. 847.
Calhoun, *Cl. Phil.*, 13 (1918), pp. 170-171, argues that "the
separate hearing of special pleas was not unknown prior to the
passage of the law of Archinus . . . to some of these special pleas
the name *paragraphē* was given. . . ." For Hellebrand, "Das
Gesetz des Archinos scheint mir kaum bedeutsame prozessrechtliche Neuerungen gebracht zu haben" (*RE*, s.v. *paragraphē*, c.
1178). But the testimony of the ancients here seems preferable
to the opinion of the moderns: Εἰ μὲν καὶ ἄλλοι τινὲς ἦσαν ἠγωνι-
σμένοι τοιαύτην παραγραφήν, ἀπ' αὐτοῦ τοῦ πράγματος ἠρχόμην ἂν

As it develops in the fourth century the *paragraphē* is encountered most often in the emporic courts.[86] Study of the jurisdictional problems in the commercial maritime courts hence is impossible without a corresponding investigation of the *paragraphē* as employed in these courts—for the *paragraphē* when raised in the *dikai emporikai* is precisely a plea against jurisdiction.[87] It is not at all surprising that of the five emporic cases (*dikai emporikai*) preserved in our sources four are attested by so-called paragraphic speeches (παραγραφικοὶ λόγοι).

Even a cursory glance at the historical development of the special pleas during the post-Aigospotamoi democracy goes far to explain the apparent prevalence of the *paragraphē* in the commercial maritime courts. Moreover the development of the special pleas involves special considerations of separability of process in Attic law—and especially in the *dikai emporikai*. Specifically, when a *paragraphē* was offered, was there a possible requirement of two separate hearings in the commercial courts? Finally, the *paragraphē*, seen in maritime legal context, explains why the Athenians wished to limit the jurisdiction of the *dikai emporikai* to disputes arising from written agreements concerning the Attic market.

τοὺς λόγους ποιεῖσθαι· νῦν δ' ἀνάγκη περὶ τοῦ νόμου πρῶτον εἰπεῖν καθ' ὃν εἰσεληλύθαμεν, ἵν' ἐπιστάμενοι περὶ ὧν ἀμφισβητοῦμεν, τὴν ψῆφον φέρητε, καὶ μηδεὶς ὑμῶν θαυμάσῃ διότι φεύγων τὴν δίκην πρότερος λέγω τοῦ διώκοντος (Isocrates 18.1). A procedural innovation that might strike an Athenian audience as a θαῦμα must certainly have involved "bedeutsame prozessrechtliche Neuerungen."

[86] Paoli, *SPA*, p. 106.

[87] Here there must be noted again the phraseology at Dem. 32.1, 33.1, 34.4 and 42, 35.45. In 34, the payment is not itself the basis of the *paragraphē*, but the basis of the claim that the maritime courts cannot admit the case through lack of jurisdiction.

It is to these problems of development, separability, and jurisdiction that we now turn.

Historical Development of the Paragraphē

For comparative purposes, the history of the *paragraphē* best begins with the ἀντιγραφή (*antigraphē*), a "special plea" known from Lysias 23, Kata Pankleōnos. Chronological difficulty results from the impossibility of dating the speech exactly, but it is clearly early among the extant Attic orations.[88] What is important, however, is not the speech's specific date, but the type of special plea it presents. The *antigraphē* is here, as the *paragraphē* can also be, a "plea to the jurisdiction," but it exhibits not only a different name but also different characteristics.[89] Having

[88] No specific time is assigned to it by Blass (I, p. 619) or Jebb (*Attic Orators from Antiphon to Isaeus*, I, London, 1893, p. 299), both of whom posit only "uncertain date." Gernet, *Budé Lysias*, finds the speech necessarily "assez près de 403," while Lamb, in the Loeb *Lysias*, guesses that it was "probably delivered some little time before 387."

[89] The lexicographers have difficulty with *antigraphē*: its technical sense of "special plea" collides with its colloquial meaning of "reply in writing"—cf. Caesar's *Anticato* answering to Cicero's *Cato* and termed ἀντιγραφή (Plutarch, *Caesar* 3). Still Pollux (8.58) notes its technical sense: ἀντιγραφὴ δέ, ὅταν τις κρινόμενος ἀντικατηγορῇ. καὶ ἡ παραγραφὴ δὲ ἀντιγραφῇ ἔοικεν . . . ὁ δ' ἀντιγραψάμενος μὴ κρατήσας τὴν ἐπωβελίαν προσωφλίσκανεν. He goes on to tell us, as we would expect, that τίθενται δὲ τὸ τῆς ἀντιγραφῆς ὄνομα καὶ κατὰ τῶν ἀπαντώντων πρὸς τὰς γραφάς, καὶ ἔστι πρὸς τὴν γραφὴν τὸ τοῦ φεύγοντος γράμμα ἀντιγραφή. . . . To see how the lexicographers handled the non-paragraphic *antigraphē*, cf. Pollux 8.33; Harpocration, s.v. *antigraphē*; Lexica Segueriana, p. 410.7. The double citation in Pollux (and cf. 8.54) is another example of his habit of citing the same term in different context, and thus preserving evidence from different

referred to his opponent's *antigraphē* (§5: μοι ἀντε-
γράψατο μὴ εἰσαγώγιμον εἶναι), the speaker deals only
with the special plea and does not allude to matters of
equity and justice, or to the circumstances of the case.
The plaintiff here seeks only to show that the case is
indeed actionable in the particular jurisdiction. Our difficulty in dating Lysias 23 derives from this very phenomenon; there is no reference to factors external to the
antigraphē. This austerity is never duplicated among
the *paragraphikoi logoi* proper. The speech, accordingly, is extremely short, its brevity again in contrast
with the adequate, and sometimes more than adequate,
length of the speeches in the paragraphic *dikai emporikai*. Moreover the plaintiff speaks first, whereas later the
normal speaking roles are reversed in the paragraphic
hearing and the defendant who offers the special plea
opens the debate. *Excipiendo reus fit actor.*[90]

---

periods (see below pp. 191 ff.). The great difficulty, for ancient
and modern scholars, in defining Attic legal terms, lies in this du-
ality of terminology: the same word is used now in a technical,
now in a non-technical sense. *Paragraphē* itself, and we might say
especially, was subject to this ambivalent employment. But
Hellebrand goes too far in concluding that "Indes dürfte dieses
sonst nicht belegte Wort kein technischer Ausdruck des klassischen attischen Prozessrechts gewesen sein, vielleicht gar nur
eine späte Parallelbildung zum allerdings festen Ausdruck *diamarturia* des attischen Prozessrechts" (*RE*, s.v. *paragraphē*, col.
1169).

[90] Calhoun considers that the "right" of first addressing the
jury was of advantage to the defendant (*Cl. Phil.*, 13 (1918),
p. 178). He may have imbibed this notion from Dem. 18.7, where
the great orator, speaking second in the litigation on the crown,
does say ἐκ τοῦ πρότερος λέγειν ὁ διώκων ἰσχύει. But where something must be proven, as the competence or incompetence of a
court, there is clear advantage in the right to close the discussion.
Thus in the Anglo-American legal system, with burden of proof

It is in Isocrates 18 (*Pros Kallimachon*) that the first clear example of *paragraphē* is encountered. The time is after the archonship of Eukleidēs—probably shortly thereafter, for the catastrophe of 404 seems a fresh impression and the functioning of the amnesty a welcome, almost astounding success.[91] Says the speaker: εἰπόντος Ἀρχίνου νόμον ἔθεσθε, ἄν τις δικάζηται παρὰ τοὺς ὅρκους, ἐξεῖναι τῷ φεύγοντι παραγράψασθαι, τοὺς δ᾽ ἄρχοντας περὶ τούτου πρῶτον εἰσάγειν, λέγειν δὲ πρότερον τὸν παραγραψά-μενον, (3) ὁπότερος δ᾽ ἂν ἡττηθῇ, τὴν ἐπωβελίαν ὀφείλειν. [On the motion of Archinos you passed a law that the *paragraphē* should be open to the defendant if someone in violation of the oaths should bring an action, and that the magistrates should introduce this question first, and the party pleading the *paragraphē* should speak first, with the loser liable to the *epōbelia*.] Here one encounters the *paragraphē* in full terminology and functioning with its later characteristics. The defendant begins the debate, and discussion runs the full gamut of legal and ethical questions.

And yet the only certain historical factor about the *paragraphē* is that it did in fact develop. For the rest,

---

on the prosecutor, the prosecutor is given the final rebuttal— the same situation and the same distribution of advantage holds even in Anglo-American collegiate debate. Nor is the Civilian concept different, for as Paoli points out, *SPA*, p. 114: "(In paragraphic cases), il convenuto aveva per primo la parola, e lasciava perciò all'attore quel vantaggio, che tutte le legislazioni antiche e moderne attribuiscono al convenuto o all'accusato, di poter chiudere il dibattito."

[91] The event alluded to is the first or at least an early utilization of the law of Archinos. Since the amnesty is praised, the speech should have been delivered before the difficulties with the partisans of the Thirty and the final conflict at Eleusis (401/0). Cf. Xenophon, *Hellenica*, 2.4.43.

our reconstruction is hazardous.[92] It is tempting to see a straight-line progression from the period of the Herodēs Murder Trial, when no special plea or proceeding was available, to the time after Aigospotamoi when the *antigraphē* had developed, and finally the years of the *paragraphē* proper, created by Archinos in the narrow context of particular public need, but extended by utility and legislation to encompass a wide spectrum of private actions, and in particular the emporic cases. That the *antigraphē* and *paragraphē* functioned at the same time seems certain, because of the nearness in date of Isocrates 18 and Lysias 23. As the *paragraphē* expanded its scope, the *antigraphē* likely fell into disuse. But the sources do not permit chronological certainty.

Contrasting with the disappearance of the *antigraphē* is the continued existence of the διαμαρτυρία (*diamarturia*), defined by Harpocration as "a certain type of *paragraphē*" that differed from the usual, according to Harpocration, in that it was available to *both* plaintiff and defendant.[93] The only clearly ascertainable separation of the two, however, derives from the absolute inadmissibility of the *paragraphē* in inheritance cases.[94] The belief that differences in practical effects led to the use of one or the other in particular cases remains only a belief; no statutory enactment requiring the use of one or the other is cited in our sources.[95] Pollux possibly may

[92] See Wolff, pp. 106-135.

[93] τρόπος τις παραγραφῆς . . . πρὸ γὰρ τοῦ εἰσαχθῆναι τὴν δίκην εἰς τὸ δικαστήριον ἐξῆν τῷ βουλομένῳ διαμαρτυρῆσαι ὡς εἰσαγώγιμός ἐστιν ἡ δίκη ἢ οὐκ εἰσαγώγιμος. διαφέρει δὲ τῆς παραγραφῆς τῷ τὴν διαμαρτυρίαν γένεσθαι οὐ μόνον ὑπὸ τῶν φευγόντων, ἀλλὰ καὶ ὑπὸ τῶν διωκόντων. Harpocration, s.v. διαμαρτυρία καὶ διαμαρτυρεῖν.

[94] E. Leisi, *Der Zeuge im attischen Recht*, Frauenfeld, 1908, p. 29; Beauchet III, p. 596, n. 2.

[95] Calhoun, *Cl. Phil.*, 13 (1918), p. 178, argues that "In plead-

be right after all in his statement that they were the same thing (παραγραφὴ δ᾽ ἦν ἡ αὐτὴ καὶ διαμαρτυρία).[96] The connection of the *paragraphē* with the amnesty of 403 suggests, incorrectly, the possible utilization of the *paragraphē* in public cases,[97] i.e. *graphai*.[98] There is no evidence for such an employment of special pleas, and it is likely that neither the *diamarturia* nor the *paragraphē* could be utilized in public actions.[99] But the

---

ing an exception of merely interlocutory effect, or in opposing a bar to ordinary civil suits, where in general the right of action was reposed in a single individual, *paragraphē* sufficed, and was uniformly preferred to *diamarturia* because it was easier and attended with less risk, while it gave the original defendant the right of first addressing the jury." (On the right of opening debate, see above, p. 140, n. 90.) The *epōbelia* in a major case however could constitute a major punishment and certainly entailed considerable risk. Cf. Thalheim, *RE*, s.v. *epōbelia*, col. 226 (1907); Lipsius, *AR*, pp. 937 ff.

[96] 8.57—"a" reads ϖαραμαρτυρία.

[97] The equation of *dikai* with "private" and *graphai* with "public" cases is sometimes decried, but universally accepted in legal scholarship. "Public law" did however permeate the "private law," despite the classic separation of the two at Plato, *Laws*, 767B. Equation of *dikai* with "civil" and *graphai* with "criminal" litigation is certainly false. But the basic division of private *dikai* and public *graphai* seems necessary. See Pringsheim, *GLS*, pp. 1-3; R. Bonner, *Lawyers and Litigants in Ancient Athens*, Chicago, 1927, p. 44; Jones, *Legal Theory*, pp. 116-119.

[98] E. Platner, *Der Prozess und die Klagen bei den Attikern*, I, Darmstadt, 1824, pp. 138 ff.; C. R. Kennedy, *Orations of Demosthenes*, III, London, 1894, p. 379. Both believed that the Law of Archinos was stated in general terms, and that its implementation depended on the defendants' privilege of pleading the *paragraphē* against public indictments violating the conditions of amnesty.

[99] Cf. Lipsius, *AR*, p. 858; Calhoun, *Cl. Phil.*, 13 (1918), pp. 184-185.

143

public amnesty did in fact affect private matters. To prevent "sycophancy" (μηδὲ ἐξῇ συκοφαντεῖν μηδενί), the Athenians voted τὰς δὲ δίκας καὶ τὰς διαίτας κυρίας εἶναι, ὁπόσαι ἐν δημοκρατουμένῃ τῇ πόλει ἐγένοντο, τοῖς δὲ νόμοις χρῆσθαι ἀπ᾽ Εὐκλείδου ἄρχοντος . . . ὅπως μήτε χρεῶν ἀποκοπαὶ εἶεν μήτε δίκαι ἀνάδικοι γίγνοιντο ἀλλὰ τῶν ἰδίων συμβολαίων αἱ πράξεις εἶεν (Andocides I.86-88). [that actions and arbitrations be binding which occurred under the democracy, but that they use only the laws passed since the archonship of Eukleidēs . . . so that there should be no abrogation of obligations or actions but an enforcement of private contracts.] Indictment for public actions prior to the amnesty was clearly prohibited except against the Thirty and a few others unless they cleared themselves (διδῶσιν εὐθύνας).[100]

But in private matters, the past had been reaffirmed. Those prevented from seeking redress against individuals through public prosecution might have been inclined to proceed in private cases (dikai), as did Kallimachos in Isocrates 18. Here was a legitimate use for the paragraphē. Where such private prosecutions were motivated by political considerations, there would have been, without the paragraphē, no adequate defense for an individual whose previous suits or arbitrations had been under the Thirty, for the amnesty specifically affirmed private rights only under the democracy (ἐν δημοκρατουμένῃ τῇ πόλει). The law of Archinos thus would have been publicly motivated to make viable the public amnesty, but privately utilized. At any rate, the paragraphē is not invoked by the defendants accused at their dokimasiai of complicity with the Thirty,

[100] τῶν δὲ παρεληλυθότων μηδενὶ πρὸς μηδένα μνησικακεῖν ἐξεῖναι, πλὴν πρὸς τοὺς τριάκοντα καὶ τοὺς δέκα καὶ τοὺς ἕνδεκα καὶ τοὺς τοῦ Πειραιέως ἄρξαντας (Ath. Pol. 39.6).

nor is it introduced by Andocides, by Agoratos, or by Philōn[101] in their defenses against similar public charges. It is this "public" origin but "private" utilization of the *paragraphē* that partially explains its predominant position in the *dikai emporikai*, private cases of manifestly public interest for the great commercial market of the Peiraeus and for food-importing Attica. The original, narrow-purposed legislation of Archinos must have been extended and expanded in scope, but in execution its form remained unchanged. It is here that the question of separability of procedure affects the *dikai emporikai*.

Separability of Procedure in Paragraphic Cases

Isocrates' testimony is vital to the belief that, when a *paragraphē* was raised, the special plea was considered at a separate hearing prior to the trial proper (εὐθυδι-κία).[102] *Paragraphē* upheld, there was no *euthydikia*; rejected, the main hearing began. Thus Isocrates testifies (ἐξεῖναι τῷ φεύγοντι παραγράψασθαι, τοὺς δ᾽ ἄρχοντας περὶ τούτου πρῶτον εἰσάγειν, 18.2), and thus modern scholarship has in the main concurred.[103] Like the other special

[101] See Lysias 16; 25; 26; Andocides I.81-99; Lysias 13; Isocrates 18.22. Calhoun considers possible public use of special pleas in some detail, *Cl. Phil.*, 13 (1918), pp. 179-185.

[102] Descriptive terms such as "special plea" or "trial" when applied to Attic legal procedure must be understood in Attic context free of their technical notation in other legal systems. The Anglo-American term "demurrer" thus conveys to many readers the essential meaning of *paragraphē*, even though in its technical application in the common law it does not involve a denial of the facts. Cf. Wolff, p. 10.

[103] Bo.-Sm. II, p. 75, express the prevalent opinion: "If . . . the defendant claimed that in law the issue was not actionable, he was privileged to enter a special plea which, in fourth-century

pleas, the paragraphic speeches in emporic proceedings (Dem. 32 through 35) would have been delivered at "preliminary" hearings.

Since antiquity, however, it has been noted that the *paragraphikoi logoi* are not in fact limited to issues arising from or dealing with the special plea; in fact, appeals to justice and equity,[104] narrations external to the *paragraphē*,[105] statements of far-reaching scope, all are introduced by the speakers at these supposedly "preliminary" hearings of a purely procedural question. Thus the hypothesis to Dem. 37 points out that the speaker begins and ends "with the *paragraphē*" but "in the middle" argues substance.[106] Similar observations appear in the hypotheses to Dem. 32, 34, and 36.[107] The same phenomena have been noted recently by modern scholars, in particular U.E. Paoli and A. Biscardi, and this observation has led to the promulgation of a doc-

practice at least, was tried separately." Paoli, the chief proponent of "inscindibilità del processo in diritto attico," recognizes this general judgment: "È, infatti, opinione generale che: quando veniva elevata una *paragraphē*, il giudizio principale veniva messo da parte sinchè la questione preliminare sollevata da quella eccezione non fosse decisa" (*SPA*, p. 77). Paoli gathers conveniently (*SPA*, p. 78) the concurring opinions of Beauchet, Glotz, Meier-Schömann, Lipsius, Thalheim.

[104] Dem. 35.56: ὑμῶν δεόμεθα, ὦ ἄνδρες δικασταί, βοηθεῖν ἡμῖν τοῖς ἀδικουμένοις. . . .

[105] Dem. 32.13: τὸ μὲν οὖν πρᾶγμ' ὑπὲρ οὗ τὴν ψῆφον οἴσετε, ὡς εἰπεῖν ἐν κεφαλαίῳ, τοιοῦτόν ἐστιν.

[106] (7) . . . καὶ ἀρχόμενος ἀπὸ τῆς παραγραφῆς καὶ λήγων εἰς ταύτην. ἐν δὲ μέσῳ τὴν εὐθυδικίαν πεποίηκεν, ἧς μέγιστον καὶ ἰσχυρότατόν ἐστιν, ὅτι μηδ' ἐπιδημῶν ἐτύγχανε τότε Νικόβουλος, ὅτ' <ἔπα-σχεν> Πανταίνετος ἐκεῖνα . . . .

[107] E.g. 32.4: καὶ ὁ μὲν ἀγών ἐστι παραγραφικός, ὁ δὲ λόγος, ὡς τῆς εὐθυδικίας τοῦ πράγματος εἰσηγμένης, οὕτως εἴρηται περὶ τοῦ μὴ Ζηνοθέμιδος εἶναι τὸν σῖτον, ἀλλὰ τοῦ Πρώτου . . . .

trine of "inseparability of process in Attic law" (*in-scindibilità del processo nel diritto attico*). It is claimed that no separate hearings of special pleas did in fact take place, although from such *exceptiones*, "certain important procedural consequences resulted," namely that the defendant spoke first and was subject to the *epōbelia* if he failed to capture one-fifth of the votes.[108] The arguments on the substantive question ($\pi\rho\hat{a}\gamma\mu a$) and the appeals for justice in the paragraphic speeches force Paoli to the conclusion that the *paragraphē* could not possibly have been delivered at a separate procedural hearing.[109]

But it is not Isocrates alone who testifies to the separate hearing of special pleas. Defining $\delta\iota a\mu a\rho\tau\upsilon\rho\acute{\iota}a$ and $\delta\iota a\mu a\rho\tau\upsilon\rho\epsilon\hat{\iota}\nu$, Harpocration, as we have seen,[110] records that $\tau\rho\acute{o}\pi o\varsigma$ $\tau\iota\varsigma$ $\mathring{\eta}\nu$ $\pi a\rho a\gamma\rho a\phi\hat{\eta}\varsigma$ $\mathring{\eta}$ $\delta\iota a\mu a\rho\tau\upsilon\rho\acute{\iota}a$ · $\pi\rho\grave{o}$ $\gamma\grave{a}\rho$ $\tau o\hat{\upsilon}$

[108] See Paoli, *SPA*, pp. 113-114. The theory of inseparability has been criticized by A. Steinwenter in *SZ*, 54 (1934), pp. 385 ff., who finds that our evidence is insufficient to support any conclusions. Paoli replies: "Sull' inscindibilità di processo nel diritto attico," *Rivista di diritto processuale civile*, 12 (1935), pp. 253 ff. Hellebrand (*RE*, s.v. *paragraphē*, cols. 1178 and 1179) finds Paoli's arguments convincing. Gernet believes that "l'état procédural qui est indiqué par Paoli est vrai en effet des *dikai emporikai*. . . . Dans les autres procès, il n'en est pas de même: le demandeur qui a fait repousser l'exception doit intenter l'action à nouveau" ("L'institution des arbitres publics à Athènes," *REG* 52 (1939), p. 413, n. 3). Cf. Gernet & Bizos, *Budé Lysias*, pp. 95-96. Wolff devotes the greater part of his book to a refutation of Paoli's view (see Wolff, pp. 17-86).

[109] "Gli scrittori di diritto attico hanno ricostruito, fondandosi su di un passo di Isocrate, un istituto processuale inesistente, che non possiamo ammettere senza far sì che tutte le orazioni paragrafiche conservate ai tempi nostri e la stessa orazione isocratea *Contro Callimaco* divengano piene di incongruenze e di espressioni incomprensibili" (*SPA*, p. 113).

[110] Above, p. 142.

147

εἰσαχθῆναι τὴν δίκην εἰς τὸ δικαστήριον ἐξῆν τῷ βουλομένῳ διαμαρτυρῆσαι ὡς εἰσαγώγιμός ἐστιν ἡ δίκη ἢ οὐκ εἰσαγώγιμος. [The *diamarturia* was a certain type of *paragraphē*: because it was possible before the case was introduced to the court to plead the *diamarturia*, (viz.) that the case is or is not admissible.] Harpocration and Isocrates thus are in agreement about the possible separability of procedure in Attic law.[111]

It has been urged even that such a dual procedure would run counter to the basic philosophy of Attic law; the Athenians were so impatient with extended trials that they would never have permitted two hearings in one case.[112] In capital cases, not even a night's delay was allowed between the hearing of the case and the decision of the judges (Plato, *Apology*, 37A-B).

Nonetheless the fact remains that the Athenians did require separate hearings in the great bulk of cases, through the institution of public arbitrators. Virtually

[111] The meaning of the Isocrates passage seems clear. Even Paoli agreed that τοὺς δ' ἄρχοντας περὶ τούτου πρῶτον εἰσάγειν would normally require "two separate hearings" but he presses for an interpretation, in his own opinion "non così evidente, ma corretta," that would require two separate votes at the conclusion of one trial, the first ballot concerning the special plea. See *SPA*, pp. 107-108.

[112] *SPA*, pp. 105 ff. Paoli however is not correct in terming the procedure against Socrates "un processo capitale"—the case was simply an ἀγὼν τιμητός that unexpectedly led to the death penalty. Only a small majority favored simple conviction—had Socrates proposed for himself even a moderate punishment he would no doubt have escaped a harsh penalty. Probably the outcome was equally a surprise to the prosecution, whose "object was simply to frighten away from Athens a person whose influence (was) believed to be undesirable" (A. E. Taylor, *Plato: The Man and His Work*, 1948[5], p. 159). The procedure is typical of ἀγῶνες τιμητοί, not of capital cases.

all private litigation (except the *dikai emmēnoi*, which were open to voluntary private arbitration) was subject to this compulsory separate procedure.[113] The trial of Socrates was no "capital case" but an ἀγὼν τιμητός (see note 112). It demonstrates the inherent requirement of divided procedure in Athenian courts, for in hearing the case against Socrates the judges listened to separate pleas and held separate votes, deciding first the question of guilt and then the punishment. Necessarily this was normal procedure in an ἀγὼν τιμητός. Similarly the procedure in homicide cases extended over a four-month period and involved numerous hearings and divided processes, and this in a case category renowned for its conservatism and preservation of the "ancestral laws."[114]

Nor would separate hearings, *paragraphē* and *euthydikia*, necessitate any significant delay.[115] The same

[113] *Ath. Pol.* 53.1: κληροῦσι δὲ καὶ <τοὺς> τετταράκοντα . . . πρὸς οὓς τὰς ἄλλας δίκας λαγχάνουσιν. By τὰς ἄλλας δίκας Aristotle apparently referred to suits other than those introduced by the *eisagōgeis* and ἀποδέκται, of whom he has just been speaking (52.2-3). See Lipsius, *AR*, p. 82, n. 116; R. J. Bonner, *Cl. Phil.*, 2 (1907), pp. 407-418. Of this wide range of cases, καὶ τὰ μὲν μέχρι δέκα δραχμῶν αὐτοτελεῖς εἰσι δ[ικ]άζειν, τὰ δ' ὑπὲρ τοῦτο τὸ τίμημα τοῖς διαιτηταῖς παραδιδόασιν (*Ath. Pol.* 53.1). Suits dealing with family relationships and property may also have been exempt from public arbitration. Cf. Harrison, *Procedure*, p. 19.

[114] There were three preliminary investigations in each of three successive months, and finally a hearing conducted within the last three days of the fourth month (Antiphon 6.42; Pollux 8.117). The length of this hearing is uncertain. See D. M. Mac-Dowell, *Athenian Homicide Law*, Manchester, 1963, p. 34.

[115] Paoli, after observing that paragraphic cases are known especially from the emporic courts, adds, "Orbene, se vi è un campo nel quale un procedimento dilatorio ci appaia in contrasto con tutte le informazioni che abbiamo sul sistema, è proprio il campo dei rapporti giuridici commerciali" (*SPA*, p. 106).

149

Athenians "who would not hear of even a night's interval in capital trials" fixed the penalty in the proceedings against Socrates at a separate sitting. But there was no delay.

In short it would be no exaggeration to state that the Athenian juridical system was *based* on a plurality of hearings. With exceptions, the concept of divided trial prevailed. Even broad political hearings show the same dichotomy. Official investigation was divided into examinations at the beginning and end of the term of office, *dokimasia* and *euthynai*. In the public sphere, discussion by the People was subject to preliminary consideration by the Council.[116]

There can be then no *a priori* assumption against separability of procedure. The references in Isocrates and Harpocration indicate that in at least some instances special pleas were separately heard. Since the other provisions of Archinos' legislation on *paragraphai,* viz. the opening of debate by the defendant and the *epōbelia,* were universally extended, there is every reason to suppose that the third provision, the separate hearing, also was widely employed.[117]

[116] The contention that the procedure involving a *paragraphē* before the διαιτητής was an undivided one is unsubstantiated. Lipsius holds that *paragraphai* were never heard by an arbitrator but went straight to court (*AR,* p. 835, cf. p. 845). Harrell hedges—see *Public Arbitration,* pp. 31-32. If this is so, then the two hearings would duplicate the normal procedure. Virtually all cases decided by public arbitrators were appealed. See *ibid.,* p. 35; Dem. 40.31, where the speaker indicates how rarely an arbitrator's decision was accepted without further reference to other jurisdiction.

[117] The defendant opens the debate in all the paragraphic speeches, except the early Lysian oration (23) Kata Pankleōnos. The *epōbelia* is considered by Paoli to have been among the

Nor should it be ignored that Lysias 23 actually provides us with a special plea separately heard. The speaker discusses only the merits of the *antigraphē*—since he establishes nothing as to the liability of his opponent (nor does he attempt to do so), it is patent that, the *antigraphē* rejected, he must speak again on the merits. Although the case is not by name a *paragraphē*, Lysias 23 not only demonstrates the inherent preference for dual hearings in Attic law but provides a particular example of a separately heard special plea.

The content of the *paragraphikoi logoi* does in fact illustrate a central characteristic of Attic law: its insistence on the necessary sympathy between technicality and justice. It is not enough for an apparently guilty man to find legalistic salvation; an acquittal will depend on his persuading the judges that Right is on his side.[118] In making a special plea, the defendant seeks to show that justice, not legalism, favors him, and that the technical motion fortuitously allows equity to prevail. This the hypotheses noted; this the speakers in the *paragraphikoi logoi* tell us. This explains the breadth of argument in the paragraphic hearing.

Thus the commentator in Dem. 36 points out: ὁ δὲ Φορμίων παραγράφεται, νόμον παρεχόμενος τὸν κελεύοντα περὶ ὧν ἂν ἅπαξ ἀφῇ τις καὶ διαλύσηται μηκέτ᾽ ἐξεῖναι δικάζεσθαι. ἅπτεται μέντοι καὶ τῆς εὐθείας ὁ ῥήτωρ, δεικνὺς

"notevoli conseguenze procedurali" of a *paragraphē* (see SPA, pp. 113-114).

[118] The general importance of equity in Greek law is well-discussed by Jones, *Legal Theory*, pp. 64-67. In a technical sense Meyer-Laurin has attempted to show, in my opinion unconvincingly, that the principle of equity did not exist until Ptolemaic times. See A. Biscardi, "La 'gnome dikaiotate' et l'interprétation des lois dans la Grèce ancienne," *RIDA* (3rd Ser. 17) (1970), pp. 219-232.

ANCIENT ATHENIAN MARITIME COURTS

ὡς οὐκ εἶχεν ἡ τράπεζα χρήματ᾽ ἴδια τοῦ Πασίωνος. τοῦτο δὲ πεποίηκεν, ἵν᾽ ἡ παραγραφὴ μᾶλλον ἰσχύῃ, τῆς εὐθείας δεικνυμένης τῷ ᾽Απολλοδώρῳ σαθρᾶς (Hyp. 3). [Phormiōn pleads the *paragraphē*. . . . However the speaker also seizes the equities by showing that the bank did not hold Pasiōn's private funds. He did this to strengthen the *paragraphē*, with the equities being shown as unfavorable to Apollodōros.] In the same way, the hypothesis to Dem. 32 explains the defendant's strategy: οὐ γὰρ βούλεται δοκεῖν ῥήματι τοῦ νόμου μόνον ἰσχυρίζεσθαι κατὰ τὸ πρᾶγμ᾽ ἀδικῶν, ἀλλὰ δείκνυσιν ὡς θαρρεῖ μὲν καὶ τῇ εὐθείᾳ, ἐκ περιουσίας δ᾽ αὐτῷ καὶ παραγραφὴν ὁ νόμος δίδωσι (4). [He does not wish to seem to rely on the letter of the law only, while being substantively in the wrong; rather he shows that he is confident even in the equities, and additionally the law allows him also the *paragraphē*.] Nor need we rely on scholiasts. The orators themselves say the same. Dem. 36.2: τὴν μὲν οὖν παραγραφὴν ἐποιησάμεθα τῆς δίκης, οὐχ ἵν᾽ ἐκκρούοντες χρόνους ἐμποιῶμεν, ἀλλ᾽ ἵνα τῶν πραγμάτων, ἐὰν ἐπιδείξῃ μηδ᾽ ὁτιοῦν ἀδικοῦνθ᾽ ἑαυτὸν οὑτοσί, ἀπαλλαγή τις αὐτῷ γένηται παρ᾽ ὑμῖν κυρία. [We offered the *paragraphē* in bar of the action not so that by delaying we should waste time but so that if this man shall prove that he has done nothing wrong at all, he may have from you some binding release from the matter.] Only a separate hearing would imply a "waste of time" (although not an appreciable delay)—the aim is to gain endorsement for the "release," premised on the innocence of the party seeking that confirmation from the court. The *actio* might be technical and special, but the justice of the matter is allegedly clear.

Strategy too could dictate arguments on the merits in supposedly special hearings. νομίζω πάντας ὑμᾶς εἰδέ-

152

ναι, ὅτι οὐχ ἧττον τὰ πεπραγμέν᾽ εἰώθατε σκοπεῖν ἢ τὰς ὑπὲρ τούτων παραγραφάς· περὶ δὴ τῶν πραγμάτων αὐτῶν τὰ ψευδῆ καταμαρτυρήσαντες οὗτοί μου ἀσθενεῖς τοὺς περὶ τῆς παραγραφῆς ἐποίησαν λόγους (Dem. 45.51). [I think that you all know that you are accustomed to consider the actual facts no less than the *paragraphai* relating to them. By falsely testifying as to the facts, they have weakened my arguments as to the *paragraphē*.]

In a system lacking the technical objectivity of the Roman law or the binding formality of the early common law, in a society where popular courts were roused by sympathy and inflamed by rhetoric, a litigant perilously limited himself to legal questions, leaving to his opponent morality and justice. Hence, broad appeals were made on narrow questions. Victory in an Athenian court required, or the orators thought it required,[119] the apparent possession of Right. And the paragraphic hearings, separate and preliminary, were worth winning.

Importance of the Paragraphic Hearing

Justice is dispensed not only in the trial proper (εὐθυδικία).[120] A preliminary paragraphic hearing was of considerable importance, if only through the *epōbelia*. The immediate conquest of one-sixth the sum in litigation easily might compensate the plaintiff for the trouble of an "extra hearing." Disdaining the judges, he

---

[119] Isocrates 18.4: βούλομαι δ᾽ ἐξ ἀρχῆς ὑμῖν διηγήσασθαι τὰ πραχθέντα· ἂν γὰρ τοῦτο μάθητε ὡς οὐδὲν ὑπ᾽ ἐμοῦ κακὸν πέπονθεν, ἡγοῦμαι ταῖς τε συνθήκαις ὑμᾶς ἥδιον βοηθήσειν καὶ τούτῳ μᾶλλον ὀργιεῖσθαι.

[120] Citing remarks such as Dem. 35.56, ὑμῶν . . . ἀδικουμένοις, Paoli has contended that judges in paragraphic hearings could not effectively aid the plaintiff unless the main issue also was being heard at the same time (*SPA*, pp. 112-113).

might find himself not only without compensation for the alleged wrong but another one-sixth aggrieved. Further, the winning of the preliminary decision by the plaintiff necessarily had some influence on the court's decision in the *euthydikia*. The defendant's basic, or sole substantial, defense might be involved in the *paragraphē*. A failure to win the *paragraphē* might mean the necessary loss of the *euthydikia*.

The full legal effect of a successful employment of a *paragraphē* is not made clear in our sources. Most scholars, however, have concluded that in some situations, for example where a *paragraphē* had been based on prescription, the plaintiff was barred from further litigation on the same matter.[121] For the prosecutor in such categories a favorable decision on the *paragraphē* would be a necessary preliminary to redress; for the defendant a favorable decision would eliminate his opponent.

In an effort to establish the impact as *res adjudicata* of a successful special plea, *paragraphai* have been separated by modern scholarship into "interlocutory" (provisional) and "final" categories. Thus Glotz differentiates "1. les exceptions de valeur absolue, permanentes, capables d'éteindre toute action généralement quelconque, en un mot, analogues aux *exceptiones peremptoriae* du droit romain, *quae perpetuo valent nec evitari possunt.* . . . 2. les exceptions de valeur relative . . . n'excluant pas tout recours à une autre procédure, comparables en un sens aux *exceptiones temporales et dilatoriae.*"[122]

The effect of a final *paragraphē*, e.g. the so-called

[121] Harrison, *Procedure*, p. 123.

[122] G. Glotz, *DS*, s.v. *paragraphē*, p. 323. Cf. G. M. Calhoun, *Cl. Phil.*, 13 (1918), pp. 174-176.

exceptio rei transactae, ὧν ἂν ἀφῇ καὶ ἀπαλλάξῃ τις μηκέτι τὰς δίκας εἶναι,[123] is clearly substantial. It would bar all recourse.

The differentiation between interlocutory and final *paragraphai* has, however, arbitrarily been drawn on grounds of terminology. Final exceptions are said to have been governed by formulas such as μὴ ἔστων δίκαι, μὴ δικάζεσθαι, μὴ ἐξέστω δικάζεσθαι, μὴ ἀρχὴ εἰσαγέτω. Special pleas from which interlocutory decrees derive are supposedly based on the legislative formula ἐὰν δέ τις παρὰ ταῦτα δικάζηται, μὴ εἰσαγώγιμος ἔστω ἡ δίκη.[124] The concept of interlocutory *paragraphē*, however, has not been sketched in a consistent nor reasonable fashion. This the functioning of the *paragraphē* in the emporic courts makes clear.

The special plea sustained in the *dikai emporikai* is generally used as an example of an interlocutory *paragraphē*.[125] And an interlocutory *paragraphē* is generally considered not a great hindrance to further action. Thus Bonner and Smith comment in regard to this decree: "Now it is manifest that if the *paragraphē* is sustained by the verdict of the court it does not mean that the original plaintiff had no recourse. All he had to do was to bring his case in the proper category and before the proper court."[126]

What has not been realized is that the proper court

[123] Dem. 37.19, cf. 38.5. For this type of special plea, cf. Dem. 17.1, 16 ff., 58 ff.; 38.1, 3, 9, 27; 45.5, 40. Cf. Harpocration, s.v. ἀφεὶς καὶ ἀπαλλάξας.

[124] Cf. G. M. Calhoun, *Cl. Phil.*, 13 (1913), pp. 175-176.

[125] Cf. G. Glotz, *DS*, who illustrates an interlocutory *paragraphē* by "l'exception pour inapplicabilité absolue de l'action à l'espèce," citing the *dikai emporikai* pleas in this category (Dem. 32.1; 33.1; 34.4; 34.42; 35.45). Cf. Wolff, p. 145, n. 12.

[126] II, p. 91.

might have been the body granting the so-called inter-locutory decree. Thus at Dem. 34.43, the speaker pleads against Phormiōn's *paragraphē*: παραγράφονται δὲ ὡς οὐκ εἰσαγώγιμον τὴν δίκην οὖσαν. ἀλλ᾽ εἰς ποῖον δικαστήριον εἰσέλθωμεν, ἄνδρες δικασταί, εἰ μὴ πρὸς ὑμᾶς. . . . [they plead the *paragraphē*, (alleging) that the action is in-admissible. But to what tribunal should we go, o dicasts, if not to you? . . .] The refusal of a case, clearly and solely emporic by nature, is also feared by the speaker opposing Lakritos' *paragraphē* who enumerates the various courts to which he could not go if his suit were rejected by the emporic court: ποῦ χρὴ λαβεῖν δίκην . . . περὶ τῶν ἐμπορικῶν συμβολαίων; παρὰ ποίᾳ ἀρχῇ ἢ ἐν τίνι χρόνῳ; παρὰ τοῖς ἔνδεκα; ἀλλὰ τοιχωρύχους καὶ κλέπτας καὶ τοὺς ἄλλους κακούργους τοὺς ἐπὶ θανάτῳ οὗτοι εἰσάγουσιν. ἀλλὰ παρὰ τῷ ἄρχοντι; οὐκοῦν ἐπικλήρων καὶ ὀρφανῶν καὶ τῶν τοκέων τῷ ἄρχοντι, προστέτακται ἐπιμελεῖσθαι. ἀλλὰ νὴ Δία παρὰ τῷ βασιλεῖ. ἀλλ᾽ οὐκ ἐσμὲν γυμνασίαρχοι, οὐδὲ ἀσεβείας οὐδένα γραφόμεθα. ἀλλ᾽ ὁ πολέμαρχος εἰσάξει. ἀποστασίου γε καὶ ἀπροστασίου. οὐκοῦν ὑπόλοιπόν ἐστιν οἱ στρατηγοί. ἀλλὰ τοὺς τριηράρχους καθιστᾶσιν, ἐμπορικὴν δὲ δίκην οὐδεμίαν εἰσάγουσιν . . . ποῖ οὖν δεῖ ταύτην εἰσελθεῖν τὴν δίκην; (Dem. 35.47-49).

Worries such as these demonstrate the true importance of the *paragraphē* in the emporic courts and the close connection of defined jurisdiction and special plea.[127] If a maritime commercial dispute involved a con-tractual arrangement, it might well be that recourse

[127] It is interesting to note also the historical relationship between *dikai emporikai* and special pleas. In Lysias 17.5 the speaker alludes to the earliest known *dikai emporikai* (see below, pp. 176 ff.): πέρυσι μὲν οὖν διεγράψαντό μου τὰς δίκας. Hesychios defines, παραγράψαι: ὃ ἡμεῖς λέγομεν διαγράψαι. The connection is intriguing: it is not impossible that special pleas developed in the *dikai emporikai*. Cf. Hellebrand, *RE*, s.v. *paragraphē*, col. 1171.

was possible for the parties nowhere other than in the emporic courts. But if the requirements for a *paragraphē* could be sustained, that is, if the contract was not in writing or did not provide for the Athenian market, then the plaintiff could find himself without effective alternative—the "interlocutory *paragraphē*" would be final. He had brought his case in the proper category and before the only possible court. He had not met the conditions of that category and of that court. Cause he has, but legal implementation he lacks. Legal aid in the courts is denied him.

This, then, indicates the great importance of the defined scope of the *dikai emporikai* and the heavy emphasis upon the *paragraphē* in litigation before the commercial maritime court. By defining narrowly and clearly the cases actionable in the *dikai emporikai*, Athens could give added incentive for the provision of imports and the taking of exports through the great Peiraeus harbor and market. By demanding written contracts, she could introduce order and stability into the vital area of maritime commerce. And for the merchants involved in litigation, the importance of the paragraphic hearing was overwhelming—it involved financial risks for both parties and threatened possible finality. It was wise to use every argument, every pretext, anything that might be of aid in gaining or refuting a *paragraphē*. This the speakers did, and fortunately for modern scholarship one weapon was reference to the laws governing special pleas and another was reference to the definitive jurisdiction of the commercial maritime courts: οἱ νόμοι κελεύουσιν, ὦ ἄνδρες δικασταί, τὰς δίκας εἶναι τοῖς ναυκλήροις καὶ τοῖς ἐμπόροις τῶν ᾿Αθήναζε καὶ τῶν ᾿Αθήνηθεν συμβολαίων, καὶ περὶ ὧν ἂν ὦσι συγγραφαί. ἂν δέ τις παρὰ ταῦτα δικάζηται, μὴ εἰσαγώγιμον εἶναι τὴν δίκην (Dem. 32.1).

157

3

HISTORICAL DEVELOPMENT OF
THE *DIKAI EMPORIKAI*

Our concern in the previous pages has been with the accurate description of the commercial maritime courts, how they functioned and in what areas they held juridical responsibility. The picture thus presented is in one important respect misleading: cumulatively it tends to appear static. In certain particulars, to be sure, as with the *emmēnoi dikai* and the *paragraphē*, it has been necessary to pause and delineate chronological stages. Now it is time to consider the overall development of the *dikai emporikai*.

Unfortunately the nature of the evidence for the commercial maritime courts tends to distort the chronological development. The evidence of the lexicographers is often piecemeal—Harpocration defines one term in one context, and Pollux the same word in another aspect or with evidence from a different period.[1] The Attic orations are undated and in some cases undatable. They do, however, extend over a broad period—some before Aigospotamoi, others after Chaironeia. Yet their testimony has sometimes been taken indiscriminately to provide an arrested-motion outline of the commercial maritime cases. The details have been filled in with testimony from the lexicographers.[2]

---

[1] For example, the term *paragraphē*. See discussion above on pp. 136 ff.

[2] See T. Reinach in *DS*, s.v. *emporikai dikai*.

In the study of the *dikai emporikai* this procedure has often led to imprecise, and sometimes to improper and inconsistent conclusions.[3] Thus an inscription erroneously dated to the wrong century is taken to contradict a citation in the orators to which it bears no relation.[4] The *nautodikai* appear on an inscription (*IG* I².41) probably to be dated after the revolt of Euboea in 446; the same word, *nautodikai*, appears in a speech of Lysias (17.5). The connection between the two is considered implicit.[5]

There is, however, a more rewarding approach, not dependent on the discarding of one of two conflicting pieces of evidence or the blurred merging of seemingly similar statements. It is to differentiate that which is chronologically differentiated. This we shall now attempt.

THE SPECIFIC PROBLEM

Harpocration defines *dikai emmēnoi* as including emporic cases (αἲ τε ἐμπορικαὶ καὶ ἐρανικαί), citing Demos-

[3] As Rostovtzeff has noted (*SEHHW*, III, p. 1327, n. 23) the study of fourth-century economic and legal history has not been characterized by zeal for chronological differentiation. This is all the sadder, since Greek law, like Greek civilization, was a continuity of change. The problem for scholars lies in the tendency to forget "trop facilement que le droit d'Athènes n'a pas cessé d'évoluer à l'époque classique" (Gernet, *REG* 1938, p. 9). On the continuity of this same law, see W. W. Buckland, *Harvard Law Review*, 54 (1940-41), pp. 1273 ff.; F. Pringsheim, "Ausbreitung und Einfluss des griechischen Rechtes," *Sitzungsberichte der Heidelberger Akademie der Wissenschaften* 1952, Abh. I, pp. 1-19.

[4] *IG* I².16; Lysias 17.5. See further below.

[5] A. Körte, "Die attischen Xenodikai," *Hermes*, 68 (1933), p. 240; W. Schwahn, *RE*, s.v. *nautodikai*.

thenes and Hyperides. Aristotle, however, does not mention the *dikai emporikai* among his ten *dikai emmēnoi* that are under the jurisdiction of the *eisagōgeis* (*Ath. Pol.* 52.2).[6] The *dikai emporikai* occur only in his account of the *thesmothetai*: εἰσάγουσι δὲ καὶ δίκας ἰδίας, ἐμπορικὰς καὶ μεταλλικὰς καὶ δούλων ... (59.5), and there he does not cite them as *dikai emmēnoi*. Lysias (17.5) introduces a class of officials known as *nautodikai*, presiding over cases in some way connected with commerce but not subject to thirty-day limitation: (the opponents) πέρυσι μὲν οὖν διεγράψαντό μου τὰς δίκας, ἔμποροι φάσκοντες εἶναι · νυνὶ δὲ λαχόντος ἐν τῷ Γαμηλιῶνι μηνὶ οἱ ναυτοδίκαι οὐκ ἐξεδίκασαν. [Last year they had my suit quashed by claiming that they were maritime merchants; now the *nautodikai* have not adjudicated my complaint of the month Gamēlion.] Again Pollux defines εἰσαγωγεῖς οἱ τὰς ἐμμήνους δίκας εἰσάγοντες · ἦσαν δὲ προικός, ἐρανικαί, ἐμπορικαί [*eisagōgeis*: those introducing the *dikai emmēnoi* which were for dowry, *dikai eranikai* and *dikai emporikai*] (8.101).

Thus there are various groupings and definitions. The tendency of scholarship on the subject has been to choose from among the pieces of evidence that one which seems the preferable description of the true state of *dikai emporikai*. Pollux assigns the commercial cases to the *eisagōgeis*; Aristotle assigns their introduction to the *thesmothetai*. Beauchet considers the evidence necessarily contradictory and concludes that Aristotle's testimony must be preferred to Pollux'.[7]

No preference is necessary. In the study of the commercial laws of fourth-century Athens, where evidence

---

[6] See above, Chapter 1, "The Monthly Suits," pp. 12 ff.
[7] IV, p. 99. Cf. Gernet, *REG* 1938, p. 11, n. 3.

is rendered valuable by its scarcity, gratuitously to dispense with ancient information is a foolish economy.

In fact the pieces of evidence cited above, together with other testimony culled from literary and epigraphic sources, furnish a consistent record and tell a chronological story.

At some time, perhaps before Aigospotamoi, commercial maritime cases at Athens were grouped together into a category of *dikai emporikai* handled by *nautodikai*. These cases were not *emmēnos*, although even under the fifth-century Athenian Empire some concept of *emmēna* certainly existed. Prior to 355, several categories of litigation were grouped together as *dikai emmēnoi* introduced by *eisagōgeis*, a class of officials who had existed in name at least even in the fifth century.[8] The *dikai emporikai* were probably not at first among them. But after 355 the *dikai emporikai* were transferred to the *eisagōgeis* and became actionable as *dikai emporikai emmēnoi*. By the 320's jurisdiction had passed to the *thesmothetai*, and the advantages to the merchant class of litigation in this category went considerably beyond speedy procedure.[9] This chronological scheme demands detailed attention since it augments the views held by Beauchet and Lipsius and contradicts on a number of crucial points the findings of Gernet in his well-argued discussion "Sur les actions commerciales en droit athénien."[10]

[8] But perhaps the *dikai emmēnoi* were not created until later. See below.

[9] I think that this was true from the beginning, but we *know* that it was at the end.

[10] See Beauchet IV, pp. 98, 100; Lipsius, *AR*, p. 87; Paoli, *SDA*, pp. 112 ff.; Gernet, *REG* 1938, pp. 2-11. Harrison, *Procedure*, p. 122, n. 4 follows Gernet.

ANCIENT ATHENIAN MARITIME COURTS

The Nautodikai: Origin and Activities

The *nautodikai*[11] are of uncertain origin—scholarly
discussion about their initial appearance has been fre-
quent, but its basis is speculation.[12]

[11] The ancient sources for the *nautodikai* are: *IG* I².41; the
lexicographers: Harpocration, Pollux, Hesychios, *Lexica Segueriana*, Photios, Suidas; Schol. Aristophanes, *Birds*, 766; Lysias 17.5
and 17.8. The scholiast to Aristophanes provides a fragment of
Kratinos (Edmonds 233). Harpocration yields a fragment from
Aristophanes' *Daitaleis*, as well as a purported quotation from D
of Krateros' *Psēphismata*. Additionally Harpocration cites Lysias,
Πρὸς ʼΑλκιβιάδην (fr. 10, ed. Didot). On these see below.

In a curious passage, Lucian, *Dial. meretricum*, 2.2, mentions
the *nautodikai* in a commercial court context: . . . τάλαντον, οἶμαι,
ὀφείλων γὰρ τῷ πατερὶ οὐκ ἤθελεν ἐκτίνειν, ὁ δὲ παρὰ τοὺς ναυτοδίκας
ἀπήγαγεν αὐτόν. It is generally agreed that the passage is an
anachronism (see Lécrivain, *DS*, s.v. *nautodikai*; Gilbert, p. 424,
n. 1; Beauchet IV, p. 97, n. 4; *MSL*, p. 97, n. 163). The dialogue
itself is of course humorous after Lucian's fashion. Whatever the
explanation, the reference is interesting, although in its isolated
position not important for this study.

Modern comment on the *nautodikai* goes back at least to A.
Baumstark, *De curatoribus emporii et nautodicis apud Athenien-
ses*, Freiburg, 1828: he imaginatively suggested that the *nautodikai* were a jury of specialists presided over by the *thesmothetai*. Among the more important commentators on the *nautodikai*
following the discovery of the *Ath. Pol.* are Gilbert, pp. 423-424;
Wilamowitz, *A & A*, I, pp. 223 ff.; Lipsius, *AR*, pp. 86-88, p. 633;
Bu.-Sw., pp. 1094 ff., 1114 ff.; Paoli, *SDA*, pp. 111-112; Ziebarth,
Beiträge, p. 44; A. Körte, *Hermes*, 68 (1933), pp. 240 ff.;
W. Schwahn, *RE*, s.v. *nautodikai*, cols. 2053-2063; Gernet, *REG*
1938, p. 13; U. Kahrstedt, *Klio*, 14 (1939), pp. 152 ff.; Wolff,
p. 28, n. 24.

[12] Thus G. F. Schömann (*Die Verfassungsgeschichte Athens
nach Grote's History of Greece. Kritisch geprüft*, Leipzig, 1854,
pp. 42 ff.) argues for their institution in the time of Solon. See
MSL, p. 53. Lipsius, *AR*, p. 86, sees their origin after the Persian
Wars "als Athen sich zu einem Handelsplatz von hoher Bedeutung

Their area of activity is made reasonably clear by the lexicographers. In the most general citation, that of Hesychios (s.v. *nautodikai*), they are termed οἱ ἐπὶ τοῦ ἐμπορίου δικασταί, ἐφ' ὧν καὶ αἱ τῆς ξενίας ἐκρίνοντο δίκαι [judges (*dicasts*) for the *emporion*, by whom the *dikai xenias* were also judged]. Pollux (8.126) defines them only in the context of the *dikai xenias*, as does Harpocration. Suidas and the *Lexica Segueriana* (1.283.3) note both functions; Suidas calls them ἄρχοντες ἐπὶ τοῖς ναυκλήροις δικάζοντες καὶ τοῖς περὶ τὸ ἐμπόριον ἐργαζομένοις [*archons* judging over the *naukleroi* and those working in the *emporion*], and then gives Harpocration's definition. The dual definition immediately suggests the possibility that the homonym *nautodikai*, used in two periods of two different officials, has from the time of Hesychios been lexicographically united in a single false definition. However Körte has offered the chronological explanation that would historically unite the two duties in one magistrate; viz. an already constituted class of *nautodikai* was assigned the duties of the *xenodikai* sometime between 442 and 437.

Nautodikai as Xenodikai

In *Inscriptiones Graecae* (I².41) there appears:[13]

---

entwickelt hatte." Schwahn, *RE*, s.v. *nautodikai*, posits the necessity of their origin in the sixth century: "im 5 Jhdt. bezeichnet man nicht mehr einen Import- oder Exportkaufmann als ναύτης." This last point illustrates the danger inherent in the argument from nomenclature. It is possible, for example, that their name stems not from ναύτης but from some word connected with naval loan, such as ναυτικόν. Cf. Liddell-Scott Lexicon, s.v. ναυτικός. Or more likely, a *neut*-derivative could connect them with the empire in the dress of imperial officials.

[13] *IG* I.28.29; *SEG* X.37; G. F. Hill, *Sources for Greek His-*

4 . . . καὶ ἐ]ν τôι αὐτôι μενὶ Hοι ναυτοδ[ί]-
5 και μὲν τ]ὸ δικαστέριον παρεχόντον πλ-
6 ἐρες ἒ εὐ]θυνέσθω(ν) Hαι δὲ πράχσες ὄντον

[. . . and in the same month let the *nautodikai* provide the court fully manned or let them be punished.] Hiller von Gaertringen here postulates a stoichedon pattern of 31 spaces. Apparently containing regulations for Hestiaia, the decree must be dated sometime after the revolt of Euboea in 446.

Thus the *nautodikai* are clearly attested for the Athenian Empire and appear to have been judicial officials even before Aigospotamoi: οἱ ναυτοδίκαι τὸ δικαστήριον παρεχόντων.[14]

---

tory, Oxford, 1951, B54. Cf. *SEG* XXI.26. See Lipsius, *AR*, p. 83, n. 119; p. 827, n. 83. For context, see A. W. Gomme, *Historical Commentary on Thucydides*, I, Oxford, 1944, pp. 346-347.

[14] The precise judicial duty of the *nautodikai* is uncertain. Were they preliminary magistrates, trial judges, or jurors? Of the lexicographers, Harpocration terms them an ἀρχή, Pollux speaks of οἱ εἰσάγοντες, while Hesychios calls them δικασταί. Lysias 17.5 with its ἐξεδίκασαν seems to require some concept of judgment. But *IG* I².41 as restored by von Gaertringen argues for a status of introductory magistrates who furnish a *dikastērion*. Always there remains the possibility that our sources are not in reality writing of one and the same office. However some judgment power on the part of the *nautodikai* seems called for—their being termed *archai* is paralleled by the reference in Dem. 32.9 and 14 to officials (ἄρχοντες) at Kephallēnia who made decisions (32.14, γνόντων τῶν Κεφαλλήνων), although that passage too is highly debated. (For its importance, see P. S. Phōtiadēs, ʼΑθηνᾶ, 36 (1924), p. 111.) To the contrary, there must be after 450 some presumption against magistrates in Athens who make binding judgments. See H. T. Wade-Gery, "The Judicial Treaty with Phaselis," *Essays in Greek History*, Oxford, 1958, p. 183: "In classical Athens it is the jurors, the Dikastai, who give judgment." Still, critical judgment on this point is interesting if incon-

But the value of the *Inscriptiones Graecae* I² text, which with its slight restoration has been widely cited (Körte, Schwahn, Hignett, *et al.*), is questioned by Meritt and Raubitschek, who "recognoverunt" that so-called *IG* I².40/41, 42, 43, 48 belong to one and the same stone.[15] Meritt, in notes quoted in Hill, restores the inscription on the basis of a stoichedon pattern of 48 letters,[16] and the result is:

4 [. . . c. 24 . . . ἐ]ν τοῖ αὐτοῖ μενὶ Ηοι ναυτοδ[ί]-
5 [καὶ . . . c. 21 . . .]ο δικαστέριον παρεχόντον πλ-
6 [. . . c. 22 . . . εὐ]θυνέσθο Ηαι δὲ πράχσες ὄντον

From Meritt's restoration only two vital points of evidence remain: (1) the testified existence of *nautodikai* sometime after 446; (2) the phrase ἐ]ν τῷ αὐτῷ μηνὶ οἱ ναυτοδ[ίκαι], which itself is open to variant interpretation—(A) in a lost part of the inscription officials X were to do something in month A, and ἐν τῷ αὐτῷ μηνὶ [in the same month] the *nautodikai* were to do something else; (B) "in the same month" refers to an *emmēnoi* prescription. The more natural interpretation

---

clusive. Baumstark, as noted above, p. 162, n. 11, believed that they were actually jurors and that the cases were introduced by the *thesmothetai* (pp. 67 ff.). Gilbert, I, p. 423, n. 3, inconclusively terms them "eine Instructionsbehörde und für Richter zugleich," in this following Schömann, *Verfassungsgechichte Athens* (cited above, n. 12), pp. 47-48. Cf. Beauchet IV, p. 97.

[15] See *SEG* X.37: valde desideramus novam editionem totius decreti. A further fragment attributed to the same stone was published by E. Vanderpool, *Hesperia*, 21 (1962), pp. 399 ff.

[16] "The letters of *IG* I².41 are more crowded than those of *IG* I².40 suggesting a stoichedon line of c. 48 letters (Meritt)" (G. F. Hill, *Sources for Greek History*, Oxford, 1951, p. 303).

seems to be (A), although no very close parallel is offered in *IG* I².[17]

If inscriptional evidence tells us little about the *nautodikai*,[18] it tells us less about the *xenodikai*. In *IG* I².342.38 ff. and *IG* I².343.89 we read:

342.38: .. XXHΔΔΔΔΓ†††$\overset{\pi\alpha\rho\grave{\alpha}\ \chi\sigma\epsilon\nu[o\delta\iota\kappa\grave{o}\nu\ \text{Ho}\hat{\iota}s..]}{\underset{\hphantom{..}}{\dot{\epsilon}\gamma\rho\alpha\mu\mu\acute{\alpha}[\tau\epsilon\nu e......]}}$

343.89: .... $[\pi]\alpha\rho\grave{\alpha}\ \chi\sigma\epsilon[\nu o\delta\iota\kappa\grave{o}\nu]$

Meyer noted soberly that it was impossible to determine what type of magistrates the "$\chi\sigma\epsilon\nu$ [$o\delta\iota\kappa\alpha\iota$]" were.[19]

But Cavaignac did not so despair and in 1908 wrote, "Je reconnaîtrais volontiers dans cette magistrature le tribunal chargé des nombreuses *graphai xenias* qui se grefferent sur la loi des bâtards en 444 (Philoch. Fr. 90) et dans l'argent versé par lui le produit des ventes d'esclaves au profit du Trésor."[20] The attribution of

---

[17] The famous inscription *IG* I².929, anno 459/58, "Ηοίδε . . . ἀπέθανον . . . τοῦ αὐτοῦ ἐνιαυτοῦ," is not of time-limit but of time-parallel: "they died the same year," but the genitive construction is a different matter. To Lipsius (*AR*, p. 87, n. 130), "Es scheint also dass die Nautodiken in gewissen Fällen das Verfahren binnen Monatsfrist zu Ende zu bringen hatten. Aber die Handelsklagen waren damals noch nicht *emmēnoi*." But if Lipsius be right about "some monthly limit" being required by this inscription, then his *ex cathedra* statement on the time-limit for commercial cases ("die Handelsklagen") is somewhat contradictory. We will do better to posit that if *emmēnos* were meant, *emmēnos* would have been written, as it is in *IG* I².65.

[18] Cf. Meritt's emendation, *Hesperia*, 14 (1945), pp. 110-112.

[19] E. Meyer, *Forschungen zur alten Geschichte*, II, Halle, 1899, p. 101.

[20] E. Cavaignac, *Études sur l'histoire financière d'Athènes au* Vᵉ *siècle*, Paris, 1908, p. LXVII.

Pericles' law to 444 is an error, "intelligible (though not excusable)."[21]

Körte connected Cavaignac's *xenodikai* to *IG* I².41's *nautodikai*.[22] His reasons are clear. The *xenodikai* after their appearance in 442 are not mentioned again until the fourth century: as early as 436, but no earlier, the *nautodikai* are connected with the *graphai xenias*: καὶ πρῶτον μὲν παρὰ ναυτοδικῶν ἀπάγω τρία κνώδαλ' ἀναιδῆ. [And first of all away from the *nautodikai* I lead three shameless beasts] (Kratinos, Χείρωνες, almost certainly produced between 436 and 431).[23] In Aristophanes' *Daitaleis* in 427 B.C., there appears the fragment ἐθέλω βάψας πρὸς ναυτοδίκας ξένον ἐξαίφνης . . . , [I want, "dipping," to the "naval judges" (*nautodikai*) as a foreigner immediately (to lead you?)], on which Suidas observed, βάψας: τὴν κώπην ἢ πλεύσας, ἐλθὼν πρὸς τοὺς ναυτοδίκας, οἳ τὰ τῆς ξενίας ἐδίκαζον. ["dipping" i.e. the oar, or "sailing," going to the *nautodikai* who judged the matters involving *xenia*.]

This early evidence, combined with Hesychios' definition of *nautodikai*,[24] οἱ ἐπὶ τοῦ ἐμπορίου δικασταί, ἐφ' ὧν

[21] Jacoby, *FGH*, IIIb (Supplement), Vol. II, p. 380, n. 28.

[22] A. Körte, "Die Attischen Xenodikai," *Hermes*, 68 (1933), pp. 240 ff.

[23] Edmonds Fr. 233, cited by Scholiast to Aristophanes' *Birds* 766. Körte, p. 240, n. 1, is dissatisfied with the textual reading: "An παρὰ ναυτοδικῶν ἀπαγῶ kann ich trotz Meinekes Verteidigung nicht glauben, man erwartet πρὸς ναυτοδίκας und so wird Kratinos geschrieben haben." Editors generally read παρὰ ναυτοδίκας. It seems however a dangerous practice to tailor our prime evidence to fit our preconceptions: παρὰ ναυτοδικῶν is not philological nonsense nor constitutional impossibility. For the dating of Kratinos' *Cheirōnes*, see P. Geissler, *Chronologie der altattischen Komoedie*, Berlin, 1925, p. 20; J. H. Edmonds, *Fragments of Attic Comedy*, I, Leiden, 1957, p. 105.

[24] To which add Harpocration's quotation from one of Krateros'

καὶ αἱ τῆς ξενίας ἐκρίνοντο δίκαι, [judges (*dicasts*) for the *emporion*, by whom the *dikai xenias* were also judged], led Körte to the belief that "man die Funktionen der *xenodikai* zwischen 442 und 437 an die *nautodikai* überwiesen hat, weil bald nach dem grossen Säuberungsprozess des Jahres 444 eine eigene Behörde für *graphai xenias* überflüssig erschien."[25]

In evaluating this hypothesis, it is necessary to test two separate conclusions, (1) Cavaignac's belief that the "*xen* . . ." are in fact identifiable with the *graphai xenias*, and (2) Körte's view that the *xenodikai* between 442 and 437 were replaced by the *nautodikai* in the handling of the *graphai xenias*.

1. *The Cavaignac Hypothesis.* Cavaignac's explanation for *xenodikai* in *IG* I².342 and 343 is confirmed by evidence of text, of time, of money and negated by a contradictory text, *IG* II².26. It is blunted by the lack of certainty in almost everything regarding the officials under discussion.

That "*xen* . . ." appears in the accounts only in 444 and 443 may be mere chance, but it gains in probable significance to the extent that those years were vital to the development of the *graphai xenias*, a significance almost unanimously agreed to.[26]

---

inscriptions, s.v. *nautodikai*: ἐὰν δέ τις ἐξ ἀμφοῖν ξένοιν γεγονὼς φρατρίζῃ, διώκειν δεῖ τῷ βουλομένῳ Ἀθηναίων, οἷς δίκαι εἰσί, λαγχάνειν δὲ τῇ ἕνῃ καὶ νέᾳ πρὸς τοὺς ναυτοδίκας.

[25] *Hermes*, 68 (1933), p. 240.

[26] Thus E. Meyer, *Geschichte des Altertums* IV, Strassburg, 1914, §392; K. J. Beloch, *Griechische Geschichte* II.1, 2nd edition, Stuttgart, 1912-1927, p. 192; Walker, *Cambridge Ancient History*, V, p. 502; Adcock, *Cambridge Ancient History*, V, p. 167; G. Glotz, *Histoire grecque*, Paris, 1936, II.1, p. 179; Gomme, *Essays*, pp. 85, 88; U. Kahrstedt, *Klio*, 68 (1939), pp. 152.

In 451/50,[27] on Pericles' motion, citizenship was limited to offspring both of whose parents were Athenian citizens. (*Ath. Pol.* 26.4; 42.1: μὴ μετέχειν τῆς πόλεως ὃς ἂν μὴ ἐξ ἀμφοῖν ἀστοῖν ᾖ γεγονώς.) Apparently however only in 445 did a gift of grain from Egypt, "five *medimnoi* to each Athenian," require any large-scale determination of individual citizenship.

Plutarch (*Pericles* 37) reports that as a result of this gift of 40,000 *medimnoi* there was much litigation in which 14,040 persons were found to be Athenian citizens and a little less than 5,000 persons were sold into slavery.[28] Philochoros, however, reports that the gift amounted to 30,000 *medimnoi*; that 4,760 persons were deprived of citizenship; and that 14,240 persons shared in the gift.[29]

---

ff.; Hignett, p. 345. Jacoby argues to the contrary, *FGH* IIIb (Supplement), Vol. I, p. 468.

[27] 452 B.C.: H. T. Wade-Gery, *Hesperia*, 14 (1945), pp. 221-222, nn. 21 and 22. For recent discussions of this ever-discussed legislation, see Jacoby, *FGH* IIIb (Supplement), Vol. I, pp. 471-482; Hignett, pp. 343-347.

[28] PLUTARCH: ἀκμάζων ὁ Περικλῆς ἐν τῆι πολιτείαι πρὸ πάνυ πολλῶν χρόνων καὶ παῖδας ἔχων ὥσπερ εἴρηται γνησίους νόμον ἔγραψε (451/0) μόνους ᾿Αθηναίους εἶναι τοὺς ἐκ δυεῖν ᾿Αθηναίων γεγονότας. (4) ἐπεὶ δὲ τοῦ βασιλέως τῶν Αἰγυπτίων δωρεὰν τῶι δήμωι πέμψαντος τετρακισμυρίους πυρῶν μεδίμνους ἔδει διανέμεσθαι τοὺς πολίτας, πολλαὶ μὲν ἀνεφύοντο δίκαι τοῖς νόθοις ἐκ τοῦ γράμματος ἐκείνου τέως διαλανθάνουσι καὶ παρορωμένοις, πολλοὶ δὲ καὶ συκοφαντήμασι περιέπιπτον. ἐπράθησαν οὖν ἁλόντες ὀλίγως πεντακισχιλίων ἐλάττους. οἱ δὲ μείναντες ἐν τῆι πολιτείαι καὶ κριθέντες ᾿Αθηναῖοι μύριοι καὶ τετρακισχίλιοι καὶ τεσσαράκοντα τὸ πλῆθος ἐξητάσθησαν.

[29] PHILOCHOROS: φησὶν οὖν ὁ Φιλόχορος αὖθις ποτὲ τετρακισχιλίους ἑπτακοσίους ξ ὀφθῆναι παρεγγράφους, καθάπερ ἐν τῆι προκειμένηι λέξει δεδήλωται. . . . μήποτε δὲ περὶ τῆς ἐξ Αἰγύπτου δωρεᾶς λέγει, ἣν Φιλόχορός φησι Ψαμμήτιχον πέμψαι τῶι δήμωι ἐπὶ Λυσιμαχίδου (445/4) μυριάδας τρεῖς, πέντε ἑκάστωι δὲ ᾿Αθηναίων μεδίμ-

169

The numerical differences are of little concern: Plutarch's 5,000 is a rounded confirmation of Philochoros' 4,760; Plutarch's 14,040 probably results from Philochoros' numeral "two hundred" having fallen out of the text. The 30,000-40,000 *medimnoi* conflict is inexplicable but of no decisive concern. We do not know why Plutarch omitted the five bushels per head.[30]

But in substance Plutarch and Philochoros say very different things about the 4,760 or almost 5,000. Plutarch enslaves them (ἐπράθησαν ἁλόντες); Philochoros only deprives them of citizenship (ὀφθῆναι παρεγγράφους). To disenroll a "citizen" is not necessarily to sell him as a slave.

The vast number involved has led to a rare unanimity in denying Plutarch, either his report of the action taken or his numbers, or both.[31] But the importance for

νους· τοὺς γὰρ λαβόντας γενέσθαι μυρίους τετρακισχιλίους διακοσίους μ̄. (Müller 90. Cited from Schol. Aristophanes, *Wasps*, 718.)

[30] See Jacoby, *FGH* IIIb (Supplement), Vol. I, p. 463.

[31] Beloch thunders, "die schauderhafte Mär, dass damals 1/4 der bürgerliche Bevölkerung Attikas entrechtet oder gar in die Sklaverei verkauft worden sei, ist aus der griechischen Geschichte zu streichen" (*Die Bevölkerung der Griechisch-Römischen Welt*, Leipzig, 1886, p. 79). "The dreadful tale" that "must disappear from Greek history" virtually has. The figure itself has lately been called into constant question. See Gomme, *Essays*, p. 80, n. 2; Hignett, p. 345 ("the number 4,760 for those now excluded from the lists must be an exaggeration"). The probable explanation is that some 5,000 were removed from the lists, but a far smaller number were sold into slavery. The regular procedure is described by Aristotle: ὅταν δ᾽ ἐγγράφωνται, διαψηφίζονται περὶ αὐτῶν ὀμόσαντες οἱ δημόται . . . εἰ ἐλεύθερός ἐστι καὶ γέγονε κατὰ τοὺς νόμους. ἔπειτ᾽ ἂν μὲν ἀποψηφίσωνται μὴ εἶναι ἐλεύθερον, ὁ μὲν ἐφίησιν εἰς τὸ δικαστήριον, οἱ δὲ δημόται κατηγόρους αἱροῦνται πέντε ἄνδρας ἐξ αὑτῶν, κἂν μὲν μὴ δόξῃ δικαίως ἐγγράφεσθαι, πωλεῖ τοῦτον ἡ πόλις (*Ath. Pol.* 42.1). More explicitly the fourth-century

the Cavaignac theory lies in the very existence of the exceptional events of 445-444, more so than in their interpretation.[32] *Inscriptiones Graecae*, I².342.39, ἐγραμμά[τενε] follows the rubric *para xenodikōn*, but in *IG* I².343 there is no secretary mentioned and no space for one, in Cavaignac's opinion probably because the group of *xenodikai* who at first were expected to require a number of years accomplished their task in some months.[33] Evidentially and chronologically, then, the parallels of a sudden rise in *graphai xenias*, of the sudden appearance of officials known as *xenodikai*, of a sudden and possibly temporary contribution from that source to the Parthenon accounts, seem important, although certainty in such fragmentary matters is impossible.

---

procedure at the time of an extraordinary scrutiny is described in the hypothesis to Dem. 57: τοὺς μὲν ἀποψηφισθέντας καὶ ἐμμείναντας τῇ ψήφῳ τῶν δημοτῶν ἐξαληλίφθαι καὶ εἶναι μετοίκους, τοῖς δὲ βουλομένοις ἔφεσιν εἰς δικαστὰς δεδόσθαι, κἂν μὲν ἁλῶσι καὶ παρὰ τῷ δικαστηρίῳ πεπρᾶσθαι, ἐὰν δ' ἀποφύγωσιν, εἶναι πολίτας. Hence an appeal was a dangerous step, and it is likely that very few took it without extremely strong cases. Gomme misunderstands this (*Essays*, pp. 80 ff.); the penalty is not for the possibly innocent espousal of citizenship, but as a bar to a multitude of appeals. Plutarch knew apparently of the sale into slavery of Athenian "citizens" who had been unsuccessful in establishing before the courts their right to polity. He apparently failed to note the difference between the hearing before the deme and the ἔφεσις ἐκ δημοτῶν. Hence, Philochoros' figures are handled by Plutarch as if all those removed from the ληξιαρχικὸν γραμματεῖον had appealed. There results the incredibly large number "sold into slavery."

[32] Gomme, *ibid.*, speaks of "extraordinary general scrutiny of 445-44 B.C."

[33] E. Cavaignac, *Études sur l'histoire financière*, Paris, 1908, p. LXVIII.

The amount of money involved is also considerable, at least 9,148 and at most 32,148 drachmai in 342.38, allowing for three digit spaces to complete the sum advanced. If the money came, as Cavaignac believed, from the sale of slaves, only a small percentage of the total receipts would have gone to the goddess, if anything like 4,760 were sold—the figures available for slave-sales in 414 show an average price of 174 drachmai.[34] I would suggest that a more likely source of revenue arises from public confiscation of real estate owned by those who had previously "passed" for citizens (τέως διαλανθάνουσι καὶ παρορωμένοις). Not holding citizenship, they could not hold property, and the land would be available for public sale. Property would be no less readily sold by our *xenodikai* than persons.

Yet even if the external conditions required for the Cavaignac hypothesis actually were met historically, there remains the possibility that neither the scrutiny of citizenship (διαψηφισμός) nor the resultant *graphai xenias* had anything to do with the *xenodikai*. It has long been contended that wherever they appear the *xenodikai* in fact have to do with disputes involving foreigners, not necessarily with Athenian *graphai xenias* or the equivalent case category outside of Athens.[35]

[34] W. K. Pritchett, "The Attic Stelai," *Hesperia*, 25 (1956), pp. 276-277. For the fourth century, slave sale prices were somewhat higher. Cf. W. L. Westermann, *RE*, Supp. VI, 1935, s.v. *Sklaverei*, cols. 915-916. Of course, the "dumping" of so many slaves in so short a period might have temporarily depressed the market—but on the other hand former Athenian citizens, or those who had passed for such, might bring premium prices. The point is academic, for the Plutarch passage seems unacceptable. Cf. Gomme, *Essays*, p. 80, n. 2: "It has long been recognized that Plutarch's account . . . is untrue."

[35] In addition to the inscriptions treated below (*IG* IX(1).333

An inscription of Oianthea dated c. 450 and legibly preserved indicates that at a parallel time in Lokris officials known as *xenodikai* existed for the trial of cases involving foreigners.[36] Although the matter of residence may have mattered in the Lokrian decree, the question of citizenship is not germane.

In two Attic inscriptions (*IG* II².46; *IG* II².144) the *xenodikai* also appear.[37] Both inscriptions are highly fragmentary; both are probably from about the same period in the fourth century.[38] It is clear that the two

and *IG* II².46), there are relevant *IG* IX(1).32, ll. 38 ff. (in Phokis during second century B.C.) and the text of Lydus, *de magistratibus populi romani*, I.38 (as equivalent for *praetor peregrinus*). As early as 1886, P. Monceaux, *Les Proxénies Grecques*, Paris, p. 174, notes, "Les inscriptions font mention de juges speciaux pour les étrangers."

[36] *IG* IX(1).333.10; M. N. Tod, *A Selection of Greek Historical Inscriptions*, Oxford, 1946, #34: Αἴ κ' ἀνδιχάζωντι τοὶ ξενοδίκαι. The inscription is in early Lokrian script, for which see A. Kirchoff, *Studien zur Geschichte des griechischen Alphabets*, Gütersloh, 1887, pp. 144 ff. H. F. Hitzig ("Altgriechische Staatsverträge über Rechtshilfe," *Regelsberger Festschrift*, Zurich, 1907, pp. 59 ff.) argues on the basis of this inscription that in all cases tried before the *xenodikai*, the jury was chosen by the foreign plaintiff. Such an argument illustrates the manifest extent to which this inscription provides evidence for *xenodikai* not concerned with citizenship matters.

[37] For improved text of *IG* II².46, see *SEG* XIII.38 and *SEG* XVIII.10. Cf. A. G. Woodhead, *Hesperia*, 26 (1957), pp. 221-229 (*SEG* XVII.17 and XVII.18) for additional fragments of both inscriptions.

[38] The precise date is disputed. *IG* II².46 is dated in the Corpus "paullo post 400." Woodhead would like to date 46 to "375 or thereabouts" and 144 "to date between 368 and 364," *Hesperia*, 26 (1957), pp. 228, 224. *IG* II².144 is included by Kirchner in the Corpus among that group of inscriptions dated "propter scripturae rationem a. 353/52 antiquiora."

documents are of similar content. As Woodhead observes, in both there "appear *xenodikai*, references to death, damage, punishment and sums of money, and to the overall similarity of content may be compared the size and comprehensiveness of both documents."[39] Here we have *xenodikai*, but their task is jurisdiction in litigation under *symbolaia* involving foreigners.

From this perspective Kahrstedt argues powerfully against the Cavaignac-Körte concept.[40] Relying on *IG* II².46 he sees the *xenodikai* as "Fremdenrichter," whose income is derived from actions against foreigners unrelated to ξενία. The juxtaposition of money and officials is impressive, as in fragmentary *IG* II².46 Aa, lines 11 and 12:

$$\tau]\hat{\omega}\nu\ \xi\epsilon[\nu o\delta\iota\kappa\hat{\omega}\nu$$
$$\delta\rho\alpha\chi\mu\grave{\alpha}s$$

Kahrstedt concludes: "die grossen Summen, über die Behörde [the *Xenodikai*] zur Zeit des Baus des Parthenons verfügt, sind keine Illustration zu der Reinigung der Bürgerschaft unter Perikles, sondern für die wirtschaftliche Bedeutung des vielverschrieenen Prozesszwanges."[41]

In effect, the problem of the *xenodikai* of *IG* I².342 and 343 is insoluble on the basis of the information presently available, for the evidence allows of various solutions—more than one key will meet the conditions. Kahrstedt can explain the officials by parallel nomenclature and can justify their providing money to the

[39] *Hesperia*, 26 (1957), p. 225. Kirchner in the Corpus: "Argumentum simile est atque t. 46."

[40] U. Kahrstedt, *Klio*, 32 (1939), pp. 152 ff. Jacoby (approvingly), *FGH* IIIb (Supplement), Vol. II, pp. 380-381.

[41] *Klio*, 32 (1939), p. 153.

goddess.[42] But Cavaignac's hypothesis, despite his error in assigning the Periclean law to 444 and his belief in the unlikely sale of 4,700-odd citizen-slaves, may still be correct; at any rate, it is not impossible, and the chronological parallels seem to me more striking than coincidental.

2. *The Körte Hypothesis.* And what of Körte's belief that sometime between 442 and 437 the *xenodikai* were replaced by the *nautodikai* in the hearing of *graphai xenias*? This hypothesis is still more perilous than Cavaignac's, to the extent that to the uncertainties of the history of the *xenodikai* must be added the uncertainties of the history of the *nautodikai*. Its basic weakness lies in its necessary appeal to *argumenta e silentio*. We do not hear of fifth-century *xenodikai* after 443; we do not hear of the *nautodikai* before 437. But why should we? And in fact there is abundant evidence (viz. IG IX (1).333 and the fourth-century Attic inscriptions) on the nature of the *xenodikai* both later in Athens and contemporarily elsewhere. Further it must be noted how the probabilities fall: if Cavaignac is right, Körte may still be wrong; but if Körte is wrong, then Cavaignac is necessarily wrong. That is, if before 442 the *nautodikai* handled *graphai xenias*, then the *xenodikai* could not possibly be magistrates charged with the hearing of *graphai xenias* in 443.

It is quite possible to postulate that the *nautodikai*

[42] It should be noted however that in the well-known Phaselis decree (IG I².16), foreigners involved in disputes under *symbola* are to appear not before *xenodikai* but *para tōi polemarchōi*. The decree is certainly more closely connected chronologically with the Parthenon accounts than are the fourth-century decrees IG II².46 and 144. So the argument from nomenclature cuts in more than one direction.

handled these cases from the beginning.[43] The *xenodikai* then would be from their beginning concerned
only with litigation involving foreigners, and from these
suits they would derive the funds they are known to
have presented to the goddess in 444 and 443. The
evidence fits, and the hypothesis is simple.

As to the Cavaignac-Körte view, the final word must
be Jacoby's: "Körte's theory has not been refuted definitely and in all parts, but it has not been proved nor
is it credible as to its main point."[44] . . . Not credible,
but still not impossible.

The question raised at the beginning remains: have
the lexicographers actually united two different magistrates of different centuries homonymously titled? The
possibility remains. The *nautodikai* in their role as
judges of the commercial courts appear only in the
fourth century. Their role as judges of the *graphai
xenias* may have been limited to the fifth. But it is their
commercial task that connects them to the *dikai emporikai*.

THE NAUTODIKAI AND THE DIKAI EMPORIKAI

Lysias 17.5: πέρυσι μὲν οὖν διεγράψαντό μου τὰς δίκας,
ἔμποροι φάσκοντες εἶναι · νυνὶ δὲ λαχόντος ἐν τῷ Γαμηλιῶνι
μηνὶ οἱ ναυτοδίκαι οὐκ ἐξεδίκασαν. [Last year they had
my suit quashed by claiming that they were maritime
merchants; now the *nautodikai* have not adjudicated

----

[43] Wilamowitz, *A & A*, I, p. 223, n. 75; Lipsius, *AR*, p. 86;
G. Busolt, *Griechische Geschichte*, III.1, p. 503n. Kahrstedt believes that they handled these cases only when skippers and
sailors were involved.

[44] Jacoby, *FGH* IIIb (Supplement), Vol. II, p. 381, n. 29.

my complaint of the month Gamēlion.] Delivered in 397, this and its companion passage (17.8) constitute the sole reference to *nautodikai* in the extant corpus of Attic orators.[45] Added to the definitions of the lexicographers (Hesychios, Suidas, *Lexica Segueriana* I.283.3), this statement has led to the conclusion that the *nautodikai* had in their jurisdiction the *dikai emporikai*.[46] From the remark νυνὶ δὲ λαχόντος ἐν τῷ Γαμηλιῶνι . . . οὐκ ἐξεδίκασαν, it has been deduced further that the *dikai emporikai* were not yet *emmēnoi* in 397. In a further reference in the same speech, the *nautodikai* appear as an annual board: μάρτυρας ὑμῖν παρέξομαι . . . τούς τε πέρυσιν ἄρξαντας, πρὸς οὓς αἱ δίκαι ἐλήχθησαν, καὶ τοὺς νῦν ναυτοδίκας (8). [I will furnish for you as witnesses . . . those in office last year, with whom the suits were filed, and the present *nautodikai*.]

So much for prevailing authority. Gernet, however, believes that *dikai emporikai* did not exist prior to the middle years of the fourth century, and for three reasons:[47]

1. The text of Dem. 7.12—"où il est dit, non pas que, dans l'ancien état de choses, les actions commerciales n'étaient pas encore pourvues d'une procédure expéditive, mais *qu'il n'existait pas encore* (italics Gernet's) —vers 350—de *dikai emporikai* (dont c'est un des caractères d'être emmēnoi)."

2. Lysias 17.5 must be applied *ratione personae*, not *ratione rei*. The *nautodikai* had jurisdiction only over *emporoi*—"siégeant peut-être au Pirée"—not ἐμπορικά.

[45] A fragment from the Πρὸς 'Αλκιβιάδην is preserved by Harpocration, εἰ γνήσιος ὁ λόγος the lexicographer adds.
[46] C. Lécrivain, *DS*, s.v. *nautodikai*; Beauchet IV, p. 96; similarly; cf. Lipsius, *AR*, pp. 86-88.
[47] *REG* 1938, p. 13.

3. The *nautodikai* in Lysias 17 "président au jugement des causes intéressant des citoyens"; foreigners
appear before the polemarch. The later *emporikai dikai*
however are open to all merchants without regard to
nationality.

We will examine these arguments individually:

1. The text of Dem. 7.12:[48] ὑφ' ἡμῖν γὰρ ἦν ἡ Μακεδονία καὶ φόρους ὑμῖν ἔφερον, καὶ τοῖς ἐμπορίοις τότε
μᾶλλον ἢ νῦν ἡμεῖς τοῖς ἐκεῖ κἀκεῖνοι τοῖς παρ' ἡμῖν ἐχρῶντο,
καὶ ἐμπορικαὶ δίκαι οὐκ ἦσαν, ὥσπερ νῦν, ἀκριβεῖς, αἱ κατὰ
μῆνα ... κ. τ. λ.

The editor of the *Budé Demosthenes*[49] translates the
passage correctly and in the correct context: "Car la
Macédoine était alors sous notre autorité et nous payait
tribut; nous nous servions de leurs ports et ils se ser-
vaient des nôtres plus que maintenant, et il n'y avait
pas à cette époque, comme à présent, une jurisdiction
commerciale régulière [*dikai emporikai*] fonctionnant
tous les mois . . . ." The editor of the *Loeb Demosthenes* renders: "For Macedonia was under our sway
and tributary to us, and we used each other's markets
more freely then than at present, and mercantile suits
were not then, as now, settled strictly every month...."[50]

In both translations "à cette époque" and "then"
clearly refer to a period when Macedonia was under

[48] The most satisfactory treatment of this passage is that of
A. R. W. Harrison, *Classical Quarterly*, 10 (1960), pp. 248-252.
De Ste. Croix's remarks on *forum contractus* appear to me sen-
sible ("Notes on Jurisdiction in the Athenian Empire I," *Classical
Quarterly*, 11 (1961), pp. 105-106 and especially Appendix C,
p. 111).

[49] M. Croiset, *Harangues*, II, Paris, 1925, p. 47. However he is
ambiguous on "καὶ . . . ἐχρῶντο."

[50] J. H. Vince, *Demosthenes I*, Cambridge, 1954, p. 156.

Athenian influence, if not truly tributary to Athens. This time manifestly was not "vers 350"—it could not have been after the battle of Amphipolis and the resultant Peace of Nikias. In fact, Gernet alone renders the passage as he does, and it constitutes the sole piece of positive evidence for his contention that *dikai emporikai* exist only *after* the period of the *nautodikai*.[51]

Even if Gernet's interpretation of the Halonnesos passage is possible (and I do not believe that it is), no less possible is the interpretation otherwise universally accepted. Certainly the text of Dem. 7.12 is not a barrier to existence of *dikai emporikai* at any time after Aigospotamoi.

2. Lysias 17.5 remains. But Gernet contends that even this passage is no evidence for the existence of *dikai emporikai*, for "la compétence des *nautodikai* a lieu *ratione personae* et s'étend à des litiges tout à fait étrangers au commerce maritime."[52] So sweeping a statement is based on the phrase ἔμποροι φάσκοντες εἶναι and the real estate dispute apparently involved. But no certainty is possible. Thus Gernet in his *Budé* edition

[51] Gernet attempts to justify this translation in a footnote (*REG* 1938, p. 12, n. 2): "L'absence d'article et le contexte justifient la traduction: '*Il n'y avait pas d'actions commerciales régulières (ou spécifiques), qui se jugent dans le délai d'un mois*' " (Gernet's italics). But the context has appeared to all others to refer to the time specified in the text, when ἐφ' ἡμῖν ἦν ἡ Μακεδονία. The absence of the article in ancient Greek is not generally considered the determinant of the precise meaning of the notoriously ambiguous verb *einai*. If it were, Plato's Kratylos would have had less trouble with nomenclature. Gomme, in fact (*Commentary on Thucydides*, Oxford, 1944, I, p. 238, n. 3), cautiously mentions the period "before the middle of the 4th-century," but his footnote is to Thucydides 1.77.1.

[52] *REG* 1938, p. 13. In agreement is Harrison, *Procedure*, p. 23.

of Lysias observes, "Mais l'allusion est bien rapide, et le texte peu explicite."[53]

His latter statement is correct. Land is involved (§5), but this does not preclude the litigation's being actionable as a *dikē emporikē* even by later fourth-century standards. It is the purpose of the original loan (§2) that would determine even after 342 the possibility of including the resulting litigation in the category *dikai emporikai.* The original transaction might well have been for maritime purposes—there is no evidence against such a suggestion, and the people involved are in fact *emporoi.*[54] At least they claim to be.

In the later fourth century, cases occurred where the precipitating factor in court action under *dikai emporikai* litigation was far removed from the question of a commercial contract. *Pros Apatourion* (Dem. 33) was brought as a *dikē emporikē,* although the precipitating factor in the actual suit was the question of surety in arbitration proceedings. *Pros Lakriton* (Dem. 35) involves the question of testamentary responsibility. Both cases however *originated* from commercial maritime loans; both cases appear in our sources as *dikai emporikai.* In both cases the defense offered is the *paragraphē,* contending that the suit is not admissible as a *dikē emporikē.* It is quite credible that the same would have

[53] II, Paris, 1926, p. 22, n. 1.

[54] Lipsius (*AR,* p. 633) notes the possible relation of the real estate dispute to the original loan: "Nahe liegt zu vermuten, dass auch diese Änderung mit dem Wechsel des Forum in Beziehung gestanden hat." Similarly W. Schwahn, *RE,* s.v. *nautodikai,* col. 2055, considers the original loan to have been connected with trade: "Ihre Zuständigkeit war offenbar dadurch begründet, dass die Beklagten sich selbst als *emporoi* bezeichnet hatten, dass es sich also um die Rückerstattung eines Darlehns handelte, das zum Zwecke der Emporie gegeben war. . . ."

held for the litigation mentioned in Lysias 17. The speaker's opponent would allege that the case fell into the category of *dikai emporikai*; the speaker would deny it on the grounds that no longer did there exist an agreement for a maritime loan between the litigants. The result would be a *paragraphē* and a hearing on the question before the *nautodikai*, the judges of commercial maritime cases in the early fourth century.

The important point is not the procedure followed in this particular dispute; what matters is the clear existence of a category of cases known as *dikai emporikai* and heard by *nautodikai*. There is no reason to assume that this category was decided *ratione personae* in the early fourth century. It is possible, but unlikely, and is not demanded by the text of 17.5. It must be noted that, in the same way in the later fourth century, it is possible that *ratione personarum* was the determining factor in the commercial courts—possible but unlikely, and yet not absolutely inconsistent with our evidence.[55]

In short our knowledge does not allow us to determine the precise nature of the early *dikai emporikai*. But it is not their nature but their existence that is in dispute. Gernet's speculative objection to their constitution does not even semantically render them nonexistent.

3. Gernet's final objection is that foreigners "qui ont affaire à la justice d'Athènes pour des opérations commerciales comparaissent devant le polémarque" and thus "on voit comme nous sommes loin de la généralité et du concept même des *dikai emporikai*, surtout si l'on tient compte de la forte proportion des étrangers parmi les *emporoi*." However, the early *dikai emporikai* were

[55] See above, Chapter 2, pp. 114 ff.

not necessarily limited to citizens simply because the litigants involved in Lysias 17 are citizens. Gernet believed that the appearance of foreigners before the polemarch at this time in commercial matters had been "bien reconnu" by Hitzig in 1907.[56] Hitzig's basis of proof is the Phaselis decree.

But this decree would establish no basic rule for litigation under *dikai emporikai* provisions—it is binding for Phaselites only, and has in fact been considered a special privilege granted to the citizens of that state.[57] More importantly *dikai apo symbolōn* are rigorously to be differentiated from *dikai emporikai*: an essential factor in the *dikai emporikai* is their admission of foreigners *without* the existence of *symbola*. The establishment of *dikai emporikai* did not lead to the destruction of *symbola* arrangements.[58] Regardless of where the Phaselites appeared, no general rule could therefore be established for aliens in general, or for trade in particular.

Yet why does Hitzig relate this decree to the *nautodikai* at all? Because he believed that the Phaselis agreement dated from the early years of the fourth century. Thus the first edition of the Corpus (*IG* II.1) and the then-current editions of Dittenberger (#72) and Michel (#6) stated in 1907.[59]

[56] H. F. Hitzig, "Der griechische Fremdenprozess," SZ, 28 (1907), p. 228. Hitzig makes this point exactly, "Während unter Bürgern die Nautodiken kompetent waren, erschien in den Prozessen gegen Fremde der Polemarch."

[57] See H. T. Wade-Gery, *Essays in Greek History*, Oxford, 1958, pp. 188-189.

[58] *Ath. Pol.* 59.5-6. Cf. Paoli, *SDA*, pp. 96-99.

[59] Cf. Köhler, *Hermes*, 7 (1873), pp. 159 ff., who dates the decree to 394-387; Judeich, *Kleinasiatische Studien*, Marburg, 1892, pp. 98 ff., esp. n. 21, where the decree is dated 388. Tod

But the true approximate date, the mid-years of the fifth century, had in fact been calculated as early as 1898 by Wilhelm working from the script: although the text is Ionian, the letter forms date from about 450.[60] There is thus no real connection between the Phaselis decree and the *nautodikai* mentioned by Lysias. There is no reason, either logical or chronological, for the separation of jurisdiction between *polemarch* and *nautodikēs* in commercial cases affecting citizens and aliens.

There remains then only the clear indication that in the early years of the fourth century *dikai emporikai* existed and were presided over by *nautodikai*: special courts with special magistrates concerned with the affairs of commerce.

THE DURATION OF THE NAUTODIKAI

The duration of the office of *nautodikai* has been widely discussed, but the discussion has been properly limited to two terminal points, the early or the middle

---

discusses the earlier dating briefly, Vol. I, p. 59 (M. N. Tod, *A Selection of Greek Historical Inscriptions*, Oxford, 1933).

[60] A. Wilhelm, *Goettingische Gelehrte Anzeigen*, 1898, p. 204; later, A. Wilhelm, *Attische Urkunden*, IV, Vienna, 1939, p. 60. P. S. Phōtiadēs offers discussion and photograph, 'Εφημερὶs 'Αρχαιολογική, 1922, pp. 62-65, 79. H. T. Wade-Gery, "The Judicial Treaty with Phaselis," *Essays in Greek History*, Oxford, 1958, pp. 180-200, wishes to date the decree between 469 and 462. He says justly (p. 182), "The approximate date, somewhere not very far from the middle of the fifth century B.C., is not open to question." Mattingly's attempt to date it later, based on its short datives, is not convincing: H. Mattingly, *Proceedings of the African Classical Associations*, 7 (1964), pp. 37-39.

years of the fourth century.[61] The *nautodikai* never again are mentioned after 397 in an extant Attic oration, which has been taken as proof of their non-existence. But the paucity of sources for the first half of the fourth century is such that no special importance need be attached to this absence of reference. In 355 however Xenophon (*Poroi*, 3.3) alludes to the ἀρχὴ τοῦ ἐμπορίου [harbor magistrate or magistrate of trade], suggesting that prizes should be offered to the magistrate ὅστις δικαιότατα καὶ τάχιστα διαιροίη τὰ ἀμφίλογα [who most justly and quickly resolves disputes]. This ἀρχὴ τοῦ ἐμπορίου is probably the *nautodikēs*—the contest could not take place unless a number of officials was involved; the dispensing of justice to merchants in some judicial capacity is clearly indicated.

Hence we are dealing with a board concerned with the regulation of commercial disputes. The only other magistrates who are reported anywhere ever to have had jurisdiction over the *dikai emporikai*—the *eisagōgeis* and the *thesmothetai*—cannot be described as the ἀρχὴ τοῦ ἐμπορίου. Their powers were too far-reaching, and their concern touched too many other areas. The *nautodikai* then continued to preside over the *dikai emporikai* until after 355.

Reform of the Dikai Emporikai

Between 397 and 322 great changes took place in the commercial maritime courts. Perhaps the most im-

[61] Early years: Lécrivain, *DS*, s.v. *nautodikai*; Gilbert, p. 424; Paoli, *SPA*, p. 185, "al massimo." Middle years: *MSL*, p. 97; Lipsius, *AR*, pp. 85-86; Beauchet IV, p. 98; Schwahn, *RE*, s.v. *nautodikai*, col. 2063; Gernet, *REG* 1938, p. 12, n. 1; Harrison, *Procedure*, p. 24.

portant of the alterations were the imposition of the monthly limitation on the filing of the *lēxis* and the transfer of these cases to the *thesmothetai*. These two reforms however appear to some extent inconsistent. The vast majority of case classifications handled by the *thesmothetai* (*Ath. Pol.* 59.1-5) are *graphai*, not *dikai*. They are public, not private. They are subject to no time limit. In contrast, the class of officials known as *eisagōgeis* are intimately and basically connected with *dikai emmēnoi* of the most varied types (*Ath. Pol.* 52.2).[62]

There can be no doubt however that at the time of composition of the *Constitution of the Athenians* the *dikai emporikai* were both *emmēnoi* and under the jurisdiction of the *thesmothetai*. Although it has not been to my knowledge observed, the *Pros Apatourion* (Dem. 33) provides evidence both that the *dikai emporikai* are within the jurisdiction of the *thesmothetai* (πρὸς τοὺς θεσμοθέτας) (1) and that they are "monthly" (αἱ δὲ λήξεις τοῖς ἐμπόροις τῶν δικῶν ἔμμηνοί εἰσιν) (23). This speech is quite close in time to the date of composition of the *Constitution of the Athenians*.[63]

Again, Dem. 34.45 gives evidence of *dikai emporikai* under the control of the *thesmothetai*; the speech dates to late in the history of Aristotle's 11th Constitution, probably in the year 327/26.[64]

[62] See above, pp. 12-15.

[63] See Gernet, *Budé Demosthenes*, Notice to Dem. 33; Blass, III.1, p. 574. The date of composition of the speech is probably late in the reign of Alexander, at least ten years after the failure of the Herakleidēs bank. Since this bank is known to have been operating in 343 (Dem. 48.12, 26) the speech cannot be earlier than 331, and may be sometime later.

[64] See Gernet, *Budé Demosthenes*, Notice; Paley-Sandys' introduction to Dem. 34; Blass III.1, p. 578.

Thus all our evidence for the assignment of the *dikai emporikai* to the *thesmothetai* falls into one decade, the 320's. Yet the period in which the *dikai emporikai* became *emmēnoi* is between 355 and 342.[65] Hence *dikai emmēnoi emporikai* existed during a twenty-thirty-year period for which we have no definite magisterial assignment. In all probability the *dikai emporikai* upon becoming *emmēnoi* were under the jurisdiction of the *eisagōgeis,* not the *thesmothetai,* and it was not until the commercial crisis of 330-326 that jurisdiction over these courts was transferred to the *thesmothetai.*[66]

THE EISAGŌGEIS AND THE DIKAI EMMĒNOI

The connection between the *dikai emmēnoi* and the *eisagōgeis* is close. In fact, upon the appearance of the *Constitution of the Athenians* with its revelation in 52.2 that the *eisagōgeis* presiding over the *dikai emmēnoi* actually did exist, as Pollux had previously testified (see below), and its parallel testimony in 59.5 that the *thesmothetai* preside over the *dikai emporikai,* at least one scholar felt compelled to deny that the *dikai em-*

[65] Cf. Xenophon, *Poroi* 3.3, and Dem. 7.12, which date respectively to those two years.

[66] Clerc long ago felt compelled by the ancient evidence to see a chronological differentiation in the *dikai emporikai.* Cf. *Les Métèques,* p. 96, where he assumes that the *thesmothetai* were succeeded by the *eisagōgeis,* but with "le jugement restant toujours, pour les affaires importantes, entre les mains des Thesmothètes" (p. 96). His discussion is brief and confused—his main interest was not the *dikai emporikai.* But he at least saw the problem. E. Caillemer (*DS,* s.v. *Foenus,* p. 1223) speaks parenthetically of the *dikai emporikai* as having been "successivement confiée à diverses magistratures," including the *eisagōgeis.* He cites Pollux 8.101, but says nothing further.

porikai could any longer be *emmēnoi* in the time of Aristotle.[67]

From all that is known of the *eisagōgeis* in the fourth century it seems clear that their prime and probably sole purpose was control of *dikai emmēnoi*. Aristotle so describes them: κληροῦσι δὲ καὶ εἰσαγωγέας ε̄ ἄνδρας, οἳ τὰς ἐμμήνους εἰσάγουσι δίκας (*Ath. Pol.* 52.2).

It is however necessary to separate these technical "*eisagōgeis*" from the non-technical meaning of the word. Every magistrate is an "introducer" when he is in the act of "introducing," i.e. he is an εἰσαγωγεύς when he εἰσάγει. This is implicit in their jurisdictional power (ἡγεμονία δικαστηρίου). Thus the *thesmothetai* are *eisagōgeis* for the actions under their competence; they are not for other actions. In a different sense the *eisagōgeis* constitute a special board of magistrates presiding over *dikai emmēnoi*.[33]

Nor are these *eisagōgeis* of the fourth century to be connected with those of the fifth century mentioned in *IG* I².63,[69] which are cited only in this inscription, never

[67] Gilbert, p. XII. This conjecture is false, since Aristotle does not claim that all *dikai emmēnoi* were assigned to the *eisagōgeis*. Specifically in 52.3 he mentions the *apodektai* as charged with *dikai emmēnoi* for tax-cases. But cf. Gilbert, p. 422, n. 3.

[68] See E. Caillemer, *DS*, s.v. *eisagōgeis*.

[69] In the tribute assessment for 425/24 there appear the lines:

6 —Ηοῦτ[οι δὲ ἀϝειπόντον ἐν τōι] κοινōι
 Η[εκάστες τε̄ς πόλ]ε̄ος πα[ρε̄ναι πρέσβες τō Μαι]

7 μακτεριōν[ος με↗ός· κυαμεῦσαι δὲ ἐ]σαγογέα[ς
 τριάκοντα· τού τ]ος δὲ [Ηελέσθαι καὶ γραμμα]

8 τέα καὶ χσυ[γγραμματέα ἐχς Ηαπάντ]ον·

The text above is that of *ATL*, II, A9, corresponding to *IG* I.37. The authors of the *Athenian Tribute Lists* explain the restoration τριάκοντε, "We posit 30 because considerable litigation must have been anticipated and because τριάκοντα allows a

187

again elsewhere in literary or epigraphic sources from the fifth century. They are clearly a group concerned with imperial matters, manifestly with the introduction of tribute disputes.[70] Working from this inscription various scholars have attempted to pinpoint the date of introduction and purpose of the fourth-century *eisagōgeis*.[71] But more salient is *IG* I².65.[72] Here the concept of *emmēna* prescription appears, but the cases are handled πρὸς τὸς ἐπιμελετάς.[73] Thus the *epimeletai* have an attested connection with *emmēnoi* cases in the fifth century. The *eisagōgeis* do not.

In view of the wide popular use of the word *eisagōgeis* in reference to magistrates in Athens, we should be surprised perhaps if the homonym of the fourth-century

---

credible restoration of the passage" (*ATL*, III, p. 74). But there is no reason necessarily to posit a large number of *eisagōgeis* here. Their homonyms of the fourth century numbered only five and handled the large jurisdiction and probably correspondingly large litigation described at *Ath. Pol.* 52.2. The restoration must be taken as purely *exempli gratia*.

[70]

12 ν αὐτὲν ζεμ[ίαν· τὸν δὲ διαδικασιὸν Ηοι]

ἐσ[α]γ[ογὲς ἐπ]ιμε[λεθέντον τὸ φόρο καθάπερ ἂν φσε]

13 φίσεται Ηο [δêμος. . . .

[71] Thus Lipsius (*AR*, p. 84) opts for a mid-fifth century date and the purpose of handling the monthly suits. Similarly, Bu.-Sw., p. 113, n. 4. Wilamowitz (*A & A*, I, p. 223) agreed on the date of foundation, but thought, reasonably, that their *raison d'être* in the fifth century was the direction of imperial, not *emmēnoi* cases. Gernet (*REG* 1938, pp. 3-4) argues strongly against Lipsius.

[72] *ATL*, II, D8; *IG* 38. The *locus classicus* for discussion of this inscription is still B. D. Meritt, *Documents on Athenian Tribute*, Cambridge, 1937, pp. 3-42.

[73] Ηο[ι δὲ ἐπιμελεταὶ ἐσαγό]ντον ἔμμενα ἐς τὸ δ[ικαστέριον ἐπειδὰν Ηοι κ]λετêρες ἔκοσι (*ATL*, II, D8, 11.47-49).

188

officials did *not* appear in the fifth. But in purpose the two types of *eisagōgeis* have no similarity, and in time they are separated by the gulf of a full century. It will be better to seek the genesis of the *eisagōgeis* of non-imperial Athens in a non-imperial context.

At precisely what period the *dikai emmēnoi* were ranged together is uncertain. It seems certain that at some time a number of *dikai emmēnoi* were brought together under the direction of the *eisagōgeis* and that for this purpose the *eisagōgeis* in the technical sense were created.

Gernet has attempted to show that during the first half of the fourth century *dikai emmēnoi* did not exist.[74] Citing Dem. 49, 50 and 40, he has sought to demonstrate that these cases would have belonged to the category of *dikai emmēnoi* as δίκη τραπεζιτική, δίκη τριηραρχική and (possibly) δίκη προικός, respectively, in the time of Aristotle, whereas in 362, 358, and 347 they had not yet become *emmēnoi*. However these proofs are subject to doubt on many counts: the lack of precise information on the nature of the later δίκαι τραπεζιτικαί[75] and δίκαι τριηραρχικαί; the impossibility of ascertaining in Dem. 49 and 50 the essential grounds for bringing the case; the improbability (in reference to 40) of the δίκη προικός itself being actionable in cases of inheritance. Furthermore it should be noted that δίκη τραπεζιτική and δίκη τριηραρχική are mentioned last of all in Aristotle's enumeration of the *dikai emmēnoi* in 52.2[76]—they of all the case classifications mentioned

[74] *REG* 1938, pp. 5-10. In accord is Harrison, *Procedure*, p. 21.

[75] Thus M. I. Finley, *Land and Credit*, Rutgers, 1952, p. 265, n. 17, "the *dikai trapezitikai*, about which nothing is known from the sources." Cf. Bogaert, pp. 399-400.

[76] This is not to suggest that he is necessarily following a chronological arrangement.

would be the only ones likely to develop for the first time in the fourth century. The others, e.g. αἰκείας and ἐρανικαί, arise from inherent human relations. The *trierarchy* and the *trapeza* are among the glories of fourth-century Athens, and litigation in these categories must have increased rapidly as the century progressed. The development of the law of these institutions must have waited on the development of the institutions. Hence any evidence based on the trierarchic or trapezitic cases is necessarily prejudiced. And on the δίκη προικός even Gernet has to say "peut-être." In contrast, the δίκη αἰκείας itself was still in 346 under the jurisdiction of the Forty (Dem. 37.33), and Lipsius admits that it was only later "added" to the group of *dikai emmēnoi.*[77] The total weight of Gernet's argument, however, is probably greater than the sum of his particular proofs on individual points.

If then Gernet is right in his contention that *dikai emmēnoi* certainly did not exist at all prior to 358, we would conclude that sometime between 355 and 342 the *dikai emmēnoi* were created as a group and that the *dikai emporikai* were at this time transferred from the previously existing *nautodikai* to the *eisagōgeis* created for the purpose of presiding over the newly established *dikai emmēnoi*. Correspondingly, if the *dikai emmēnoi* actually existed as a group prior to the *dikai emporikai*'s becoming "*emmēnoi*," it seems likely that, during the same period and in the same way, control of the *dikai emporikai* was likewise transferred from the *nautodikai* to the *eisagōgeis* of the *dikai emmēnoi.*[78] This would be the period to which Pollux bears

[77] Lipsius, *AR*, pp. 85 ff.

[78] The belief that the *eisagōgeis* of the fifth century are one with those of the fourth has led to the conclusion that the *dikai*

witness in his testimony of 8.101: εἰσαγωγεῖς οἱ τὰς ἐμμήνους δίκας εἰσάγοντες. ἦσαν δὲ προικός, ἐρανικαί, ἐμπορικαί. [*Eisagōgeis*: "introducers" of the "monthly cases," viz. dowry, "friendly loan," and commercial maritime (suits).] Pollux' testimony however has generally been considered valueless. Thus Gernet disregards it, observing "Ce n'est pas la seule fois que Pollux s'est trompé."[79] However, if this citation is to be considered "just another error" of Pollux, an incredible incompetence must be assigned to the author of the *Onomastikon*, sufficient to call into question the value of his entire eighth Book, but an incompetence not justified by an evaluation of the nature of Pollux' scholarship or by his testimony on this particular point.

THE EISAGŌGEIS AND THE DIKAI EMPORIKAI

Pollux' statement is not, *prima facie*, totally absurd. Only because of the habit of telescoping legal developments into static pictures has this testimony been treated with a scorn it does not merit.

Thus before the publication of the *Constitution of the Athenians* and especially before that of *Inscriptiones Graecae* 37,[80] Pollux' total testimony on the *eisagōgeis* was questioned. They are not mentioned as a special office by the Attic orators. They existed only on the basis of Pollux' testimony at 8.101. Hence Meier and

---

emporikai were "added" to the already existing class of *dikai emmēnoi*. See Beauchet IV, pp. 98-100; Lipsius, *AR*, p. 87; Paoli, *SDA*, pp. 112 ff.

[79] *REG* 1938, p. 11, n. 3.

[80] U. Köhler, "Urkunden und Untersuchungen zur Geschichte des delisch-attischen Bundes," *Abhandlungen der Preussischen Akademie*, Berlin, 1869, pp. 63 ff.

others concluded that they had not existed at all[81]—Pollux was confused.

The publication of the text of the tribute assessment of 425/24 proved the existence of the *eisagōgeis*; the publication of the *Ath. Pol.* proved the exactness of Pollux' defining them as the magistrates charged with the *dikai emmēnoi*.

Cases of a similar sort can be multiplied. For example: Pollux 8.87 contains the statement that the *thesmothetai* laid the εἰσαγγελίαι [public denunciations] before the *Dēmos*. The statement was doubted.[82] *Ath. Pol.* 59.2 proved it true.

Pollux 8.90 was an incredible statement contradicting Pollux' own testimony at 8.120. At §90 he characterized the King Archon as the "judge" of trials involving inanimate things (βασιλεύς: δικάζει τὰς τῶν ἀψύχων δίκας). At §120 he seems to assign the same jurisdiction to the tribal kings (φυλοβασιλεῖς : προειστήκεσαν δὲ τούτου τοῦ δικαστηρίου φυλοβασιλεῖς, οὓς ἔδει τὸ ἐμπεσὸν ἄψυχον ὑπερορίσαι). The *Ath. Pol.* confirms both of Pollux' statements by assigning concurrent jurisdiction to the King Archon and the tribal kings: δικάζει ὁ βασιλεὺς καὶ οἱ φυλοβασιλεῖς καὶ τὰς τῶν ἀψύχων καὶ τῶν ἄλλων ζῴων.[83]

In regard to 8.101, the case is somewhat different, for this citation is seemingly inconsistent with the *Ath. Pol.* itself. But it has not been observed how inconsistent it is with Pollux' own text. For at 8.93 Pollux offers a variant interpretation of *eisagōgeis*, or so it would seem: εἰσαγωγῆς: ἀρχῆς κληρωτῆς ὄνομα· οὗτοι δὲ τὰς δίκας

---

[81] M. H. E. Meier & G. F. Schömann, *Der attische Process*, Halle, 1824, p. 214, W. Wachsmuth, *Hellenische Altertumskunde*, II, Halle, 1846, p. 250.

[82] Cf. Boeckh, *Kleine Schriften*, V, Leipzig, 1858-1874, p. 163.

[83] *Ath. Pol.* 57.4.

εἰσῆγον πρὸς τοὺς διαιτητάς. [*Eisagōgēs*: name of an office selected by lot. These men introduced the cases to the arbitrators.] This seems nonsense, for the essential saving of time in the *dikai emmēnoi* has been generally considered to result from its bypassing the arbitrators (διαιτηταί).[84] When on top of all this, Pollux proceeds to cite Aristotle's own definition of *thesmothetai* (Pollux 8.88; *Ath. Pol.* 59.5) and assigns the *dikai emporikai* to the *thesmothetai*, one must wonder not at his ability but at his sanity, or else wonder what Pollux is really trying to do in the *Onomastikon*.

To me it seems clear that what he is trying to do is precisely what he states as his purpose in his opening remarks to Commodus Caesar: to give information on the meanings and usage of words, τὸ μάθημα τῆς φωνῆς. He is not writing a systematic textbook of Attic law in the eighth Book, which he devotes to judicial terms—he is illustrating certain categories of terminology, admittedly in an organized, but certainly not in a legally consistent fashion. In fact it seems likely that in illustrating his terms he did no more than copy. If so, the consequences are important for the history of the *dikai emporikai*. And it is likely that it is so.

That within five pages of text Pollux could assign the *dikai emporikai* both to the *eisagōgeis* and to the *thesmothetai*, and that he could define *eisagōgeis* in two different ways is incredible if explained solely by his carelessness or foolishness.[85]

[84] See Bo.-Sm. II, p. 116; Reinach, *DS*, s.v. *emmēnoi dikai*. Cf. above, Chapter 1, "Fundamental Steps in Monthly Procedure."

[85] The situation is not materially affected even if, as Bethe feels sure, we possess only a lengthy epitome of a longer original *Onomastikon*. In that case we should have to say, perhaps, "ten" instead of "five" pages.

Pollux himself gives insights into his working methods, for example, the opening of Book VI, where he appears sensibly concerned with problems of authenticity.[86] Again in his opening letter of VIII, the very book dealing with judicial terms, he apologizes to Commodus Caesar for his delay in its production—teaching duties had interfered with scholarly publication.[87]

Having apparently gained his necessary leisure, could Pollux not see how mixed-up his text was? For the problem does not result from later contamination. Despite the variant textual readings to be found at places in his text[88] the essential "contradictions" are in the manuscripts soundly witnessed and securely based.

The explanation then is that of source and purpose: Pollux is illustrating the use of language, and he quotes different sources for different words.[89] For us it is reasonable to make use through Pollux of the multifold

---

[86] ἐνίοις δὲ τῶν ἀμφιβόλων προσέθηκα τοὺς μάρτυρας, ἵνα τοὺς εἰπόντας εἰδῇς, ἔστι δ᾽ ὅπου καὶ τὸ χωρίον ἐν ᾧ τοὔνομα, ἐπὶ δέ τινων καὶ τὴν λέξιν αὐτήν.

[87] ταῦτα ἐγὼ μὲν συνελεξάμην, ὅτι μὲν διὰ ταχέων, αὐτὸ δηλοῖ, πλὴν οὐκ ἔστιν ὅτε ἀποστὰς δι᾽ αὐτὰ τῆς συνουσίας τῆς πρὸς τοὺς νέους καὶ τῶν δι᾽ ἔθους ἀγώνων ὁσημέραι δύο λόγους (ἐξειργασάμην;) [OM. FS] τὸν μὲν ἐκ τοῦ θρόνου λέγων, τὸν δὲ ὀρθοστάδην · ἔδει δέ, ὡς εἰκός, κἀκείνοις παρασκευῆς καὶ τούτοις σχολῆς.

[88] Consider, for example, the variants at 8.101: ἐπαγωγεῖς ΠΒ; ἐκμήνους Α; ἐπάγοντες ABCL; ἐρανικαὶ: γαμικαί Α where Π = P (Parisinus 2646) & S (Salamanticensis Hispan. I.2.3); A = Parisinus 2670; B = Parisinus 2647; C = Palatinus Heidelbergensis 375; L = Laurentianus 56.1.

[89] Hesychios' definition of eisagōgē offers insight into the lexicographers' sources for such definitions. The definition is virtually word-for-word that of the Scholiast to Dem. 21, 515.14 (Dindorf). Pollux' sources are not similarly extant on this point, with the exception of the Ath. Pol., but we cannot doubt that they were of the same sort.

sources now available to us only through the *Onomastikon*. There is no necessity immediately to disregard as "error" that which seems inconsistent at first glance with other sources.[90] On the particular problem, Pollux shows us clearly the nature of his sources. In defining the *thesmothetai* he is following the *Ath. Pol.* Hence he gives the *Ath. Pol.*'s definition: now the royal reader of the Attic orators is able to know what a *thesmothetēs* is when one is mentioned. (Pollux was not writing a treatise on *dikai emporikai*.) In defining the *eisagōgeis*, he excerpted another source from or based upon a time when *dikai emporikai* were *emmēnoi* under those officials. In defining *eisagogēs* at 8.89 Pollux is not even here contradicting himself—he is defining a word which differs from the one that names the introducers of monthly trials. We know of the two different concepts of *eisagōgeus*. So did he.

THE TRANSFER OF THE COMMERCIAL COURTS TO THE THESMOTHETAI

At what time the *dikai emporikai* were entrusted to the *thesmothetai* is not absolutely certain, but an event of unparalleled economic importance, the great grain shortage of 330-326, may well have been responsible.[91]

[90] See A. E. Raubitschek's remarks on the value and sources of the lexicographers, which holds as true, *mutatis mutandis*, for fourth-century law as for fifth-century history: *Classica et Mediaevalia*, 19 (1955), pp. 73-74.

[91] For evidence of the vast difficulty caused by this phenomenon, see Dem. 34.39, 42.20, 42.31; Aristotle, *Oeconomica*, 2.33A, 33E; *SEG*, IX.2. For evidence of the Athenian gratitude to benefactors of this period, see *IG* II².342, 407, 408, 409, 416, 423. It is important to note the depression in the mining in-

Before this event we know of no *dikai emporikai* under *thesmothetai*. The dates of composition of the *Ath. Pol.*, of Dem. 33, and of Dem. 34[92] follow immediately upon the grain shortage.

The crisis brought great reverberations in the commercial world. Its impact was so serious that even after the event litigants in Athenian courts spoke of their admirable behavior in the difficulty or questioned the conduct of their opponents (Dem. 34, 42). Inscriptional evidence from Africa records the amounts of grain distributed to the various cities.[93] To no city did there go more grain than to Athens.

The cause of the crisis is not vital to the possible legal reactions of the Athenians. It is difficult to determine if there was a widespread crop failure or a widespread breakdown in importation from a vital granary area.[94]

---

dustry that apparently paralleled the problem of food supply. Cf. R. J. Hopper, "Attic silver mines in the 4th century B.C.," *Annual of the British School at Athens*, 48 (1953), pp. 250-252; M. Crosby, "The Leases of the Laureion Mines," *Hesperia*, 19 (1950), pp. 189 ff., leases ##29-38. The major manifestations of the grain shortage are summarized by Michell, pp. 275-278, and discussed by Rostovtzeff, *SEHHW*, Chapter II and n. 29 on p. 1329. Cf. Schäfer III, p. 295; M. Segre, *Mondo Classico*, 4 (1934), pp. 398 ff.; F. M. Heichelheim, *Wirtschaftsgeschichte des Altertums*, I, Leiden, 1938, p. 850; G. Oliverio, *Documenti antichi dell'Africa Italiana*, II.1, Bergamo, 1933.

[92] See above, this chapter, n. 64.

[93] ὅκα ἁ σιτοδεία ἐγένετο ἐν ταῖ Ἑλλάδι (*SEG*, IX.2.11.3-5).

[94] Michell (p. 275) finds that "there is no certain evidence of a serious crop failure." But Aristotle (*Oeconomica*, II.33A) seems specific enough, Κλεομένης Ἀλεξανδρεὺς Αἰγύπτου σατραπεύων, λιμοῦ γενομένου ἐν μὲν τοῖς ἄλλοις τόποις σφόδρα, ἐν Αἰγύπτῳ δὲ μετρίως. . . . Also the widespread area to which Cyrene exported grain during the crisis argues for general climatic difficulties. Epirus, for example, is not generally known as a food-importer,

In either case the Athenians would be exceptionally anxious to control grain supplies and those commercial circles that provided food for the city. The normal legal reaction to such a situation is to transfer control of specific cases from a neutrally specified body to the *thesmothetai*.

The one characteristic that has seemed to unify the diverse functions of the *thesmothetai* has been their "charge in principle of cases in which the interests of the community as a whole were immediately concerned."[95] More specifically, "Quand des affaires privées mettaient fortement en jeu l'intérêt public, il arrivait que, par un décret spécial fondé sur la raison d'État, le peuple athénien dessaisît le tribunal compétent. Dans ce cas, il confiait volontiers aux thesmothètes la présidence d'un tribunal extraordinaire."[96]

Such was the case in 415 when the *thesmothetai* were entrusted with decisions regarding the profanation of the mysteries—a matter of special and immediate importance to the state (Andocides, 1.28).

Possibly of the same sort is the citation in *IG* XII.I.977, a decree of the fourth century favoring the Eteokarpathians, where jurisdiction is assigned to the *thesmothetai*:[97]

---

but figures prominently among the areas to which Cyrene exported grain at this time.

[95] A. W. Gomme, *Oxford Classical Dictionary*, 1st edition, Oxford, 1949, s.v. *thesmothetai*.

[96] G. Glotz, *DS*, s.v. *thesmothetai*, p. 246. Cf. Lipsius, *AR*, p. 74.

[97] See P. Foucart, *Bulletin de correspondance hellénique*, 12 (1888), pp. 153 ff.; Lipsius, *AR*, p. 74, n. 85; Wilhelm, *Goettingische Gelehrte Anzeigen*, 1903, p. 780; Dittenberger 3129. The Chalkis decree (*ATL*, II, D17) is a different matter, for there only *ephesis* to the court of the fifth-century *thesmothetai* is provided (1.75).

26 δίκην δὲ ἔνα-
27 [ι πρὸς τὸς θεσμο]θέτας ἐν ᾿Α[θ]-
28 [ηναίοις. . . ----

It seems to have been established practice in matters of special importance to the state, for whatever reason, to give access to the court of the *thesmothetai*.

In this time of crisis in the early 320's, in a matter of such importance as the provision of the city's grain supply, it may well have been decided to transfer control of the *dikai emporikai* from the "rapid-procedure" officials, the *eisagōgeis*, to the "special-crisis" officials, the *thesmothetai*, while maintaining the "rapid procedure."

Such a transfer is generally recognized by modern scholarship, but it is considered to have been from the *nautodikai* to the *thesmothetai*. If so, there is then no explanation for the rapid procedure nor for the testimony of Pollux. It seems certainly better and in accord with *all* the evidence to recognize three stages in the development of the *dikai emporikai*: 1. their introduction under the special board, the *nautodikai*, 2. their transfer to the *eisagōgeis* when the need for rapid procedure became clear, 3. their transfer to the *thesmothetai* during or after the exceptional difficulties of 330-326. Aristotle, writing shortly thereafter, so found them, and modern scholarship has so recorded them. Such a stage certainly existed, but it was not the only one. Unlike the goddess of Athens, the *dikai emporikai* of Athens were not born fully developed, nor were they virginally immutable.

Index Locorum

When a note is prolonged for more than one page, the reference given is to the first page only.

199

15 *Antidosis* 35: 135 n. 78
313-4: 92
17 *Trapezitikos*: 15 n. 32
3-4: 122
12: 81
37-8: 35 n. 75
18 *Kallimachos*: 136 n. 84,
142, 144, 147 n. 109
1: 137 n. 85
2: 145, 148 n. 111
3: 141
4: 153
22: 145 n. 101
24: 113 n. 31
19 *Aiginētikos* 12-5: 72 n.
163
20 *Lochitēs* 1: 17 n. 38

Justinian, *Institutes* 3.21: 134
n. 76

Krateros, *Psēphismata* (FGH
342): 162 n. 11
Kratinos, Fragment 233 (Edmonds): 162 n. 11, 167

Lexica Segueriana 237.33: 27,
42, 115 n. 33
283.3: 162 n. 11, 163,
177
410.8: 139 n. 89
Lucian, *Dialogos meretricum*
2.2: 162 n. 11
Lydus, *De magistratibus populi Romani* 1.38: 172 n.
35
Lykourgos, *Against Leokrates*
27: 68 n. 151
58: 7 n. 13
Lysias, 6 *Andokidēs* 21: 78

10 *Theomnēstos* 19: 18, 18
n. 43
13 *Agoratos*: 145 n. 101
23: 81
16 *Mantitheos*: 145 n. 101
17 *Dēmosiōn adikēmatōn*:
178, 181, 182
2: 180
3: 38 n. 82
5: 11, 32, 42, 49, 115
n. 33, 156 n. 127, 159,
159 n. 4, 160, 162 n.
11, 164 n. 14, 176, 177,
179-80, 181
8: 162 n. 11, 177
22 *Against the Grain Deal-
ers* 16: 68 n. 154
17: 67, 118
23 *Pankleōn*: 121 n. 48,
136 n. 84, 139, 140,
142, 150 n. 117, 151
5: 140
25 *Dēmou kataluseōs apolo-
gia*: 145 n. 101
26 *Euandros*: 145 n. 101
30 *Nikomachos* 17: 132
Fragment 10 (Didot): 162
n. 11, 177 n. 45

Old Oligarch, see Ps.-Xen. *Ath.
Pol.*
Ox. Pap. 275.18: 28

Philochoros, *FGH* (Jacoby)
90: 166, 169 f.
136: 135 n. 81
Photios s.v. ναυτοδίκαι: 162 n.
11
Plato, *Apology* 36b: 84 n. 194
37a-b: 148

205

General Index

Where an entry refers to a note, the page given is that on which the note begins.
Where an entry occurs more than once on a page, only one reference is given.

209

211

diaita, 40, *see also* arbitration
diaitētēs, *see* arbitration
diamarturia (special plea), 86, 142 f., 147-48
dicasts, 38 n. 82, 78, 173 n. 36
  nautodikai, 163, 164 n. 14, 167-68
  special judges for *dikai emporikai*, 93-95, 98, 115 n. 34
dikai (private actions), 31, 63, 143 n. 97, 160, 185
  amnesty of 403 B.C. and *paragraphē*, 144 f.
  arbitration, 149
  damages, 17 n. 41
  epōbelia, 85
  execution of judgment, 74, 77, 77 n. 180
  imprisonment, 76
  paragraphē, 142
  procedural steps, 36
dikai aikeias (assault), 13, 16-17, 20-21, 190
dikai anagōgēs (restitution), 19 n. 44
dikai ἀνδραπόδων (slaves), 14, 18, 160
dikai apo symbolōn (treaty cases), 16 n. 36, 49, 61, 80, 126, 126 n. 61, 182, *see also symbola*
dikai ἀποστασίου (patron), 156
dikai ἀφορμῆς (capital), 13
dikai βλάβης (damage), 9 n. 17, 98 n. 6
dikai daneiōn (loan), 13
dikai emmēnoi (monthly), *passim*
  apodektai, 187 n. 67

arbitration, 35, 35 n. 75, 193
  definition, 12-20, 26
  eisagōgeis, 185, 186-91, 192
  epimelētai, 188
  epōbelia, 17 n. 41, 20
  historical development, 158, 159-61
  monthly during the winter, 42 ff.
  motivation, 20-22
  procedural steps, 36-40
  significance, 23-36
  see also emmēnos procedure
dikai emporikai (commercial maritime), *passim*
  admissibility rules, 96 f.
  bail, 80-81
  chronology, 91 n. 213, 184 f., 186 n. 66
  custom, 64
  definition, 100-14 *passim*, 115 n. 33
  delivery of goods to and from Athens, 101 f.
  dikai apo symbolōn, 182
  eisagōgeis, 186, 191-95, 198
  enforcement, 77, 77 n. 178
  epōbelia, 84 f., 86-87
  historical development, 158 ff.
  imprisonment, 74-79, 79 n. 185
  metics, 121 n. 49
  nautodikai, 176-83, 198
  non-limitation to a "commercial class," 114-29
  paragraphē, 86, 136 f., 142
  phasis, 84 f.
  rapidity, 9-58
  reform, 184-86

213

emporic action, *see dikai emporikai*
emporic cases, *see dikai emporikai*
emporikoi logoi, see dikai emporikai
emporos, definition, 103 n. 15, 123 n. 54, *see also* merchant
ephesis, 197 n. 97
epimelētai, 188, *see also* harbour magistrate; ἐπιμεληταὶ τοῦ ἐμπορίου (Greek Index)
epimelētai tōn kakourgōn, 82, 82 n. 187
Epirus, 196 n. 94
epōbelia, 17 n. 41, 20, 76, 77 n. 176, 83-92, 141, 142 n. 85
paragraphē, 147, 150, 153-54
eponymos archon, 126
equity, 96, 146, 151, 151 n. 118
eranos, see dikai eranikai
Eteokarpathians, 197
Euandros, 77 n. 178
Euboea, revolt of 446 B.C., 159, 164
Eukleidēs, archonship of, 141, 144
euthydikia, 149, *see also* trial proper
euthyna (examination of accounts), 144, 150, *see also* εὔθυνα (Greek Index)
Euthyphēmos, 127 n. 63
Evergos, 124
evidence, admissibility, 11 n. 23
examination, *see anakrisis*
exceptio rei transactae, 155

exceptiones, 149, 154
special pleas, 147
exportation, foodstuffs from Peiraeus, 68, 68 n. 156

family law, 4 n. 5
family relationships, suits, 149 n. 113
fides, 64 n. 137
fines, 90 n. 211, *see also* damages; *epōbelia*
foenus, 23 n. 55, 186 n. 66
foreigners (ξένοι), as litigants, 8, 57-58, 59 f., 116-18
bail, 80 f.
nautodikai, 167
polemarch, 175 n. 42, 178, 181 f.
surety, 82
trade in grain, 68
xenodikai, 167, 172 ff.
see also xenodikai, dikai apo symbolōn
"formula," 37 n. 80
The Forty, 17, 17 n. 39, 35 n. 76, 149 n. 113, 190
forum concursus, commercial litigation, 62, 71
forum contractus, 112, 178 n. 48
French law, 4
friendly loans, *see dikai eranikai*
friendly societies, *see dikai eranikai*

general, *see strategos*
German law, 4

prosecutor, *epōbelia*, 86-87
fine for dropping suit, 90 n. 211
share in damages, 89
prosklēsis, see summons
prostatēs, 60 n. 124
prothesmia (time limitation), 11, 19 n. 44, 136 n. 84
Prōtos, 146 n. 107
proxenos, 121 n. 49
Psammetichus, 169 n. 29
public actions, see *graphai*
public denunciations, see *eisaggelia*; εἰσαγγελία (Greek Index)

rapidity, *dikai emporikai*, 8, 9-59
real estate, litigation, 180, 180 n. 54
receipts, 132 f., 132 n. 70
residence, foreign merchants, 52 ff.
Rhodes, 53, 68, 116 n. 35
Rhodian Sea Law, 5, 123 n. 54
rigor, *dikai emporikai*, 8, 74-95
Roman law, 3 n. 2, 3 n. 3, 4 n. 4, 4 n. 5
  autonomia, 73 n. 166
  contracts, 105 n. 19, 129 n. 68, 131, 134 n. 76
  imprisonment of debtors, 75, 75 n. 170
  institutions, 96 n. 1
  liability, 122 n. 52
  monetary penalization, 75
  oral stipulation, 134
Ruscaja Pravda, 3 n. 3

sacred law, 41
sale, ready-money, 133
sale and hire, 22
sample, 5 n. 6
scholarship, Athenian commercial world, 119, 119 n. 45
  bail for foreigners, 81
  citizenship scrutiny of 445/4 B.C., 170
  contracts, 108, 113 n. 31, 131
Demosthenes text, 98 n. 7
dikai emmēnoi, 16, 16 n. 35, 36, 44-45
dikai emporikai: admissibility, 96; definition, 99, 100 n. 8; historical development, 160 f., 198; *paragraphē*, 157
dikē, 98 n. 6
eisagōgeis, 180, 191 f.
emmēnos, 26, 31
epōbelia, 85
forum concursus, Macedonia and Athens, 61
graphai and *dikai*, 143 n. 97
Greek law, 9 n. 17, 23 n. 54, 44, 159 n. 3
imprisonment, 79, 79 n. 185
"inseparability of process," 146 f.
juridical determination of class, 115 n. 33, 116 n. 36
marine law, 94
nauklēros and *emporos*, 123 n. 54
nautodikai and *xenodikai*, 165 ff.
paragraphē, 136 n. 84, 154
Pollux, 91

221

Greek Index

Where an entry refers to a note the page given is that on which the note begins.

www.ingramcontent.com/pod-product-compliance
Lightning Source LLC
Chambersburg PA
CBHW030940150426
42812CB00064B/3077/J